D0622218

West Virginia Tough Boys

Publisher's Cataloging-in-Publication
(Provided by Quality Books, Inc.)

Davis, F. Keith.
  West Virginia tough boys : vote buying, fist fighting
and a president named JFK / by F. Keith Davis ;
introduction by Lieutenant Governor and Senate President
Earl Ray Tomblin
   p. cm.
   Includes bibliographical references and index.
   LCCN 2003112047
   ISBN 0-9724867-2-0

   1. Chafin, Raymond, 1917- 2. Dahill, Dan. 3. Ellis,
   Claude. 4. Presidents--United States--Election--1960.
   5. Primaries--West Virginia—History--20th century.
   6. West Virginia--Politics and government. 7. Politicians
   --West Virginia--Biography. 8. Kennedy, John F. (John
   Fitzgerald), 1917-1963. I. Title.

   F245.4.D38 2003   975.4'043'0922
                              QB133-1602

Woodland Press, LLC

Copyright © 2003 Woodland Press, LLC / F. Keith Davis

Published In Beautiful Chapmanville, West Virginia
By Woodland Press, LLC
www.woodlandpress.com
Appalachian Stories. Appalachian Authors. Appalachian Pride.
SAN: 2 5 4 – 9 9 9 9

West Virginia Tough Boys

Vote Buying, Fist Fighting And
A President Named JFK

By F. Keith Davis

Foreword

West Virginia, for good or for bad, has long been regarded by politicians from across the country as having some of the most memorable and colorful political figures, worthy of characterization in any novel. That's why this book is appropriately titled *"West Virginia Tough Boys,"* because the lives they have lived, if reduced to print, would read more like political fiction than political fact.

There's no question that in Logan County, where I was raised, and where I live and serve in the Legislature today, the history of politics would and should be more about the men and women who engaged in politics more than the issues which surrounded them. Tradition and leadership meant more than issues to many, who owed much to a political organization and its top man.

In his book *"The Making of the President 1960,"* the historian Theodore White wrote that in southern West Virginia politics, at the time of John F.

Kennedy's election to the presidency, school board members spent five minutes discussing curriculum and five hours trying to determine who would drive the school bus on "Pea Pot" ridge. He was pointing out that politics in this region was based on personalities, political patronage (jobs or the lack of them during lean coal production periods) and strong precinct organization, based mainly on the use of large families or the influence of local political leaders.

While our political culture in Southwestern West Virginia has steadfastly and significantly moved away from this stereotype, this book is about those people who were able to organize and sustain some of the strongest local and regional political organizations anywhere in the country. They were able to do it without formal political training, yet understood the nature of the average voter and citizen and knew what it took to motivate them to go to the polls and vote.

The events and personalities, some now mere shadows, while others have dimmed with the passage of time, helped to frame a tradition of voting and campaigning, which has captured the imaginations of writers from all over the world. And, there's little question that the brand of politics practiced in the 1960s and earlier by these men and women, did as much as anything to propel one of the most popular presidents of our time into national office — John F. Kennedy.

As we reflect on our role in U.S. Presidential History and our own unique historical perspective, some might have legitimate reason to question the means, but no one can question the positive and outstanding contribution West Virginia has made in this venue of government and political development. We demonstrated to the world that while life in the hills may not be as complex as that of the big city or other areas of the country, at least we judged the candidate on his merits and not on his religious beliefs. We helped to tear down the walls of prejudice and establish an independence not seen in politics anywhere else in the United States.

This work backs up that thesis and with remarkable candor, makes it a personal walk through the immediate past history of a noble and proud people and their passionate relationship with the West Virginians who led them through such memorable and unforgettable times.

Earl Ray Tomblin
West Virginia State Senate President
Lt. Governor of West Virginia

Table Of Contents

WEST VIRGINIA TOUGH BOYS

Introduction
Concerned With Posterity

"Look at the people below us. You know I can help these people, Raymond."

These were the hypnotic words that gently rolled off the tongue of charismatic presidential candidate John F. Kennedy while he stood next to Raymond Chafin, Chairman of Logan County's Democratic Executive Committee, as they gazed out the finger-smudged second-floor window of the Aracoma Hotel. These carefully selected syllables resonated in Chafin's thoughts as he fretfully contemplated the future of the 1960 campaign for his group of candidates in Logan County.

All the years of grooming by some of the best political minds in the Mountain State and his own controversial decades of public service and campaign strategizing had not prepared Chafin for an anxiety-laden moment like this.

Up until this secret rendezvous at the downtown Logan hotel, it was John Kennedy's formidable opponent, Hubert Humphrey, who had the complete support of this middle-aged West Virginia political boss and his faction of local incumbents.

Humphrey, with his comparatively limited resources, had already financially compensated the faction boss, Chafin, and therefore expected him to use his political muscle to bring him victory in the county. Humphrey had every right to expect to get top billing on the political slate for the upcoming election. However, Humphrey forgot one small detail: this was Logan County, West Virginia — the infamous hotbed of political corruption.

We know from history that Humphrey's presidential expectations were never achieved. In the last moments before the primary election, his campaign completely unraveled. He lost in Logan County. He lost the West Virginia primary.

What changed things? Money. The remaining incidents that transpired are legendary. Chafin boasted:

> You'd be surprised how many local and state elections have been decided on the back deck of my home. In times gone by, we have argued and nearly fist-fought in my yard over the strategy and outcome of primary elections.

Even in 2003, from his modest command center, the 86-year-old continues to oversee, in an advisory role, the course of the Democratic Party within the borders of Logan County, West Virginia.

Whether one agrees with his brand of old-school politics or not — because of his amusing personality, his backwoods mannerisms, and his smooth-talking demeanor — in the Logan County region around Omar, Barnabus, and Cow Creek, it seems that nearly *everybody loves Raymond*.

But that's not always true elsewhere in the county. From past political clashes, there are more than a few individuals and past candidates who have vivid negative memories and have stored up a great deal of animosity for this elderly man. Maybe the bitterness stems from suspicious election maneuvers and alleged double-crosses, which changed the

1

course of certain primary elections of former years. Maybe it's because of the old-fashioned jealousy of political wannabes.

In 1994, the Cow Creek native authored his autobiography, *Just Good Politics*, with the help of Topper Sherwood, and the title sold well across the country. Chafin talked about his book:

> I've been told that book is used in classes at West Virginia University and at Marshall University. Young kids find out what politics – *real politics* – is all about. Well, as I look back, I didn't really want to write that darn book. There is so much I wanted to say at the time; however, I couldn't reveal too much. For one reason, Kennedy people had asked me not to. The finished product touched on the John F. Kennedy campaign in our state. However, there was plenty more to tell about that story and about my life in the Appalachian Mountains of southern West Virginia than just what was printed then.

Raymond Chafin, although now in his twilight years, is concerned about posterity and wants to set the record straight about his public and private life. Thus, in this volume, we attempt to do that. More than half of the pages focus on the struggles of everyday life in Appalachia. Chafin openly talks about his early days of poverty and explains how he grew in political power during a peculiar time in state history.

He speaks candidly about John F. Kennedy and the 1960 campaign.

Additionally, Chafin's main factional opponent in 1959 gives his own account. For the first time, Claude "Big Daddy" Ellis, who is now 77-years-old and who was a political big wheel in his own right, adds his own vivid memories of the Kennedy campaign to these pages, along with other stories of political tomfoolery.

Ellis handled JFK's campaign in Logan County. He worked closely with brothers Teddy and Robert Kennedy and state JFK Campaign Chairman Bob McDonough. He has firsthand knowledge of powerful "moneymen" who came to the area in behalf of the famous family.

Ellis was a rough and tough individual in 1960, and he exercised his own particular brand of politics, which often involved his clenched fist or the influence he commanded by carrying a crowbar.

Finally, amongst this compilation you'll become familiar with Dan Dahill, another former politician who is still a local practicing attorney. Dahill recalls his own childhood in Appalachia and his wild and cantankerous ways as a young man in the Marine Corps.

Dahill later served in the West Virginia House of Delegates, and then as a state senator. In the 1950s and '60s, he held an enormous amount of political control in Appalachia.

All of these men, who have hobnobbed with one another from time to time, are revered in southern West Virginia, as they represent some of the most admired and the most powerful politicians. Collectively, they have influenced the course of local and state politics for more than half a century. They have all — in one way or another — rubbed shoulders with many of the icons of our era.

***

Rather than being just another report of the Kennedy family's manipulation of the Mountain State, or a rehash of old material, this is intended to be a far more intimate effort that attempts to reveal a unique glimpse into West Virginia's quaint lifestyle and the making of a country politician. It is the story of mountain politics as it once was — and will never be again. It is history as told by those who lived it — as Chafin, Ellis, Dahill and others remember it.

Besides recorded interviews, previous oral history manuscripts, and newspaper records, I have utilized a number of other sources, which are all named in end of this work.

I would like to personally thank these men, and others, who have graciously allowed me to come into their homes, speak to them on the phone, or chat with them in my office. Over the course of time, I have asked hundreds of personal questions about the past, while each person patiently endured the procedure.

Though I don't condone the Election Day actions or unorthodox high-jinks of these kingpins, I would like to think that now, after spending many hours with each man in preparation for this project, I better understand the times in which they lived and their root motives a bit better.

In the book *Billy The Kid, A Short And Violent Life*, author Robert M. Utley vindicated a few of Billy Bonney's shortcomings by explaining, "all around him he saw corruption, both personal and institutional."

It would certainly be unfair or unfounded to compare the acts of the men in this book with those of the notorious "Kid;" however it is true that these men, like Bonney, saw corruption in their times and their environment as the norm. They thrived in a time when many politicians — even most leaders — served their own selfish interests and thus perverted primary and general elections through a variety of unlawful actions.

Are all the colorful stories in this volume true in every detail and facet? In most cases, only those who were interviewed for this project really know for sure, but I suspect most of the accounts are accurate — and that even the most seemingly farfetched tale by Raymond Chafin must contain a remnant of truth. One thing is certain: these individuals were extremely important in politics for many, many years. Through their years of control, the complexion and countenance of southern West Virginia has forever changed, mostly for the good.

Join me and meet individuals who have changed my preconceived notions of politicians and political affairs. If you can hang on with me, I assure you that you'll learn at least a few lessons in *vote buying, half-pints, and fistfights ... from Kennedy's West Virginia Tough Boys.*

F. Keith Davis
October 2003

Chapter One
A Politician's Humble Beginning

"If you have a couple thousand dollars, a copper still, and a crooked smile, you can still win yo'self an election in Logan County," one white-haired retired coalminer boasted to several of his buddies who were seated in Hardee's Restaurant in the little hamlet of Chapmanville, West Virginia.

The group of elderly men, who meet each morning for biscuits-and-gravy and a hot cup of coffee, looked at their fellow retiree and chuckled for a moment before continuing their discussion concerning the upcoming primary election. The community affectionately, unofficially, calls this assembly of old-timers the *Chapmanville Coffee Club*. Nearly a dozen strong, they meet to discuss current events, swap corny jokes, argue religion, confer over the weather, and of course, talk mountain politics. Although the offhanded statement about United States currency and moonshine was made in jest, the joke wasn't that far off the mark, especially if one is describing southern West Virginia.

There's always been a dark, portentous cloud of controversy lingering over the green southern West Virginia countryside. If someone even mentions the words "Logan County" elsewhere in the Mountain State, he or she is likely to get a negative response.

Positioned in the cradle of the Appalachian Mountain range, Logan County, West Virginia is a unique region with a longstanding reputation for tough, tumultuous union struggles, blood feuds, and political-machine rivalries. Religious fervor and passionate politics walk hand-in-hand here in this secluded area of the state.

In bygone days, Logan gained notoriety through the corrupt leadership of men like Sheriff "Dapper Don" Chafin and his political allies. The region is ill-famed for its strong-willed candidates and for what some believe were underhanded political shenanigans and clannish fights, dating all the way back to the days of Anderson "Devil Anse" Hatfield and later by at least two of his sons, Joe and Tennis, who controlled Logan County local elections for many years. Another son of Devil Anse, Cap Hatfield, who has been called the most dangerous of all Hatfield & McCoy feud participants, was also a powerful deputy for many years in the county. He was considered an excellent shot with rifle or pistol; he was sometimes called unpredictable and measured as a powerful force to be reckoned with.

Power Factions

Traditionally, the Democratic and Republican parties in Appalachia are made up of several groups or factions that strive to nominate and elect their specific roll of candidates to office. These bands of politicians are associated with a political party, which binds them together in order to support and struggle for the same cause, and are organized and controlled by a main politician, officeholder, or businessman. In the wooded hills of the southwestern region of the state, these faction leaders are generally known as bosses, kingpins, or big wheels, and they exhibit an enormous amount of power and influence, especially when it involves primary elections.

Through the years, there have been many powerful Democratic cliques in the county, headed by equally authoritative individuals, including Don Chafin, George C. Steele,

Claude Gore, Everett Workman, Lester "Bus" Perry, Earnest "Red" Hager, Jack Ferrell, Claude "Big Claude" or "Big Daddy" Ellis, Earl "Roundhead" Tomblin, and Raymond "Cathead" Chafin.

There have been effective Republican factions within this predominantly Democratic region, too. A listing of successful GOP bosses from the past might include names such as Tennis Hatfield, Jack Rayburn, Dr. Noah Steele, Ose Richey, Bob Samson, Robert McCormick, and T. K. Killen.

To validate the extreme passion that sometimes erupts in county political fighting, Lester "Bus" Perry wrote in his memoirs, *Forty Years, Mountain Politics, 1930-1970*, that in the mid-1930s, George C. Steele, who was the Democratic county chairman of the executive committee, and Dr. Noah Steele, the influential GOP chairman of the Republican executive committee — although brothers — ruthlessly fought one another in several heated election battles over the years, yet remained close as siblings.

Nowadays in Logan County, dominant political machines still exist, such as the "Triple A Team," controlled by individuals such as Rick Abraham, son of the late political powerhouse Bill Abraham; Rick Grimmett; Joe C. Ferrell; Alvis Porter; and Art Kirkendoll. In the first years of the 21st century, the countenance of politics has changed a great deal and calmed itself considerably when compared with the backdrop of state history. Yet, political factions remain and creative wheeling and dealing behind the scenes is still said to be the standard.

Besides the new visages in politics, there are a few remaining political warhorses from Logan's past who continue to influence the direction of primary and general elections in the region — specifically, Claude Ellis, Dan Dahill, and probably the most involved of the three, Raymond Chafin. Although these fellows are officially retired politically, they each continue to dabble in the affairs of the Democratic Party.

The Region

It's best to understand the region — southern West Virginia and Logan County — if you want to fully comprehend the behavior and goings-on of politicians such as Ellis, Dahill, and Chafin during their public lives.

West Virginia, a rather small state, is located in the Appalachian highlands of the continental United States. From east to west, its length is 266 miles; its width, from north to south, is 237 miles; its area is 24,231 square miles. Charleston became the permanent capital in 1885. West Virginia is governed under its second constitution, adopted in 1872.

Approximately 68 miles southwest of the capitol building, the City of Logan, the county seat of Logan County, was a hustling and bustling community by the time Raymond Chafin was born, in 1917. It was an active neighborhood built along the muddy Guyandotte River, with a population of approximately 3,900. Its quaint business district was limited to four or five city blocks on two primary streets — Stratton and Main. The county courthouse had been built in the center square of town — a grand post-Civil War design — making it the hub of activity for the people and the nucleus of mountain politics. Logan became a boomtown when the coal and timber industries gained momentum; by the turn of the century, it was also considered a rowdy and lawless community.

Until recently, the county was divided into three voter districts — Triadelphia-Man District, Chapmanville District, and Logan District, often called Guyan District.

Triadelphia-Man District, which is sometimes described as Man District, included many small towns and rural communities: Town of Man, Gilbert, Amherstdale, Accoville, Rita, Becco, Mallory, Kistler, Crites, Lorado, Buffalo Creek, and Crown.

Small communities surrounding the county seat in Logan District included West Logan, Aracoma, Slab Town (also called Central City), Holden, Peach Creek, Stollings, Rita, Yolyn, Dehue, Sunbeam, Dingess Run, Verdunville, Yuma, Whites Addition, Mt. Gay, Cherry Tree, Draper, Whitman, Ellis Addition (also called Black Bottom), and McConnell.

A few of the regions in Chapmanville District included the Town of Chapmanville, Harts Creek, Big Ugly, Barker's Fork, Big Creek, and Garrett's Fork.

Chafin's stomping grounds, Main Island Creek, included communities such as Omar, Barnabus, Chauncey, Switzer, Sarah Ann, Maysburg, Crystal Block, and Pine Creek, situated in some of the most remote and beautiful acreage in the state. Actually, by driving past Cow Creek altogether, you'll eventually head into the former timberlands of Devil Anse Hatfield, the beared patriarch of the Hatfields of Hatfield and McCoy feud fame.

The People

From the beginnings of statehood through the first half of the twentieth century, Main Island Creek was made up of predominantly blue-collar workers — reflecting a variety of nationalities — who were coal and timber workers living in company-owned housing camps and mining towns.

The people who created this immense ethnic hodgepodge had moved to West Virginia from various regions of the Old World — Yugoslavia, Italy, Poland, Germany, Hungary, and Wales — in search of good-paying jobs and American opportunity. Instead, most breadwinners held backbreaking positions, slaving under extremely hazardous circumstances. The majority of these men were digging bituminous coal from beneath the Appalachian Mountains for relatively little pay and few prospects for the future.

Being that this melting pot of cultures had moved into the region, clannish behavior was not uncommon. Certain nationalities and kinfolk often lived near one another in camps or close-knit neighborhoods and defended one another's interests against the perceived outside world.

In Island Creek, particularly, day-to-day life revolved around the coal industry, where coalmines or timber businesses owned nearly everything — housing, power plants, medical clinics, movie-theaters, recreation centers, barbershops, and general stores.

Citizens from each of the county's districts were somewhat alienated from one another by the rugged mountainous terrain. The limited roadway system, excessive poverty, and the unavailability of modern forms of travel added to this isolation. Educational opportunities were just as limited in the outreaches of the county. Creature comforts such as clean water, electricity, and indoor plumbing were still hard to find in the 1920s and '30s in remote hollows of West Virginia.

Then, There's the Politics

Today's Logan County, for the most part, is conservative in its thinking. Yet, the majority of citizens are loyal Democrats, constituting a one-party county.

"My Momma and Daddy were die-hard Democrats; if it was good enough for them, it is good for me, too. Besides, Democrats have always been for us little people, the common man; Republicans are only for themselves and the rich," one elderly resident recently stated when asked about his political persuasion. Such a comment as this would be a typical response in the southern part of the state.

The county brand of politics is inimitable and seems highly exaggerated in comparison to other regions in the state. Maybe it's because the county was born in the rural seclusion and deprivation already mentioned. Regardless, the influential politician of the early twentieth century was often an unhealthy mixture of astute organizer, hillbilly hooligan, and carnival barker. Wealthy officeholders found the poor and impoverished easy prey — using political promises, kickbacks, and blatant payoffs to move their often-selfish agenda forward.

For years, the region was held back economically and culturally because of self-centered politics and self-absorbed power mongers. Alas, many believe that some of these characteristics have overflowed into the twenty-first century, as well.

The early 1900s were a challenging time to grow up in Logan County. It was in such a time as this — toward the end of the first decade of the 20th century — that Raymond Chafin was born.

Chapter Two

Raymond Chafin, Cow Creek Resident

Today Raymond Chafin lives in the same modest ranch-style cinderblock and wood structure he's lived in for decades.

To find his residence, one must travel along the rural countryside toward Chauncey, West Virginia, going on up past the town of Omar to Cow Creek hollow. Once you circle toward Cow Creek, drive another mile or so up the indentation between two mountains and prepare to cross a rickety, fifteen-foot wooden bridge that covers a lazy-running creek animated with small suckerfish and frogs. The weathered boards on the bridge have warped, discolored, and broken over the years, but the crossing is still usable. Chafin's home is situated directly on the other side of the bridge.

The exterior of his house is painted a flat canary yellow with dull brown trim, surprisingly conservative, simple, and seemingly uncharacteristic for a man with Raymond Chafin's legendary past, boisterous charm, and monetary success.

The front yard is small, with a flower garden, surrounded by an electric fence to scare off pesky neighborhood dogs. There's a crude sign, which has unevenly printed letters — "Car Wash Here" — that his teenage grandson, Jesse, painted and erected a while back, in order to earn extra money. There are three or four birdhouses hanging from tree limbs and landscape timbers along the property line to attract and feed wildlife.

Some time ago, Chafin hung wood-slat porch swings outside, suspended by oxidized chains. There are simple plastic patio fixtures under a separate shelter house by the creek bank that offers privacy and cool shade in the summer.

Two flagpoles stand in the forefront of his yard, displaying a United States and a West Virginia flag; each flaps proudly in the wind as if to mark the home of a man who has devoted his adult life to the game of politics. The word "game" must be especially emphasized; for Chafin's focused planning of a political campaign is much like calculating a strategic checker jump or a critical chess move.

Once Raymond Chafin opens his front screen door and begins to talk, one realizes that this unpretentious block home with its level grounds, carved out of a mountainside, fits this gentleman perfectly — to a T. Although Chafin has been called "cunning" and "crafty" by many of his friends and foes alike, he remains a likable good ol' boy at heart with a genuine love for people — especially folks from his beloved Barnabus and Cow Creek hollow.

He still has his famous, nearly uncontrollable gift for gab, which has sometimes been described as his piece of good fortune that has opened many doors of opportunity over the years. However, this same attribute has also shown itself to be little more than a family curse — or Chafin's thorn in the flesh — placing him in harm's way on more than his share of occasions.

Son Of A Coalminer

It was springtime 2002 in Barnabus, West Virginia. Winter had been especially long, but finally the snow melted and buds began bursting forth, casting a light green hue on

9

the trees. Wildflowers were in full bloom and there seemed to be a renewed sense that Mother Nature was finally resurrected from her long winter's sleep.

Unfortunately, though spring was beginning and new life could be seen everywhere, on this particular day it was gloomy and overcast. It was much too chilly to sit outside in one of the swings; therefore, Chafin slowly tottered into the kitchen, turned up the thermostat knob on the electric heater, and decided the first interview for this volume should take place indoors. Returning to the living room, he impulsively expelled a low grunt as he leaned back and plopped into his seat; he crossed his legs and relaxed on his favorite side of the maroon crushed-velvet sofa. Chafin coughed several times and finally cleared his throat before beginning. Once he had completed this ritual, he tilted his head back and began to talk about his life in Logan County. He smiled as he reminisced about his roller-coaster public life, and he obviously seemed to enjoy explaining how he came to be a prominent individual in southern West Virginia politics.

Chafin came from meager circumstances. He was born during a blizzard — January 29, 1917 — and his mother later told him that it was so "blue-cold" on the night of his birth she feared Cow Creek would freeze over. Chafin snickered as he spoke about his humble beginnings. Chafin chuckled, and stated:

> I was born during a frightful snowstorm. Since that night, I've been raising a ruckus — and plenty of storms — ever since.

Chafin also pointed out that the date of his birth was only a few days after the death of William F. "Buffalo Bill" Cody. Buffalo Bill, the famous chief of scouts, frontier Indian fighter, and Wild West showman, died quietly at his sister's home in Denver, Colorado on January 10, 1917 and a nation deeply mourned his passing. Chafin explained that he didn't particularly think Cody's death was relevant to his own life; but he thought it gave a timeline for one to consider. The wild frontier days were coming to an end by the time Chafin was born.

Raymond Chafin was the firstborn of Elbert and Lucinda Curry Chafin. His Aunt Sally Curry acted as midwife and helped Lucinda with birthing her first young'un. Elbert waited in the living room — nervously pacing back and forth — as his wife quietly endured the pain of natural childbirth in the connecting room of the coal-camp house.

The frame house was small, three rooms in all, with no electricity or indoor plumbing. An old iron coal-burner sat in the far corner of the living room and barely generated enough heat to keep the front room and bedroom warm. After sundown the Chafin home was illuminated by the golden glow from several intentionally placed oil lamps. Other than the light from the lamps, translucent moonbeams peeked through the front windows, adding a mellow luminosity, which formed a dim contrast of long dark shadows and soft natural highlights throughout the front room of the dwelling. This particular night, the lamplight merged with the natural lighting to form an eerie, surreal appearance.

In the early morning hours, when Raymond was finally born, young Lucinda held the pudgy child close to her bosom and thanked God that he was healthy. Elbert, standing near the bed, looked down at his son with amazement and pride. He wondered what this little child would someday become — maybe a timber worker, a miner, a salesman, or even a moonshiner.

"Mrs. Chafin, this is quite wonderful," Elbert said softly. "Very good; very good indeed."

Though Raymond was the first to be born, he definitely wasn't the last child for Elbert and Lucinda. Eventually they had a full house, with seven additional children — Bessie, Ester-May, Verna, Willie, Junior, Kenneth, and Clifton.

Chafin's first years were spent playing in the mountains, along creek banks, or near the coalmines with his brothers and sisters and other children in the neighborhood. Chafin grinned and recalled:

> We boys all dressed the same and probably all looked 'bout alike. We started out clean in the mornings, but it sure didn't last long. We were probably black from playing in coal dust and dirt piles long before noon.
>
> As for me, my face was fresh-washed or spit-shined every mornin', and Momma raked a comb through my matted hair. However, once I ran out the screen door, my friends and I seemed to wind up with scraggly mops in no time. Our faces were soon dirty from play; and when we finally came home, we were usually all in trouble for being filthy. Most moms bathed their kids in a No. 3 washtub every other night or so. We were no different. By the next mornin' we'd start the process all over again.
>
> I guess all of us boys wore ol' worn-out knickers or britches, which were rolled up to our shins and flimsy cotton shirts. We were always barefoot. You couldn't bribe us into wearing a pair of leather shoes. Some of us wore wide-brimmed straw hats on real sunny days. I guess the little girls on the creek didn't look much different than we did, except they usually wore sloppy play dresses.

Chafin started school at Barnabus Grade School, a two-room schoolhouse, around 1924; he was seven years old. His dad was a coalminer at Omar No. 4 Mine when he started class. Chafin commented:

> All the mines were numbered back then, ya' know — still are. I don't think Dad ever cared for mining too much. However, that same year he lost his job after a mine fire closed the entire operation down. School ended for me at the same time. A short time after that we moved up Pine Creek Hollow and Dad started working in the lumber business, hauling lumber for Peytona Lumber Company. I then started back to school, being promoted to the third grade.

By the time Chafin was eight or nine, he was expected to help load lumber, sand, and gravel for his father and for customers of the lumberyard. He explained:

> Dad also taught me how to drive a team of workhorses by then. Like all kids at the time, I had to do my part. The horses were stocky and muscular, but I was able to keep them under control, most of the time.

Chapter Three
KKK Leaves Switches

According to historical accounts, there were two organizations known as the Ku Klux Klan. The first was organized by veterans of the Confederate Army initially as a societal organization, and then as a secret means of resistance to Reconstruction after the war, with the ultimate goal of restoring white supremacy over the newly freed blacks.

Dressed in flowing white robes and pointed masks, and carrying around great amounts of resentment and racial prejudice, Klansmen flogged and often killed freedmen and their white supporters and cohorts in nighttime raids through the South. History tells us that this cruel organization had largely run its course by the 1870s, then gradually faded away.

The second KKK arose from those smoldering ashes of animosity around 1915, partly out of a particular group of Southerners' wistfulness for the Old South, but also out of their fear for the changing character of American society. It is said that this version of the KKK enlarged its scope of hatred to include Jews, Catholics, foreigners, labor unions, as well as African-Americans, among its adversaries.

Its membership peaked in the 1920s, with over four-and-a-half-million members, but then weakened with the advent of the Great Depression and with the organization of the Federal Bureau of Investigation.

The Ku Klux Klan was at its peak in Logan County when Raymond Chafin was a youngster, living up Pine Creek. Chafin recalled:

> When I was about nine or ten years old, they had the Ku Klux Klan right around here and throughout the county. A lot of times when someone did something wrong or immoral, home folks would threaten to turn them over to the KKK. It was a type of bullying organization back then. The KKK enforced *their* law. Sometimes it may have been good; sometimes it was bad.

By now, Chafin's father, Elbert, and a relative, John Curry, were partners in a small contracting business of their own, supplying timbers for area coalmines. Once the timbers were cut, the two of them took the logs to various mine sites in horse-drawn buck wagons. Along the way to the job site, they often overheard gossip from residents in the coal camps of the Klan's vigilante behavior.

It wasn't that unusual for Elbert to come in from a long day at work, sit down at the kitchen table, and tell his wife that the KKK was after somebody the night before.
"What fer and why?" Lucinda asked her husband. "How come the KKK is huntin' ol' Jimbo?"

"Well, the fellar wasn't workin' as he ought," Elbert said, shaking his head before he took another sip of his cold coffee. He was able to sympathize with the man's needy family.

There was little governmental assistance for poor families. So when a healthy head of the house wasn't working, "his wife and children were left to do without" — being forced to scavenge the hills for wild game, nuts, and berries. As Chafin explained, out of concern for the woman and her youngsters, neighbors might notify members of KKK chapter, which in turn would take domestic matters into their own hands   through intimidation, usually, and force, if necessary. Chafin spoke about his childhood memories of the KKK in more detail.

Dad wasn't a member — at least I don't think he was. However, he told me that if a Klansman were somehow notified that a fellow wasn't carin' for his family, they'd go to that man's home late at night and leave a short note on his door. The letter, which was straight to the point, usually said somethin' like, "Hey, if you refuse to go to work and take care of your family, the KKK will take care of YOU!"

The KKK was a whole lot of the law 'round these parts back in those days. The county deputies didn't take care of those kinds of cases back then. The Klan sure would, though. People here didn't have a telephone to call the law, either. So, the Klan *became* the law.

If the fellar didn't listen to the note and obey the warning, then the KKK would leave switches [thin tree branches, skinned of their leaves, often used for whippings] on his porch. When someone found a tied bundle of switches, he knew he had been warned. Now, if that didn't work, they'd use the switches.

Twenty-five or thirty stout men — dressed in menacing white gowns and masks — would go over to the perpetrator's home, drag the lazy one out into the yard, give him a good thrashing, and then turn him loose. Then, if he didn't go to work after that, he'd most likely leave the area out of fear of greater chastisement.

There were other things that you could do that would get you in trouble with the Klan, too. A man that was beatin' his wife might get a note pinned to the screen door, too; or a father who was especially mean to his children might face a circle of masked men and give an account for his actions.

At that time, we had several black folks living on Pine Creek. We never had any trouble with them, and they had no problems with us. Everybody at Pine Creek got along good, as far as I know. Maybe a few blacks would drink a little too much around the mine tipple on occasion, shoot pistols a little bit, and horse around. But the whites and blacks never did fight each other.

The KKK around here didn't seem to be opposed to blacks at that time — around here at least. They were more often after white folks who were irresponsible or plumb cantankerous.

Although, I will confess that I don't believe they would have ever allowed a black member. The Ku Klux Klan would often dress up in their uniforms and have a march — called the snake-tail march. They'd march from Pine Creek down to Omar, and they'd form a line and swagger along like a snake, weaving from one side of the road to the other in formation. I've seen as many as a hundred at a time in these marches.

During the march, some Klansman rode horses that were also draped in white cloth. The sight of one hundred or more robed members of the secret society marching along the narrow, unpaved roads of Pine Creek was undoubtedly disturbing for most residents.

Oftentimes, Chafin, as a youngster, would barely peek out from behind living room curtains as hooded men strutted past his home. It was at times like this that the community worried and questioned one another about who would be the next target of this underground society. Chafin explained that when "they marched the snake-tail, it usually meant that they were after somebody. They were letting people know that they were active. Believe me, everyone listened!"

Numerous cross burnings and public whippings — as well as many instances of bundled green switches being dropped on doorways as forewarnings — were documented in the 1920s and '30s. Chafin stated:

> In this region, all you had to say to somebody that was bothering you was something like, "Hey, the Ku Klux Klan will get you!" and a wayward soul would straighten right up in a hurry. As far as I'm concerned, there was not a lot wrong with the KKK that met around here in those days. They did their job, and they did it well. The big problems between the KKK and the colored folks may have happened at other places, but not 'round the communities like Stirrat, Cow Creek, Omar, or Pine Creek in this county.

> What do I know about the Klan? Did they exist? I sure remember them and I still know more than I'm tellin'. We heard rumors of who many of them were, too.

Although many of the men of Island Creek were believed to be passionate members at the time, it seems that the actual identities of most of them remain forever hidden beneath the white robes and masks that they wore.

Another individual who recalls the activities of the KKK in this area, confirming Chafin's recollections, is Ben Hale, now 92-years-old and living in Chesapeake, Ohio. Hale grew up in the small town of West Logan, near the city of Logan. He married at the age of 26. His late wife, Bessie Hale, was the daughter of Lillian White and A. D. (Kiser) Hale, of Slabtown, Central City, in Logan. Hale reminisced:

> There were many [average] citizens in the Klan at the time. Most of the merchants and businessmen of Logan were members. Many boys wanted to be members, but you had to be 18. At the time, they were not particularly against race, so much here. They dealt with other things. It was not uncommon for the KKK to go to a specific church service, which was underway. They might enter the church doors in white robes and masks and walk up the aisle to the front and drop an envelope in the offering plate.

At other times a couple dozen or so might show up for a tent revival or evangelistic service — and most likely sit in the last row of pews or stand along the back wall — and listen to the pastor, shouting "Amen!" when they agreed with a particular point in his sermon. If they liked what they heard, they left a generous gift at the altar or in the collection plate. If they disagreed with the message, they might jump up and shuffle out the front exit during the middle of the service while muttering cross words and pointing accusingly toward the minister.

Tough Boys

The late James Major, a highly respected black man and community activist who lived nearly all of his eighty years in Superior Bottom and passed away in September 2003, agreed in a 2002 interview that the KKK in Logan County was not particularly against "Negroes" in those days. Major added:

> I suspect the KKK were not particularly supporters of the black communities, although I never ever knew of them giving any of the black residents of Island Creek any problems when I was growing up.
>
> Additionally, it was amazing that in the coalfields there was little difference between black and white, especially when it came to the workplace and income. All nationalities and races made the same kind of money for the same job. Most had the same opportunities in the mines.
>
> Socially, there were differences made between blacks and whites; however, blacks weren't specifically targeted by the Ku Klux Klan or by anyone else, for that matter, at that time period. The Klan was horrible in other regions of the country, though. I would guess our problems in this area came sometime later.

According to Chafin, there were other lodges besides the KKK in the region. He recalled: "There were the Independent Order of Odd Fellows, Grand Lodge Knights of the Pythias, and the Red Man. Women had their lodges, too. That's about all folks had to go to in those days; and we had a lodge hall that was built by the coalmines, located in downtown Omar. The coal companies allowed lodge meetings to take place only when it didn't interfere with the men's work at the mines. A lot of fellows were working only two or three days a week in the 1920s and '30s. Lodge days had to fall around their off days."

Too Much Free Time

During the hot and humid summer months, little Raymond Chafin and other smudge-faced children from Pine Creek and Cow Creek had plenty of free time on their hands and very little to keep their hyperactive minds stimulated. There were few toys; things like scooters, wagons, and bicycles were normally too expensive for the coal-camp children. Instead, camp kids would look for simple ways to entertain themselves. At times this summer search for amusement would lead to trouble.

There was a natural spring at Slate Dump Hollow beyond the coal tipple at Pine Creek. There were several metal pipes that protruded out of the ground with fresh spring water flowing from them continuously. Residents brought their buckets to the spring daily in order to fill them up for cooking, drinking, and cleaning water. Because the stream flowed freely, there was always a large puddle of standing water beneath the rusty pipes. Chafin remembered the spring and the trouble that also flowed out from the water source. He smiled as he recalled the spring:

> I remember that sometimes a gang of the boys and girls in the holler – both blacks and whites — would get into the spring and try to dam things up [for swimming]; but area parents were pretty firm about taking care of their own and other kids, too, if need be. If I ever got into a rock-throwing fight or a fistfight with anyone — white or black — and Mom and Dad ever heard about it, I

would face a "rock throwing" of sorts when I got home — only it would be with a switch or tree limb on my rear end!

It wasn't strange for an adult to scold another person's child if he or she was out somewhere doing something wrong. You didn't have to be that child's parent to discipline them. People watched out for one another's young'uns back then.

Moms and dads didn't get mad if a sensible person from up the holler caught your child out doing something ornery and intervened. That concerned neighbor might grab a hickory switch and swat the child right there on the spot if he or she deserved it.

If the neighbor whipped your child in those days, you thanked the neighbor for doin' it — for makin' your child mind. Then when you got a hold of your child, you whipped him or her again! Nowadays, if you even talk about spankin' your own child, that child or someone else might call the law and say you're guilty of child abuse.

Chafin went on to say that the railroad used to "drop" railroad cars at the tipple — meaning the conductor released a huge steel car and let it roll freely toward the mine site. As the car rolled, the wheels would grate against the steel track, screeching, squealing, and whining at a nearly deafening pitch. He recalled that they didn't have trains with elaborate switches like they have now, so a railroad brakeman released one or maybe two empty cars by hand, letting momentum take over, as the train car headed for the tipple yard to be loaded. He added:

> I had two friends, Ray and Orel, and we all played together. We used to sneak and hop the railroad cars as the railroad man dropped them. As the cars were rolling toward the tipple, we'd take a run-and-go … and jump up and grab hold of the train car for the ride of our life!
>
> One time the train worker who dropped the railroad cars saw us and went and told our dads about it. My dad was workin' quite a bit at the time, so he sent word to a neighbor named Tusk Nichols.
>
> So, on this particular day, when we went back down to hop the train again, Tusk was waiting on us with a peculiar, devlish grin on his face. Without warning, Tusk got to me first, and he gave me a real good whippin' with a green switch. It stung straight through my worn britches and I hollered bloody murder!
>
> The conductor showed up and grabbed a hold of the other two boys while I got walloped. When Tusk was done with me, he poured it on Ray and Orel, too!

Later, Nichols walked Chafin up to his mother's house and told her, "Mrs. Chafin, I hopes I didn't stripe your boy much. I gave him a good one for hoppin' those cars."

"Thank you, thank you, Tusk!" she said, as she slapped and rubbed her hands together. She turned her head quickly and glared at Chafin, who was already blushing and expecting the worst. "Trust me, Tusk. We'll *also* take care of Raymond when Daddy comes home this evenin'."

She wiped her hands on her apron and then grabbed her boy by his earlobe and led him into the house while he squalled for mercy. When his father finally came home from work that evening, Chafin got another whipping, as promised.

Chafin said, as he laughed, that the Tusk Nichols episode immediately stopped the railroad hopping for all the children in the hollow — at least for a while. He added:

> News travels fast. We all stopped the train jumpin'. That made me respect and fear Tusk Nichols. If that man were living today, I would still have a high opinion of him and listen to him completely. I appreciate what Tusk did when he got after me. That's what made people better in those days — good old-fashioned discipline.

Chafin added that when he was older, he started thinking about what could have happened when they hopped those unstoppable multi-ton railroad cars.

Collecting Coal for Mom and Dad

Chafin had daily chores; his parents expected him, as well as every other member, to do his part for the family. He sometimes helped clean the house, scrubbed the front porch with a soapy bleach solution, or gathered leftover coal for the stove. He had to fetch water when it was needed, too.

During the Great Depression, times were tough for everyone. Chafin, like other children his age, had to hike along the train tracks with an empty white lard bucket to hunt for coal chunks. Coal would often tumble from the overloaded train cars, dropping along the tracks as the train ran through the hollow.

After the loud chugging and belching steam engine passed through the mountain camps — with its string of cars loaded down with the "black gold" — children from the communities picked up the incidental overflow from the cars. It was reminiscent of the story of the gleaners in Scripture who picked up extra grain that was purposely left along the corners of the wheat fields. The coalmines knew some coal tumbled from the cars. It's believed that some companies allowed it to continue in order to help the communities. Chafin recollected:

> My neighborhood friends and I could pick up several buckets worth of coal — large shiny black lumps and small chips — and it helped our parents. It was actually a lot of fun when I was small. We had competitions to see who could pick up the most.
>
> It made my buddies and me feel like we were working for the family. Nearly all of the camp folks heated their homes with coal during those times. Most families cooked with a coal burnin' cookstove, too. The most popular model I remember was a cast-iron stove with a large flue, firebox, and oven; it had a slide hearth plate and heavy, tin-lined oven doors.

Chafin and his friends would sometimes carry home firewood from the hills, as well. He said, "if it would burn, we'd drag it to the house." He explained that, obviously,

17

a bucket or two of coal every day, and sometimes a load of hardwood, twigs, or sticks, made a big difference [on the home budget]."

> I suspect nearly everyone in Island Creek region used a small fireplace or a stove with a cast-iron firepot. All looked farely similar, with a dumping grate, sheet steel body, and nickel-plated hinge pins and knobs. The coal-camp houses belched thick black smoke in the wintertime. The smell of burning coal would get in your nostrils and stay there all winter long.

Chafin recalled that on bitter-cold December and January evenings, his mother might have their Warm Morning heater so hot that it glowed red-orange by the middle of the night. With a roaring fire in the stove's belly, the protruding stovepipe was often so searing that she worried and quarreled with her husband about the possibility of a fire beginning where it connected into the heavily wallpapered wall. The wallpaper was actually not store-bought paper at all; it was created with layers of newsprint glued to the wall with wheat paste, offering insulation and visual creativity.

"Kids, y'all keeps away from the stove! You'll burn up alive, by getting too close to the Warm Morning," Lucinda often shouted at the children as they ran into the kitchen. Chafin elaborated:

> We definitely believed Mom, 'cause you could feel the heat radiating from that old stove! I don't think any of us kids ever got burnt. We were way too timid of that big black furnace to ever get close enough to find out if we could get scalded.
>
> Besides what coal chunks could be picked up along the tracks, coalminers or employees of the mines generally got a truckload or two of coal from the mines every so often. Regardless of how plentiful coal was, the coal company would always deduct the price of coal from the miner's next payday. They charged a premium price for the coal, too. So you had to use it sparingly.

Chapter Four

Working for the Company Store

By 1931, when Raymond Chafin was around 14 years of age, he was going to school at Omar. During that period of time his father, Elbert, was no longer working in the timber business. He was now working at the Omar company store — called the Junior Mercantile — delivering groceries to customers. Chafin explained:

> Our family eventually moved. After we moved away from Pine Creek, we moved below Omar in a house at Sandy Bottom, a nice section of Omar, for a while. Then the state decided they wanted to move the creek and the entire road that followed along the water's edge toward Maysburg. When they started changing the roadway, by first moving the creek bed, they tore down the ol' house we lived in. We had leased the place from an ol'-timer, Leif Browning. When the road construction started, we were forced to go.

In addition to working at the company store, Elbert Chafin liked to farm; so he always helped neighbors with their gardening, including the general manager of the company store, T. A. Obenshain. Chafin reminisced:

> I had an Uncle Alex who lived at the left fork of Cow Creek, where there was a lot of good bottomland and a few good farms. Alex had recently married Roscoe Conley's daughter, Effie, and decided he was moving to Chapmanville. Effie's family owned a large farm at Airport Road, and they were accustomed to the newest in farm equipment. Since we had to move and Uncle Alex was ready to move from his farm anyway, Dad bought his lease out. We bought his horse, mule, and this old dilapidated plow with two wooden handles. We kids had to drive that ol' horse and mule and the turn-plow.

For the first time, the Chafin clan was a long way from Omar, in an isolated region. There was no electricity or running water at the farm. There wasn't really much to do after Raymond Chafin finished his chores "except look at the newspaper covered walls." During the winter months, crops were already in for the year and the planting season was months away, so it was even more boring for the young Chafin and his siblings. Chafin recalled:

> My mother was a bit disgusted about it all, too. Before we moved to the farm, we had a radio at the other house, and we had gotten pretty used to it. Now we went without, because this farm didn't have electricity or anything else. Not many places around the area had electric power at the time. But we had gotten used to it when we were at Sandy Bottom. It's hard to go without it once you've had it.

Being isolated from Omar they were also unable to see the latest Tom Mix reels at the theater. Even though these were the last days of the silent screen era for Mix and Tony, his wonder horse, the children around Omar still flocked to the company-owned movie house to see his Wild West adventures and cowboy thrills. His flashy costumes, fancy stunts, and trick riding fascinated adults and children alike. Another Hollywood favorite of Chafin and his friends was rough and tumble Ken Maynard and his trusty steed, Tarzan. Then, with the advent of sound pictures, or talkies as they were called at the time, there were also new B-Western movie stars, whom Chafin idolized — including Big Bill Elliot and his painted pinto, Dice.

Radios And No Electricity

Now that young Chafin, his siblings, and parents had moved away from Omar, the Saturday matinees and radio serials were a thing of the past. Chafin recalled the frustration of living in a secluded region without the luxury of electricity.

It wasn't just Mom and us who missed Sandy Bottom, either. I believe Dad had gotten accustomed to listening to national radio shows like "Lum 'n' Abner" every evening. Lowell Thomas always did the news, and the Grand Ole Opry was just gettin' good on Saturday nights.

Before long, Elbert Chafin went to the company store because he heard about new fangled radios that operated off of batteries.

Dad started looking through the catalogs. He finally found a battery radio that took four Cs, two Bs, and an A battery. These are nothing like the alkaline batteries we have today. These were big, bulky things; you wired 'em up in a particular series. You almost had to be an electrical engineer to hook these up correctly!

Dad got the store to order us one. When we finally got the radio, we didn't know how to hook it up, and Dad was afraid to try to connect it up by himself. Fortunately, Mr. Obenshain had a son, Sonny, who had gone to radio repair school and was very intelligent. At that time, everybody wanted to be a radio repairman because of the radio's popularity. It was as big as television or computers are today. A repairman never had to worry about work; his job would never work out, or come to an end. Dad asked Sonny if he would hook up his new radio. He said that he'd have to read up on it, study the model, and then get back with him.

So, for a long time, we had the radio, along with the various batteries, sittin' in the house just waitin' to be used. We already put up our antenna — from one hillside up to the other hillside. Finally, Sonny came up and fooled with it one Saturday. It took all day, but he got it hooked up, and presto — we had perfect reception! We were all excited about it.

I remember there was an ol' Bisquick-sponsored soap opera that used to play every day around 11:30 in the morning. It started right around the time that we came into the house for lunch, after we'd been hoeing corn or working in the field all morning. My mother, sisters, and all of us boys got hooked on that show! Even though she listened, Mom always said, "I don't know if your papa would want us listening to this or not; we might run down these batteries."

Batteries cost a whole lot back then. This type couldn't be recharged, either. You just bought more batteries when the ol' ones petered out.

At this same time, several people — farmhands from the area — helped the Chafin family as they maintained the crops. As it turned out, the hired help became addicted to the daily program, too.

Our helpers were the Sergeant family, who lived near us. If we had plenty to do, Daddy would always hire them. The father, Davy Sergeant, was a short man who had two or three girls and several boys. He brought them all over with him. The women and girls hoed that corn just like us boys. One of Davy's girls was named Odessa, and I was kind of struck on her.

Another was Lela ... *and who really cares to remember those ol' boys?* There ain't no use rememberin' them anyway.

When the Chafin and the Sergeant families came in to listen to the soap opera, they all sat together surrounding the radio. No one would say as much as a peep, as they strained to hear every detail of the story. Chafin's mom would always tell the children to walk lightly inside the house so they didn't rattle any of the radio tubes loose.

When Elbert Chafin eventually found out that the family and the workers were listening to the daily broadcast, he looked at Lucinda, his wife, smiled, and said, "Miss Chafin, hon, I don't mind if'n these young'uns listen to that show. Just don't let 'em get hooked on too many of 'em — 'cause they won't want to work."

Other neighbors who lived down below the Chafin residence were Uncle Lewis, Aunt Cindy, and their son, Elvie, Curry. Elvie would eventually become one of Chafin's best political buddies. Chafin fondly remembered the evenings:

I'd say Elvie was closer than a brother when I was growin' up 'round him. They'd all come up to our house every Saturday night 'cause we all liked to play cards. Dad eventually bought one of these gas stoves that had mantles on it. You had to pump it up and hang it on the wall. We didn't burn it all the time, but we burned it occasionally, when we'd play card games like Sit Back and King Pedro.

The two boys would listen to the national programs, while shuffling and playing cards; Chafin's mother and Aunt Cindy also listened, as they stayed busy cooking in the kitchen. He recalled:

They might fry us up chicken and bake a few fruit pies or homemade cakes. So, by 12 midnight or 1 o'clock in the morning, we'd all be sittin' 'round a big kitchen table havin' fried chicken and dessert. Since no one had to work on Sunday, we didn't care how late we stayed up. We stayed wide-eyed as we listened to a bunch of half-hour shows. When the batteries were ready to run down, Dad always had another battery sittin' next to the radio — ready to hook up. Best I can remember we had the first battery radio on the creek.

Then a couple of years later, retailers came out with another kind of radio that used a six-volt battery, but it didn't last near as long. Around that same time, a fella came through this area sellin' windmills that would supposedly make electricity. The company store ordered a few of them, but when they came in, *they didn't work*! There wasn't enough wind around here to spin the dang blades. So that was a big flop!

You wouldn't believe how we all worshiped that radio. We all stared at it for hours while it was on. I remember every inch of what it looked like, with its round dial, wood cabinet, and large knobs. Mom shined it every day. We didn't bounce no balls 'round that radio; we took care of it! Yes, sir, we did!

It was obvious that the programs on the radio whisked Chafin and his family away from the doldrums and hardships of the farm world and took them to exotic faraway lands through their imaginations and the magic of radio waves.

Times Are Changing

Chafin explained that during his childhood in Cow Creek, his family had no electric service in their home until around 1942 or '43. According to Chafin, "President Franklin D. Roosevelt made 'em put power lines up these creeks and hollers."

After seventh grade, Chafin dropped out of school so that he could work alongside his father at the company store. He intended to return to school in a year or so, after he had "earned a few extra dollars" for the Chafin household. Besides the store work, he was still responsible for his own duties at the farm once he went home.

Going to school beyond junior high was extremely rare in those days in Island Creek, for it typically took every member of the family working to make the home run smoothly. Chafin recalled the time period:

> Dad took me along with him to just about everywhere he went on his grocery route. First, he started taking me to the Omar company store with him, and when the big shots – that's what we called 'em – came into the store, my job was to carry their groceries out to their cars and sweep up the floor.
>
> I used to help him bag up potatoes – ten pounds in a bag – and put a pound of beans in a brown bag and weigh 'em for customers. I think I was paid a bit less than a fifty-cent piece a day. I did that until I was a great big ol' boy.

During this time, Cow Creek was still unpaved and extremely rural and rugged. Travel wasn't particularly easy, and automobiles were scarce. Chafin added:

> We had a pack wagon and two workhorses at that time, and my dad delivered all over these hills. Being with him, I got to know everybody along the route. It was a lot different in comparison with today. Anybody who shopped at the store back in those days had his or her groceries delivered. They most likely didn't have an automobile, and they usually walked everywhere. At Omar we

had areas called Three Hundred Hill, Four Hundred Hill, Seven Hundred Hill, and Pine Creek. We delivered to all those places.

I worked with Dad and finally we got a one-horse wagon and a horse. We rented it from Mary Talip and Andy Rebar, of Cow Creek. They actually loaned us their wagon in the wintertime. We could get up the hills in the summertime, but in the winter we couldn't. This wagon and horse made it possible. When we rented the wagon, my dad talked the men at the store into giving me the sole job of running the grocery route. We kept the horse and fed him; we paid the Rebar family 'round twenty dollars a month for the wagon and horse.

My job was to get up in the mornin' and feed that horse and keep the harness shinin'. Oh, boy, Dad really made me shine it, too," Chafin chuckled. "I had to keep it clean — including the reins, bridle, and the brass knobs up on the harness. I also had to keep the wagon itself clean and the wheels clean as a pin. In my imagination, I made it look like a big locomotive engine — or passenger train — going around the hills, because it glistened and sparkled so.

That horse's name was Frank. Oh, boy, he was a smart ol' thing, too. You could turn Frank on a dime and he'd give change! He never bucked your commands.

Chafin thought he hated the daily responsibilities and the backbreaking labor at the time; however, looking back, he believes that the experiences in his youth helped him to be responsible and to "get along" in later life.

Political Revolution

When Raymond Chafin was a freckle-faced 15-year-old, the Mountain State, as well as the entire country, went through a significant political revolution, along with significant sociological changes. In 1932, Franklin Roosevelt went into the Democratic convention in Chicago as the front-runner. His main opposition was Alfred Smith. Roosevelt easily secured the party's nomination on the third ballot. History records that Roosevelt disregarded ritual by going to Chicago to personally accept the nomination.

The Roosevelt presidential campaign took place against the backdrop of the Great Depression and the last months of Prohibition. It seemed that poverty and suffering had touched every neighborhood in America. Meanwhile, organized crime and gangster activity were running rampant in the bigger cities.

Shiny copper stills, illegal liquor delivery, smoke-filled gambling halls, and brothels were commonplace in Logan County. Opportunists and the local criminal underworld had a sturdy chokehold on the poverty-stricken area.

Seemingly senseless murders and mutilations were fairly commonplace, such as the legendary Mamie Thurman murder of 1932 — a gruesome homicide that continues to baffle investigators to this day. Other assassinations happened when revenuers or rival gangsters were caught snooping too close to illegal stills in the high country.

Meanwhile, most lawful residents struggled to support themselves. Hardship was everywhere, and the unemployment rate soared above the national average. Many in Logan could hardly meet the bare essentials of life: shelter, nourishment, and clothing. Some families resorted to scavenging the hillsides for wild game. Other folks, who were able, cleared off small tracts of land on the sides of the mountains and planted meager crops, like Hickory Cane field corn, in order to survive.

It's been said that, in those days, to be employed in Logan County, with a weekly payday, was a "fortunate blessing."

Amidst this inundation of poverty and human misery, Roosevelt campaigned vigorously to prove that, despite his own physical disadvantages, he was well equipped to undertake the job of American president and that he could pull the United States out of its financial dilemma while breaking crime's stranglehold on a scared, hurting nation.

His political opponent, President Herbert Hoover and his re-election team subtly portrayed Roosevelt as physically feeble and a political extremist who would bring chaos and ruin to the nation. However, facts often speak louder than words, and it's estimated that 25 percent of the nation's work force was unemployed at the time. *People were ready for change.*

Roosevelt won in an overwhelming triumph. He received 57.4 percent of the national popular vote. In West Virginia, Roosevelt received 375,550 votes, while Hoover retrieved 263,780 votes. Although Republicans had held strong membership in the state, Democrats were able to establish dominance in Logan County. That Democratic iron grip endures to this day.

Little did young Raymond Chafin know at the time that his life would eventually be dedicated to this political party that had just won the White House by a landslide.

If You Cut Your Finger Off, Sell It

Through experiences such as delivering groceries for the Junior Mercantile, Chafin was likely gaining valuable people skills that would eventually serve as a catalyst for his future in politics.

> Before long, I knew just about everybody. When I was 14, 15, and 16 years old, I was still doing the same ol' thing — helping Daddy deliver groceries; then they moved me inside the store.

The head butcher, a strong, stocky man named R. W. "Bob" Buskirk, who lived up on the hill from the powerhouse, had a big apple orchard at the back of his place.

> In my spare time, I would go up and pick apples for him. That made him like me! Another butcher on the company payroll at the time was Ike Reed, a kindly black gentleman from the Omar area.

Together, Buskirk and Reed made sure that the meat shop ran efficiently and customers who shopped at Junior Mercantile were well tended to.

Because of the friendship Chafin had already cultivated with Buskirk, the skilled meat cutter took the young lad under his wing. Before long Chafin was working part-time in the meat department, and the two butchers taught him nearly everything they knew about their craft.

"If you go and cut a finger off, be sure you sell it, too," Buskirk would mischievously whisper to Chafin. Then the two would laugh and tease one another about the idea of selling body parts through the meat department.

Bob had a sense of humor. He ran a good butcher shop, and he trained a lot of fellows in this county. Bob lived in an area called Buskirk Addition, named after his people. I suspect he liked me a lot. He was also a friend to Dad. Luckily, I never lost any fingers during that time.

Getting a Driving License

Whether working in the general store, doing menial chores, or running errands for the boss, Chafin learned to find a certain amount of pleasure in his work. It was during this period of time that he began to admire the young women who worked at Junior Mercantile.

Chafin did little things for everybody in the store. If any of the girls wanted something, he'd run and do it. He might run to the post office or deliver groceries. Every once in a while he would even "story a little bit — tell a few white lies — for 'em, too." Any one of the teenage girls who worked with Chafin might secretly tell him that she was going to go to someone's house for a little while and ask him to cover for her while she was out. Chafin would smile shyly and say, "Ah ... well — okay. I'll do it just this one time."

Chafin recalled the days at the company store:

I loved working at Junior Mercantile, and I loved all the folks I worked with. It was like a big family. I was so loyal that if someone had as much as a can of cream in their home and it didn't come from the Junior Mercantile Store, I didn't think it was any good at all. I felt that strong about their store.

Finally, I got to makin' 'round two dollars a day. This is when I had pretty well grown up, and I first got my operator's card. I took my driving test at Logan and passed my examination the first time. I was probably 16 or 17 years old then. On the day I was old enough to get 'em — I got 'em.

Fellows at Junior Mercantile told me, "Son, we're going to let you drive our new truck now, because you've got your operator's card."

So, I started driving a delivery truck – still carrying groceries up the hollow.

In the meantime, since his father now delivered furniture, Raymond Chafin also learned how to wrap home furnishings to get them ready to be delivered.

The company store eventually had a man quit on the furniture delivery route. When he quit, Chafin started riding on the truck and delivering furniture full-time.

The Junior Mercantile furniture manager during that time was F. C. "Fred" Hensley. Chafin discussed the store in more detail:

Hensley was a good salesman and a good ol' man. He originally worked for the furniture store in Logan, and management transferred Fred to Omar to be in charge. We had the second, third, and fourth floor full of furniture, accessories, and everything else. It was well stocked. We sold anything you wanted for the house. Besides furniture, we had room-size rugs — 10 x 12s and 12 x 12s; we didn't know what carpeting was back then. We also had rolls of linoleum.

The store had cook stoves, including the ol' loaf stove. They had several different kinds of stoves. One had a warming closet in the front. You could put your water in there. Women would buy this type of stove so they could keep their water hot all the time. When their men would come in from the mine, they'd have hot water waiting for 'em. You have to remember, they didn't have any bathtubs or shower stalls in these houses back then. You used a No. 3 tub.

The other style of loaf stove had the [water] tank in the back. That was designed so you'd always have hot water, too. Most the time we sold this kind. You had to watch about that one with the tank [or warming closet] in the front because the water would get too hot from being near the fire too long," he remembered. "They also had one with a warming closet on top of the stove. It had two big levers that came down, and you could keep anything you wanted nice and warm on those. Then I remember when they came out with a new one that was called the buffet-type stove. That one was the prettiest thing you have ever seen. We got those in by the boxcar load.

The train engineer would bring a whole boxcar and back it into the store on the delivery tracks. At that time I was pretty stout, and several of us boys would take two-wheel carts and unload those heavy stoves, moving them from the boxcar to the elevator. We then took them all up to the fourth floor and set two or three of them up for demonstration.

When we delivered a cook stove, we'd take it out of the store in a wooden crate 'cause we could handle it much easier. We'd set it up for the customer, and we'd even install the stovepipe. Boy, we'd wipe it clean — it would sparkle — and then we'd give a home demonstration and made sure the woman liked it. Of course, as I think back on it, the ladies probably knew much more 'bout the stove than we did, and they just let us go through the motions anyway to entertain them. But we fancied ourselves as real salesmen at the time.

When someone was off at another company store, I would go and fill in.

The Omar manager might say, "Hey! Raymond, why don't you go down to the Rossmore Company Store today? They need a butcher!"

One day I might be the butcher, and the next time I might be the store clerk. If a store manager somewhere els e would take a vacation, they'd send me down to that location to fill in.

Chapter Five

They'd Point at the Chicken; I'd Fetch It

It might be said that a coal company store was the mall of yesteryear. It was the center of activity for a bustling coal town.

One reason the company store was so popular was that it offered free delivery to the homes in town and the surrounding area twice each day. Any size order could be delivered, from a small jar of jelly to several fifty-pound bags of pinto beans or flour.

Before the advent of the electric refrigerator, the store wagon or truck also delivered blocks of ice to the homes for iceboxes. Like a scene out of *The Pied Piper of Hamlin*, playful neighborhood children would run alongside the ice wagon in the summer months, drawn to the vehicle, hoping to catch a chunk of melting ice as the wagon bumped and jostled along the dirt roadway.

There was no such thing as self-service at the Junior Mercantile. Clerks waited on customers from the time they entered the front double doors, and the butcher cut or ground their meat to order. Floor workers filled orders and replenished the stock on the shelves. Service was foremost at the company-owned store.

In the butcher department there was a thin layer of sawdust thrown on the floor to absorb spills.

Through the 1920s and 1930s, the store was the only building in town that had a working elevator. It was normally used to hoist heavy boxes and other supplies from the basement and first floor to the upper floors.

The Boy Scouts of America, local baseball teams, lodge halls, and churches — mainly of the Pentecostal, Church of Christ, and Freewill Baptist denominations — would often hold bake sales on the wood-slat porch outside the store. Women of the town might prepare their best lemon or apple pies, chocolate cakes, sugar cookies, and other confections and take them to the porch, where they would be sold to shoppers.

Junior Mercantile also had a medical clinic and drugstore.

Meats and sale items were taken to another store location at Chauncey from the Omar company store, including pork chops and most sandwich meats. Chafin explained that it was rare for any store to sell T-bone or other steaks at the time, although the mine bosses and physicians did purchase steaks and better cuts of meat often by special order. Chafin chuckled and explained that everybody liked chicken at the time, and recalled the matter:

> In those days we didn't know what it was to have a dressed chicken [killed, plucked, packaged, and ready to be cooked]. Actually, nobody even wanted a dressed hen. They wanted to see and inspect the [live] chickens. They would choose their bird from the chicken lot. A couple of us boys would take the customer downstairs, they'd point out which hen they wanted, and we'd fetch that chicken and bring it upstairs and weigh it.
>
> Then when this area got a bit uppity in society, the Omar store started dressing their chickens. We'd go catch fifteen, twenty, or twenty-five of 'em and put them in a wooden crate. We had an old black lady working for us who lived over in Superior Bottom, a fine old woman named Miss Sawyers. She would

clean the chickens with the help of neighborhood ladies. The chickens would be plucked clean as a pin.

It was downright comical on some days to watch us boys chase those fat hens around the downstairs chicken coop. They would cluck, flap their wings, and race around in circles to avoid us. But we didn't give up. Eventually we would get our hands on the chicken as the customers stood in the corner of the chicken coop and roared with laughter at our antics.

When we started offering dressed chickens, the butcher placed the packaged fryers, wrapped in white butcher paper, in ice-cooled refrigerators, much like they do today. It wasn't too long after the Omar store started dressing their chickens that other stores in the area started taking notice and became interested in the process.

When Chafin was a child, there were many more folks in the Island Creek area than there are today. Back then, the house numbers started at 500 on the right-hand fork of Pine Creek, from Omar on up the wooded hollow, and they ended at 593 — standing for 93 houses and families in the neighborhood. No houses ever stood empty. Nearly everyone was working in the mines. Chafin explained:

When you went up the left-hand fork of Pine Creek, there was the No. 6 Mine. The house numbers started at 600, ending up at 645, meaning there were another 45 houses on the left fork. Some of the houses were double houses, or duplexes. Of course, the coalmines owned all of the houses in the area.

Four Hundred Hill started below the Junior Mercantile, and the house numbers started at 300 and ran up the hill. They ran up to about 345. Then when you came up above the town of Omar, those houses ran up to the Omar Bridge; the house numbers were in the 500s, too — and hooked into the Pine Creek numbers. When I was delivering groceries there was only a one-lane wagon road all through the area.

You wouldn't even want to see how I sometimes turned that grocery wagon around on that narrow road on a cliffside. There were four rough lanes that broke off from the main road at Four Hundred Hill, so I had to slip that wagon up the lane, drop off the groceries, and come back out to the main road again.

Nearly all of these households had large families. It wasn't strange to see a man and his wife with four or five children living in a four-room company house — sleeping on couches, on chairs, and on the wooden floor.

You'd be surprised how many families would order a one-hundred-pound bag of pinto beans back then. Now, that's a lot of beans!

At the mouth of Pine Creek, the company had a boardinghouse on each side of the road. Each boarding home housed a certain nationality of people — Italian, Hungarian, Irish, and a bunch of others.

Each of these boarding projects held some two-dozen or so boarders who were either unmarried or didn't have any other place to go. The "Boarding Miss" — the woman who was over the house — was usually responsible for the main meals and basic housekeeping. She was also in charge of ousting unruly renters and maintaining order. Chafin recalled some of the residents:

> I remember that a few of these boarders were really bad to drink. If they got too loud and out of control, they'd find themselves homeless. However, there were some landladies who would offer the drinking men in the boardinghouse one shot of their favorite liquor each night to keep down trouble. The funniest thing was that this was also going on during Prohibition. Booze and white lightnin' were plentiful in our region; alcohol flowed freely at the boardinghouses!

Once a tenant was thrown out of a boardinghouse for bad conduct, he had few options. He might be able to keep his job. However, he would never be allowed to rent another room or tract from West Virginia Coal and Coke. His only option was to search for affordable housing outside the company. This was no easy task.

Many of the foreign workers in the boardinghouses didn't have their citizenship papers. Groups of men would sit on the porches at night, smoking pipes and chatting with one another. Few could speak English when they arrived at the mines, so they immediately started trying to learn the language.

> Besides the two that I remember at Pine Creek, there were two foreign-born houses — boardinghouses — on Four Hundred Hill, also.
>
> I can remember taking two cases of Italian bread and a whole case of eggs to one Italian boardinghouse every time I went to the hill. I also took two rolls of minced ham – 'cause we didn't know what bologna was back then — just for the boarders.
>
> Mayonnaise had just come out in that time period, and they seemed to love the stuff. Besides all that, I took French's Mustard in a large glass jar, along with several one-pound bags of coffee and flour.

Red Star Flour

One time Chafin was working inside the company store with Bill Mullins, a longtime employee. Oftentimes Chafin toiled on the first floor and helped customers until his delivery list was ready. He said that at that time there were several "big shots" who regularly shopped at the store.

On this particular day, these older women walked into the store to buy pinto beans. They were always meticulously attired in expensive lace-trimmed dresses, matching dark polka-dot print turbans embellished with decorative feathers, and the finest black, high-top, shiny-leather dress shoes. Their strong perfume lingered in the air as they walked through the aisles. Their sweet-smelling cologne was so overpowering that the neighborhood dog — a flea-infested mongrel that hung around the store — would get up and walk off the porch every time they came to shop.

All the pinto beans had been bagged in brown paper sacks, ready to sell at five cents a pound. Especially suspicious of the young grocery worker, a lady named Mildred said she wanted a certain amount of beans, then snarled at Chafin, "Whoa there, sonny. I want to see the goods I'm fixin' to buy. That's my right, isn't it?"

Chafin smiled and dutifully opened the sack for Mildred, pouring a few of the hard, speckled brown beans into his hand.

"How's that?" Chafin asked. "They're A-No. 1 pinto beans, ma'am."

"Sonny, pinto beans will turn colors on ya. If a pinto bean is fresh, it's light in color. But if it's an old pinto bean, it will be dark-colored. OK, these look OK. I'll take 'em," she said.

Chafin quickly bagged up her order.

"We also want a couple of twelve-pound bags of Red Star flour, lil' sonny boy," Mildred added, with a nasal whine. After making her request, she arrogantly cocked and twisted her head as if to point her nose toward the ceiling, and folded her arms. She stood absolutely rigid with her padded shoulders pushed back and chest heaved out for emphasis as she waited for him to comply.

"What a snooty thing," Chafin thought to himself as he glanced at her.

The store carried two brands of flour: Queen Quality and Red Star. Red Star was more expensive, since it was enriched. Unfortunately they were out of Red Star, but they had plenty of the cheaper brand.

"We might be out of Red Star. Would Queen Quality do?" Chafin asked as pleasantly as he could.

"Sonny, I would *never* buy that other brand; that ol' cheap stuff ain't worth two plug nickels! We intelligent Omar women like Red Star — period. You best have Red Star or else I want to see the manager."

"Yessum," Chafin replied nervously. "Let me check in the back room one more time."

He walked back to the storeroom where Mullins was. Exasperated, he asked Mullins if the Red Star flour shipment had come in yet, saying, "Bill, I gots me a problem out on the floor. This uppity-uppity is wantin' Red Star, or else."

"Nope, Raymond, we're out — no can do," Mullins replied. "Who is the woman, anyway?" he asked, peeking his head around the door to catch a glimpse of the group of ladies. "Oh, it's MILDRED. All of those ladies give me fits. Mildred is the worst. Well, we'll just fix her wagon this time!

"Chafe, go tell Mildred and the rest of those biddies that the truck will be here in a little bit, and we'll bring their Red Star over to them within the hour," Mullins ordered as he chuckled.

Even though he was confused, Chafin went back out on the floor and told Mildred that he and another worker would deliver the flour, along with the other groceries, in an hour or so, after the warehouse truck arrived.

The ladies fussed and grumbled among themselves, until Mildred finally answered, "Fine, sonny, but it better be an hour, or we'll be back. You hear me?"

They then left the store in a huff, clomping loudly with every step against the marred pinewood flooring.

In the meantime, Mullins found two empty Red Star bags in the back room. He then got two ten-pound Queen Quality sacks of flour.

Mullins slowly poured the less expensive brand into the Red Star bags. He tied the two containers with red string. They both laughed at what they were about to do.

"But what if she can tell the difference?" Chafin asked Mullins, as the laughter died and he started to ponder the situation. "She says this Queen Quality isn't worth anything!"

"We'll face that problem later. Watch what happens," Mullins answered, as he cackled.

About forty-five minutes later, Chafin grabbed the sacks of the flour and the other groceries, with Mullins assisting him. They walked over to Mildred's house first, because it was near the store.

When they reached Mildred's, she opened the door, smiling.

"Thank you, young men. Right on time, I see," she said, as the two placed the bags of groceries on her kitchen table. "I'll split up the flour and take it to my girlfriends a little later. I just love that Red Star. Here's a penny for each of you for your trouble. Now skedaddle."

The two men looked at each other sheepishly and walked out of the house. As soon as her door closed, they both burst out laughing and walked back to the store.

"Whoa, Nelly! I hope she doesn't taste the difference, or we're sunk," Chafin said, as he chuckled. "It'll be an awful day for both of us if'n she does. Mildred will surely throw herself a fit!"

Several days later, Mildred came back up the steps to the store to pick up a few odds and ends. This time she was alone. Mullins saw her coming and nudged Chafin, who was mindlessly sweeping the pinewood floor near the vegetable boxes.

When she walked inside, Mullins greeted her, and she smiled and began looking at the produce.

"Excuse me, ma'am. Remember when we got that fresh order of Red Star the last time you were here? Do you know everybody's been braggin' on it? How 'bout you, ma'am?" Mullins said to her, with an innocent look on his face.

"Oh, my goodness, son! It's so much better than I even remembered!" she said, with a broad grin. "I want to thank you boys for makin' sure it was fresh, extra fresh! All the girls have remarked about it."

Chafin dropped his broom, ran back to the warehouse, and burst out in laughter. Several weeks later, when the ladies were ready to order again, they had real Red Star flour.

Neither of the boys ever told any of them what happened — especially not Mildred.

Exterminators

Milled flour was intermittently shipped into the Barnabus warehouse in one-hundred-pound bags. From there, the bags were taken to the company store and placed on the floor. Tall, tightly woven mesh-wire screens, framed in wood, were built around the flour display so that the rats couldn't get into the flour bags.

Store managers were in a precarious situation. Much of the food was not packaged, and it was displayed openly. The customers were afraid of buying food if they thought the store put out rat poison, fearing the possibility that a rat might carry the poison back into the food bins. Therefore, the company store operators had few options when it came to extermination efforts.

In addition to the wire screens, rattraps were placed around the store, but their effectiveness was limited. Most of the time the store used an even more interesting form of pest control, according to Chafin:

> To control the rodents, after Junior Mercantile closed every evening, the night watchman would shoot the vermin in the store with a .22-caliber rifle. Then he'd throw the carcasses in the creek before morning. For fun, sometimes residents who lived near the store would come down and shoot the mice and river rats they saw running around outside near the loading dock.

Before Collection Agencies

In the 1920s, '30s, and '40s, the company stores operated scrip offices, which simulated a credit system, of sorts, long before there were Visa, MasterCard, or American Express cards. Most miners had little choice but to buy on credit from the company store. Few other stores were available, or as well stocked, in the southern West Virginia coal camps and mining communities.

There were, by and large, two means of credit at a company store. One was the slip system, in which items purchased, along with their cost, were recorded on a duplicate sales slip kept by the company store's bookkeeping office. At the end of a pay period, all or part of the bill was deducted from the coal miner's pay. If work had been sluggish, some of the credit could be carried over to the next pay period. This process often kept the coal miner in arrears to the company store and the coal company, as was referred to in Tennessee Ernie Ford's early 1960s classic, in the line: "I owe my soul to the company store."

The second method was the company store check. The checks were issued in amounts of one dollar, two dollars, and so on up to ten dollars, and were a form of company scrip. The company store check could be punched for any purchase from one cent to one dollar. This hole was punched so that the remaining value of the check could be determined. The amounts of all the checks drawn in a pay period were then deducted from the miner's pay.

While the intent of the check was for the purchase of food and other necessary items at the company store, often miners who found themselves strapped for cash misused the checks. They could draw a check and then sell it for quick cash to someone with ready money.

In some situations a company check, metal coinage, and paper scrip were issued instead of a legitimate payday altogether. Therefore, the company store became a tidy little moneymaking venture as well as an unusual workforce control system. Chafin remembered:

> At West Virginia Coal and Coke, miners and their families had to wait until the first of the half — a two-week period of time — to see how they ended up. So on the first day of the half, I've seen as many as fifty people lined up with their scrip card at the scrip office, to see how much they could get. That came twice a month, on the first of the month and on the sixteenth day of the month.

Tough Boys

On the first of the half, the scrip writer calculated out how much a family spent for the preceding two weeks. And they took out all the stoppage and figured out how much cash one would receive on the next payday.

When an employee went to the office to have your payday calculated, the scrip writer was basically telling you how much you could draw in advance, against your payday. If you wanted that advance immediately, the company would pay you in its own paper currency — scrip — in one-dollar denominations. Chafin said:

> The way you got change was when you used your paper scrip to purchase something for an uneven amount. For example, if you bought a pound of potatoes for thirty-five cents, you would hand the clerk a dollar in paper scrip. The clerk would give you change in coal company coinage — dimes, nickels, pennies, and fifty-cent pieces in metallic scrip. Folks would stand in line in order to give their scrip card to a scrip writer. For example, the writer might figure it all out, and you might get four dollars, after your deductions. If you got four dollars, you could get a whole lot of groceries.
>
> Stoppage included other expenses to be deducted from your pay, such as your doctor bill, hospital bill, rent, and the price of a load of coal. They would also sell furniture from the company store, and they took that payment out of your payday twice a month. By the 1930s, West Virginia Coal and Coke produced its own electric power, too, so a coalminer's power bill was also deducted from the payroll. Putting it all together, miners hardly made a thing after the deductions. It was a very greedy system.
>
> Before a man could buy furniture at the company store, he would be questioned by the Junior Mercantile salesperson, somewhat like a credit check. A miner was asked whom he owed besides the company. Then he was asked about his company doctor bills and how much coal he recently bought from the mine for heating.
>
> The salesman would then figure out how much a miner made altogether. He then subtracted stoppage and other deductions from his payroll. After all this, most miners had very little money left, if any. So the salesperson might ask a miner if he could pay a dollar or two a month until the bill was paid off. A contract was signed, and if it was approved, still another deduction was made from the payroll. The salesman gave the paperwork to the store manager. Then the manager would call the mine superintendent to verify if the man was a good worker and making enough hours to make such a purchase. If everything worked out, he was able to make the purchase.

The sad part is the way the company would raise prices on furniture and other items in the store. It's been said that a miner and his family might pay four or five times what the items cost the company. So really, in the long run, the company was never paying a coalminer. A coalminer gave his payday back to the company and usually owed the employer a great deal more when it was all said and done. It had been likened to slavery before the United Mine Workers came to this area. In the early days of the UMW, it was still tough for families. But with UMW's help, it eventually changed.

If you had money on the sixteenth of the month and you didn't draw it out until the next payday, you'd draw that in cash. Sadly, most men had little if any legitimate American currency to bring home.

Chafin nervously tapped the arm of his chair and rolled his eyes in revulsion as he continued the interview:

> You might see as many as fifteen or twenty bill collectors come outside the company store each payday, like vultures circling and waiting for a meal. Their vehicles waited in the lot in the center of Omar, with large signs leaning against the front fenders. The signs told bystanders what business they represented. Local stores such as Lewis Furniture Company and Beckett Furniture, and other companies from Logan and Williamson were present. They were like daggone turkey buzzards waiting for a fresh carcass.

These traveling accountants worked for merchants in close-by towns that had extended credit to West Virginia Coal and Coke miners. They waited outside their vehicles, usually with account books lying open on the hood of the car or truck. They waited for the men to come out of the store with their paycheck, ready to nab them before they had a chance to spend.

"Hey, wait a minute there, George," a collector might yell at a coalminer as he stepped out the door of Junior Mercantile. Then the collector would run over to the worker and ask him how he did on his payday.

"Son, you need to settle up with us befo' you head to the house! You done bought our furniture; now it's time to pay fer it."

"I didn't draw nothin' this time," the miner often replied to the collector.

"Overdraft!" another miner would yell to the collection representative as he was hustled by the bookkeepers.

The collector would likely frown and nod his head in disgust while checking off the miner's name in his black book as he hollered, "Catch you next half — and you better have a payment ready!"

Chafin realized at a young age that it stole a man's dignity to have bill collectors publicly waiting at the company store as he picked up his paycheck.

A great deal of commotion surrounded the act of collecting a coalminer's hard-earned payday. With multiple collectors and bookkeepers barking out names in the parking lot, scrip writers quickly double-checking their books inside, company store clerks hurriedly filling food and merchandise orders, and the miners going to and fro in town with their families, Island Creek took on a carnival-like atmosphere for two days out of every month.

Unfortunately for many miners, they would go all the way into town to find out that they got a red mark scratched across their check, meaning that they owed money to the company — overdraft! Therefore, they would have to do without or borrow against the next pay period — digging deeper and deeper in the cavernous pit of poverty.

Stirrat and Omar were the only two places where West Virginia Coal and Coke paid its men at the time. A Logan County constable was always on duty to guard the payroll at the two sites as the men came in to collect their wages. The constable also had to keep order among the bill collectors and the mine employees. On occasion, miners who were under a great deal of stress would erupt in a flurry of words and fists when the accountants approached them. Chafin added:

> Miners worked three shifts in the early days, loading coal by hand. I remember that a couple of boards hung across the railroad track, suspended by rusty chains at the tipple. The boards hung level, horizontally, quite a few feet above the traincar. When the men loaded that car, they knew that they better fill the car up to the height that was level with that hanging board, or they were docked on their payday.
>
> The company may have paid the men a dollar a car at the time, never much more. If there happened to be slate mixed in with the coal, the company docked the workers, paying them half the normal wage. There was no overtime or time and a half for extra work until the union came in. After twelve or thirteen hours of continuous work on a busy shift, you saw the men slow way down.
>
> Up until the United Mine Workers took control, the men were paid straight time, regardless of how long they worked. It was pretty tough on the coalminers and their families.

Being a rambunctious teenager who was employed by a busy store was never easy, but it had its rewards. Chafin said that his political career might never have started if not for his position at the company store. He explained:

> You know there were at least ten of these Junior Mercantile stores back when I was a boy, all in places where West Virginia Coal and Coke had coalmines. They were all near small West Virginia communities, such as Omar, Lyburn, Rossmore, Monaville, Micco, and an especially small one at Chauncey. All of these company operations were stocked out of a warehouse near the Omar store, at little Barnabus, West Virginia.

T. A. Obenshain, the local overseer of the Omar store, was a man the young Chafin learned to love and respect. Manager Obenshain had only one arm, so Chafin would often help carry his groceries to his home on Four Hundred Hill. He would also work in Obenshain's yard, mowing his grass with an old push mower. He also pulled weeds and cleared stones from the property. Chafin chuckled, as he continued:

> That old mower weighed approximately forty-five pounds with its steel cylinder of blades, wood handle, and heavy cast-iron wheels. It was definitely a chore to push it 'round Obenshain's lot. Of course it was before the days of motorized lawnmowers. Ugly blisters turned into hard calluses as I jerked and shoved that mower across his lawn.

Young Chafin was much like his father, Elbert. He was able to do nearly everything at the company store. Elbert — before his debilitating illness – was a man with a strong work ethic and a bullheaded nature that drove him onward. He worked the family farm, delivered groceries, carried furniture, helped in the butcher shop, and was a jack-of-all-trades around the store.

Besides delivering victuals to customers, Elbert was also known for carrying ceramic jugs of moonshine on the delivery wagon, which he kept neatly covered by a worn canvas tarp. Most customers knew that jolly old Elbert always had several gallons of high-quality corn liquor stashed on the rig for any customer who wanted to pay the price. Apparently, many did. A gallon of moonshine cost around three dollars at the time. Although Chafin's father never made illegal liquor, it was well known that he delivered the product for area still owners. Chafin snickered as he explained:

They trusted ol' Dad. They knew he carried the good stuff. And a lot of the best moonshiners and rumrunners up and down the creek liked him, too, because he got them cash. Poppy never really made any money off of it, to speak of, but he sure made a lot of friends.

A Girl Loses Her Life; Chafin Blackballed

Things were going well for Chafin by the time he was 18 years old. He was working. He wasn't particularly wealthy, but he had just bought a used car — a yellow 1924 Pontiac — with wire-spoke wheels and two big spare tires, one braced on each fender. The jalopy had a convertible top and roll-up windows in the doors. It resembled something you might see Al Capone or Pretty Boy Floyd driving in a History Channel documentary.

Chafin also went to great lengths to look the part of a proud driver. Before he took the Pontiac out on the roadway, he would slick back his coarse brown hair with witch hazel and sprinkle men's cologne on his undershirt. Chafin dressed in his cleanest white shirt, pleated tweed slacks, and brown wingtips from the company store.

He sat far back in the driver's seat while cocking his chin forward. With his left arm fully extended, he tightly gripped the steering wheel and slowly cruised around the area after work hours. His right hand was free to gently shift gears as he maneuvered down the narrow streets of Omar, Chauncey, and Switzer. He was certainly something to see "on the Creek." It was during this time period that teenage girls living on Island Creek began to notice Chafin.

Then a tragedy happened that changed his run of good fortune and his future with Junior Mercantile. Chafin recalled the horrible mishap:

One Sunday in the summer of 1935, I was in an awful car accident. I was the passenger in a car with a friend. We were headed to the traveling Grand Ole Opry, which was putting on three big outdoor shows in Omar that day.

When the two arrived, the first country and western show was too crowded. So they tried to attend the second show, but arrived at Omar too late.

So we went home and started in on a gallon of white lightnin'. Later, we decided to go up the road where I could get a piece of equipment for my car, which had broken down. By this time neither one of us should have been on the highway. We were liquored up pretty good.

Tough Boys

While he and his friend were coming up over a small knoll, their car swerved and slammed into another vehicle topping the hill. The two teenagers hit that car head-on.

There was a terrible impact as the sound of scraping metal and screeching tires overpowered the dreadful shrieks from within the two automobiles. Chafin remembered bracing himself and crying out with a loud scream as the car rammed the other automobile and then rolled over on its side, skidding down the roadway. Chafin's spindly arms buckled from the impact, and his body was thrown over the front seat, landing him upside down on the floorboard of the backseat of the automobile.

> By the time the car came to a dead stop, I was the one injured the worst in our car. I got all banged and crippled up — thrown around pretty good. I hit my head terribly hard, and it instantly fractured my skull. Both of my legs were busted up badly and my neck was broken. Both of my eyes were a mess. My buddy was knocked around, too. However, he was in much better shape than I was.
>
> I later found out that a prominent doctor from the Welch, West Virginia, area had been driving the other car involved in the head-on. He had been innocently traveling through our region with his family on that day. His daughter was killed instantly when our cars collided.

At the hospital, doctors decided to put a metal plate in Chafin's head, which he still wears sixty-some years later. The surgeons were afraid that the severe damage to his eyes would blind him for life. Fortunately, they were wrong, though he still bears many of the deep scars.

The death of the girl affected Chafin a great deal once he fully realized what had happened. He deeply regretted drinking and going out with his friend that day.

> Even though it was so long ago, I still remember the emotions I felt from that time period; I felt solely responsible for that young one's death. I was the one who urged my friend to drive that day. I participated in drinking heavily. If I had refused to drink the 'shine, I figure that neither one of us would have been in that wreck and that young girl would have lived.
>
> I was off work quite a bit of time, nearly all the summer, over that, laid up in Logan General Hospital in Logan. I had plenty of time to think while I was strapped down to the bed. After a long recuperation process, I was finally released, and I tried to go back to the store. Ol' Obenshain was goin' to let me c'mon back so that I could try to help my dad and mother. We didn't have anything [savings] to live on at the time, since my father had recently become sick.

37

Chapter Six

Elbert Diagnosed With Cancer

While Chafin was in the hospital, his father had been diagnosed with prostate cancer. Because of his illness, he was unable to continue at the Junior Mercantile and was forced into early retirement. Chafin now felt that it was his duty to earn an income, to "keep food on the table and a shelter over the family's heads."

A few years earlier, Chafin had quit junior high school to devote himself to full-time employment at the company store. Now, with his father laid up at home, he must have felt even greater pressure to work, since he had become the sole breadwinner for the house. He realized that his dream of returning to the classroom was unlikely.

> I was the only source of income we had. So, yes, I recall that I went back to work by fall. While I had been laid up, there had been a change in management at Junior Mercantile. Obenshain's boss was now S.C. Pohe, an extremely heavyset man from Cincinnati who was now the vice president of all Junior Mercantile stores.
>
> Pohe came in to look over the place, then went upstairs to talk with Mr. Obenshain on the second day after I returned to work. From where I was sweeping the floor below, I could see Mr. Pohe talking and pointing down at me. I sensed there was something wrong. As soon as Pohe left – maybe thirty minutes later – the manager called me up to his office.

Chafin nervously made his way up the worn, unvarnished wood steps that led to the manager's cluttered desk. He paced into Obenshain's office, walked up to him, and smiled. A somber-looking Obenshain motioned for him to take a seat. This was one of the few times he wasn't "all smiles."

"Raymond, I'm so sorry," Obenshain said as he shook his head in true pity. "You have been like family to me. Raymond, I have to do something that I hate to do. I've got to let you go! Mr. Pohe says that due to that accident that was responsible for that girl's death, you are no longer eligible to work on these premises. So you don't work here anymore."

A stunned Chafin sat there speechless. Finally, he nodded as he hung his head low and took off his work apron. He grabbed up his few belongings and quietly left the building. Obenshain walked him to the edge of the store's property, patted him on the back, and said, "Raymond, good luck, son. Good luck. Stop by and see us every once in a while, OK?"

Chafin remembered:

> They fired me. It was that simple. Deep down I really didn't think there was any store like Junior Mercantile. I thought that it was the only place to work. So it hurt a lot. A big part of my life was over.

When Chafin got home, he told his family what had happened at the store that day. "Uh, Poppy, I really don't know what I've done," Chafin said.

"Son, come on in here and let me talk to you," Elbert said to Chafin angrily.

At that moment he hollered at his wife, Lucinda, "Get out of here, Mrs. Chafin. I want to talk to him — man to man!

"Son, I'm goin' to tell you what happened to you," Elbert continued. "Everybody in the world liked you and helped you along. One reason was because of me. I always got along with everybody and tried to satisfy everybody. The other reason was that you were humble and respectful. Well, now look at you!

"I once told you to never know more than your boss. Well, let me explain. It is actually OK to know more than your boss, but don't let him know it and don't tell other people that you're smarter. You keep it to yourself. You keep it all upstairs in your noggin! By gosh, that's what happened to you, boy! You got to knowin' more than your boss or anybody, and nobody could tell you anythin'. Strong-headed and strong-willed, that's what I call you! You're too dang irresponsible, and you think you know it all. Then you started drinkin' with the boys from up the holler. Look what happened to you in that accident. Irresponsible!" he shouted.

Chafin recalled:

This is why Dad wanted my mother out of the room. He wanted to give me down-the-road. And he really gave me a good one that day!

But after I came to my senses, I decided I wouldn't have any problem gettin' me another job. I've got all of this experience, I thought. So I started going out to mines and tipples.

My dad was always the best of friends with everybody, and I was, too. Shoot, I had delivered groceries to every mine superintendent and tipple boss around these parts. They all knew me, and they all knew how hard I worked. I went to see each of them, and each of them would say, "Come back. Come back in a month. We ain't hiring today."

Finally, I went up to No. 5 mine. This was the third time I had gone there. There was a man up there by the name of Martin Amburgey, who was the tipple boss. I went in and said, "Mr. Amburgey, I'm back. Do you have anything I can do yet?"

Mr. Amburgey motioned for Chafin to walk into a side office, for privacy, as he whispered, "Raymond, sonny, come back here for a moment. I want to talk to you for a minute or two. I'm goin' to tell you something, but if you tell this, they'll fire me sure as I'm lookin' at you."

"Well, what is it?" Chafin, now puzzled, asked him.

"Sonny, you're just wastin' your time. The company has blackballed you. Ol' Man Pohe has called all the mine owners and foremen around these parts and told everyone that you are blackballed because you were drunk and in a car wreck. He told everyone about the young girl who lost her life needlessly. You can't get a job, Raymond. You might as well know it."

Chafin later found out that Mr. Pohe had been a close friend of the Welch doctor and his family who were in the accident.

Chafin wiped his brow with his hand, and remembered:

It was a sad and awful mess of a time. I was hurtin', and I didn't know what I was gonna do. I wore my shoes out tryin' to find a job. After a while, nobody would even talk to me when I would try to apply for a job. It was a dead end.

Now that Chafin was told that he was singled out — blackballed — he felt like a man with a gigantic "X" on his forehead, a marked man. He wondered if he could ever resume a normal life and work in West Virginia again.

Keno Found Murdered

Raymond Chafin was caught in a vise of difficult circumstances. With each crisis, the pressure grew tighter. The mental load that he carried at the time was horrific.

First of all, he realized that since he was the oldest son and his dad, Elbert, was unable to work due to prostate cancer, he desperately needed to help out. Even though Chafin felt "especially responsible for keeping up the home place," the truth was that he was a scared teenager who had just lost his job and knew work was going to be hard to find. He now had an ugly reputation in the county, thanks mostly to S.C. Pohe. He become known as a reckless drunkard who killed a helpless young girl.

Regardless of whether any mine, tipple, or store in the area had a job opening, the Cow Creek teen seemed to be one step behind Pohe and his mission to undercut his job search.

Blackballed.

Because of friends, the Chafin family never went hungry. However, day-to-day living was incredibly difficult for the household. Chafin discussed the time period:

> As I remember it, I fooled around all summer, and then winter came on. The family finally got on relief with a county agency called the RFC. My mother was able to get about eight dollars a week. We tried to make that stretch.
>
> We had no car or no way to get anywhere, either. By this time my Pontiac was broke down and there was no way that I could afford to get it on the road again. I ended up selling it for extra money. We had neighbors who helped us. One was a relative named Clifton Curry, who had married Dad's niece, Marie, and they lived just below us on the left fork of Cow Creek. Clifton took my mother to the store and places she needed to go.
>
> Dad was in the bed sick and could do very little for himself. Dad was still so well liked by the doctors at the company store that they would travel up Cow Creek, some three miles from their offices, to see him twice a week.

The relief officials in the county at that time were all Republicans. They made sure that the relief check was taken to stores where they had "friends" or where they needed favors. According to Chafin, U. G. Browning was the Republican living in "his neck of the woods." Therefore, he got all the government business. To refuse to shop at a Republican friend's store could have meant denial of the assistance check, so Chafin's mother complied.

The Works Progress Administration (WPA) was starting around that time. To be eligible, somebody had to work. I knew I would have to go to work with the WPA crew. I had been a big shot down at Omar – at least I thought so at the time. I had been driving a truck, delivering furniture, and everything else. Now I was going to the WPA.

The WPA was the U.S. work program for the unemployed, created in 1935 under Franklin D. Roosevelt's New Deal. The plan behind the WPA was to energize the economy during the Great Depression and to preserve the expertise and self-respect of unemployed persons by providing them with useful work.

In all, the WPA employed 8.5 million people in the construction of 650,000 miles of roads, 75,000 bridges, 125,000 public buildings, 8,000 parks, and 800 airports. The WPA also administered a federal art project, a theater project, and a writer's project.

Artists were often commissioned to paint murals in post office facilities and state buildings. Others traveled and sketched and documented the hard times for the government. Theatrical projects and acting opportunities sprung up across the nation and traveling thespians entertained the masses.

Chafin suggested that there was a stigma connected with working for this government agency. Many working individuals "looked down on WPA workers" as if they were second-rate citizens or uneducated sluggards.

I don't remember exactly what the WPA check amount was, but it doesn't seem like it was too much. I think it might have been around seventy dollars a month. Being the oldest, I went to work on the WPA. It was my duty.

You know where the WPA put me? They put me at Superior Bottom carrying rocks. There's a rock wall standing behind Superior Bottom to this day. I helped build that wall. That was the most embarrassing time I reckon I ever had in my life. Kids can be awfully hard-hearted sometimes. You may not believe me now, but while I worked on that wall, they'd go by and point at me and laugh because I was barely employed and working a poor man's job.

"Ah, looky there, ha-ha-ha — poor boys, poor boys!" the children would holler, taunting the workers while riding their bikes by Chafin and the other men.

After one of those occasions, Chafin went home and in desperation talked to his father about it all.

"Dad," he said, "I'm gonna quit that WPA job. They're killing me! The kids are pointing and making fun of me. They call us poor boys and giggle as they ride by. It's humiliating."

Chafin's father thought for a minute and then recommended, "Raymond, when they go to laughing at you, you must wave back at them as you smile and speak to 'em. When they point and laugh, act like you like it! Grin and laugh along with them. If you call their names and speak to 'em, they'll leave ya alone."

Although Chafin decided to take his father's advice, he wasn't confident that his counsel would help.

Well, the next day the boys came back where we were working and I did exactly as Dad suggested. I waved, smiled, and acted like I enjoyed their sorry sense of humor. First thing you know they quit it. Dad was absolutely right!

Chafin said he carried rock on his back and worked on the Cow Creek Road for months. Not only was it a humbling experience just working for the agency, but worse still, he said, was the fact that hauling rock was the lowliest job the WPA had.

During Chafin's time spent on the WPA, he said he helped mix concrete for two bridges that are still used on Cow Creek. The concrete was mixed by hand. Chafin clarified that the WPA didn't have any of "them fancy mixers" at the time.

Chafin began helping mix the concrete for a third bridge. One day, Troy Perry and several younger workers were busy mixing concrete around 2 o'clock in the morning. Chafin recalled the moment:

> When you started constructing one of those bridges, you had to finish it even if it took all night. The WPA foremen would pick us younger guys 'cause we could stand the late hours and we could turn concrete with a shovel.
>
> That particular evening we had a fire built up, and we were eating our dinner around 3 o'clock in the morning. We were getting ready to finish the third bridge up Cow Creek. That's up where Logan County Sheriff Johnny Mendez now lives. I was so frustrated I blurted out, "Boys, this job is not for me! I'm gonna go get me a real job. Just watch and see!"
>
> Troy Perry scolded me and said, "We can't quit on this bridge now, Chafe. You can't let us down. We need your help."

"Well, uh ... OK, but I'm goin' to hunt me something else. Watch me," a frustrated Chafin mumbled as he strained to swallow his last bite of beans.

Workin' With One-Eyed Bill

Chafin woke up early the next morning and prepared for the day, but he wasn't dressed in his usual work clothes. As he walked into the kitchen for breakfast, his mother, puzzled over his dress, asked him if he was going to work. Chafin said, "No, I'm goin' huntin' fer work — fer a real job!"

This was around 1935, and Chafin knew that some men had started a small construction job on Island Creek. He had his eye on the group for several days and decided to go see the foreman to ask if they were signing anybody up for employment.

Chafin walked out of Cow Creek toward Stirrat, and eventually strutted all the way up to Crystal Block, a mile or more up the road. Sure enough, the company was hiring men to nap [pile] rock on the road. He walked into the company's office and asked the boss, Pat Holland, for a job. Holland stared at Chafin, looking him over from head to toe, and then said, "Where have you been workin'?"

"WPA," Chafin muttered, as he uneasily looked down at the dusty floor.

"What?"

"WPA, sir" Chafin said again in a stronger tone.

"You're awfully young to be working on the WPA, aren't ya, boy?" Holland asked.

"Yeah, I have to — for a check. My dad's really bad sick and I'm the oldest. Somebody has to support the household."

"Well, I'm goin' to give you a job nappin' rock," he told Chafin. Holland later revealed that he was surprised at Chafin's determination to support his family at his young age. Chafin pondered the time period and added:

> I remember that this small construction company was rebuilding the road from Crystal Block to the top of the hill, putting sand and gravel on the roadway. The construction boss was from Huntington, WV. He was an engineer who worked for Ira Hatfield of Hatfield Construction.

Chafin started immediately. He quickly decided piling rocks for a legitimate employer was a whole lot better than lugging them for the WPA. Even if the job was the same, at least he had his dignity back.

Every so often Holland would drive by while Chafin was in the middle of moving rocks. He'd roll down his car window, grin, and yell at the top of his lungs, "Give her hell, boy! By gosh, bust 'em, boy!"

> One day Holland came up to me and said, "Get in the car, Chafe!"
>
> I got in his car, and he asked, "You ever run a jackhammer before, Raymond Chafin?"
>
> "What is that? I never even seen me a jackhammer before," I answered.
>
> "C'mon, I'll show you, son," Holland replied, as he motioned for me to close the door of the car.

The construction boss took Chafin to a fellow by the name of Bill Chafin, a crusty old man who was no relation to the younger Chafin. They called him One-Eyed Bill because he had lost one eye in an accident on the job.

Holland got out of the car, sauntered over to Bill, chuckled, and said, "One-Eyed Bill, I've got a man here named Raymond Chafin, who can help you drill — if'n you can teach him what a drill is."

Bill was a disheveled, untidy, rough-and-tough looking character. When he attempted to look at someone, he squinted so hard that the right corner of his mouth drew up, making his entire face look lopsided and off-center. At some point in the distant past, Bill had lost an eye — probably on the worksite. But in spite of his unusual appearance, he was considered a master driller and one of the crew's best men to work with.

"Raymond, I gots to ask you one question: Will you work like a mule?" One-Eyed Bill asked Chafin somberly as he squinted at the lanky teenager.

Holland chimed in, "Raymond, it's ten cents more on the hour if you can drill, son."

"Okay," Chafin said. "Yup, I'll work all right! From now on, call me a driller!"

Chafin was making only thirty-five cents an hour piling rocks, so this represented a substantial raise. Besides, lifting rocks was not Chafin's cup of tea, and he was glad to hand that job over to someone else.

I wanted to get away from that rock pile anyway. I wanted to try that ol' jackhammer. I was determined to learn everything there was to know about drilling. I had watched these fellas before. I'd seen them drill as I went by 'em on my way to my job, even though I didn't want Holland to know I even knew what a jackhammer looked like. That ol' hammer would shake their innards out, but it looked like something I could do.

I got out of the car and helped Bill that day, and we did real good together. So we worked together from that day forward.

One day when One-Eyed Bill and Chafin had gotten ahead on the drilling, Holland happened to come by and, noticing they were resting, asked, "Raymond, have you ever been to Huntington?"

"Yes, Mr. Holland, one time," Chafin answered. "That was a while back, though."

"I have had problems sending these fellows here to get the checks," Holland said. "The payroll checks will be down at Hatfield Construction. There will be twenty-five checks, and you'll have to wait for the secretary to write 'em up. But you go get them for me, OK?"

Chafin recalled:

> He put me in a brand new Plymouth with all the extras. He scribbled out a map on a napkin, telling me precisely how to get to Hatfield Construction, which was actually at Barboursville, a few miles south of Huntington. Once I arrived, I read the totals and names off to the secretary and helped her hurry up and get them made out. Once I picked up the completed paychecks, I jumped back into that brand new car and I got myself back to Island Creek way before quittin' time.

When Holland saw Chafin return, his mouth nearly dropped as he exclaimed, "You're back this early? You turned those checks in — all twenty-five — and you're back?"

"Yessir," Chafin said smiling.

"Well, well, it looks like I got me a brand new driver! I never had anybody do that before," Holland said as he grinned. "You were careful with my jalopy, weren't cha?"

"Oh, yeah," Chafin said. "I didn't know I was breaking any records though."

Chafin Meets Keno

One morning Pat Holland walked up to Chafin and said, "Now, since you're a quick learner, I'm gonna put you with ol' Keno."

Keno was the gentleman responsible for setting iron stakes and figuring elevation for the road, using a road construction tool called a lock-level. Although Chafin didn't particularly want to leave his buddy One-Eyed Bill, he wanted to learn all he could about road construction. So he accepted the offer graciously.

Chafin recollected the circumstances:

Tough Boys

I remember ol' Keno as if this all happened yesterday. Keno was a little bit older than me and a little bit on the lazy side, as I remember. However, he was a pretty good engineer. I didn't care if he was a sluggard, because he taught me how to use that lock-level. He'd go sit down in the shade, and I'd use it for him.

We'd set stakes and put forms all the way down the hill. I not only learned how to use a lock-level, but how to cut grades, figure slopes, and so on. I took it all in.

Finally, we got that job done, the road up the hill, and Mr. Holland asked me to go with him to the next job at Kimball, WV, which is near Bluefield. It was the fall of the year, and they had a rugged camp over there.

I went with the crew over to Kimball and stayed with them in the camp. I didn't like it much there. We were there less than a week when I first realized that Keno was a gambler. He'd play poker every night that he could find a gambling place and a few people to hustle. He itched to gamble.

One morning, after several weeks, we got up for work and we couldn't find Keno. Mr. Holland and everyone on the crew looked for him. Several of us finally found him — dead. Someone had killed him, and he lay behind one of the camp tents. He was a bloody mess — with his skull bashed.

That day I said to myself, "Uh-uh, this is enough. I don't like this and I want no part in it. No more Kimball for me."

Keno was murdered under mysterious circumstances. Chafin's new buddy was hopelessly hooked on gambling, which was a fact that probably had a great deal to do with his demise. Also, the people that hung around the camp were "rough-natured," and Chafin was highly suspicious of many of them.

One can only imagine what events transpired that ended the construction worker's life. Perhaps Keno was finally lucky and won big — too big — and one of the other players decided to meet him after the game to recover his losses. Could it be that someone from Kimball mugged him after a winning streak, when he was carrying a large sum of cash? Or maybe Keno lost everything in a game of poker and, angry over his losses, picked a fight with the wrong person and was murdered.

Regardless, Keno, the engineer who had befriended Chafin, was dead. Now Chafin was afraid to stay in the little town of Kimball. Too many possible suspects made Chafin paranoid and anxious to get on the road.

"It is too dangerous here for me," Chafin told Holland. "I'm leaving and going back home. I never really left home before, and I surely don't like Kimball."

That morning he started hitchhiking back to Barnabus. He received several rides, which brought him near the head of Island Creek by that afternoon. Chafin tried to keep that final image of Keno lying in the mud out of his mind as he traveled back home, but he couldn't shake it. No matter what the circumstances were, he didn't deserve to die such a violent and gory death. As far as Chafin knows, the murder was never solved.

Chapter Seven

Chafin Works First Precinct

After returning home from Kimball, West Virginia, Chafin found himself back at square one. He was unemployed again, but still responsible for supporting his family. He headed back to work for the WPA, where he returned to carrying and stacking rocks.

One day while Chafin was working, a friend who also worked for the WPA, Andrew McClure, came along and asked what he was doing still carrying stone.

"Chafe, you can drive a truck, can't you?" McClure asked. "We need to talk to our department boss about you, because we have a truck that we drive on Saturdays. We'll drive on Sundays, too, if we can get enough men out to work."

McClure urged Chafin to ask the foreman for a driving position. Soon Chafin was transferred to a driver position for the WPA.

Mitch Robinson, a construction foreman for the county's state road department, had occasionally seen Chafin driving his truck past his house, located near No. 4 Mine.

> Someone overheard that there was a temporary opening for the county division of the West Virginia Department of Transportation, and Mitch needed a truck driver. One thing led to another; my cousin Clifton Curry went to Mitch to tell him that I could drive a truck and that I was available. After Clifton had talked in my behalf, Robinson came to me and asked if I wanted a job with the state road until his usual driver, who was sick, came back to work.
>
> I remember saying, "I'll take a chance on anything. I definitely want the job."

Chafin then started driving a truck for Robinson. The former driver never returned, so Chafin ended up working permanently for the state road crew.

> I would plow snow in the winter. They paid me around fifty cents an hour. You didn't get time-and-a-half for overtime; it was all just straight pay. However, anytime I could work all night plowing snow, I'd do it. I finally had a steady job. I didn't care how deep the snow got or how slick the roads got, for it all meant work for me.

By this time the Democrats had again established themselves in the county elections. One day while Chafin was working, George C. Steele, the Democratic county chairman and kingpin who was also Robinson's boss, politically, stopped by the state road office. He was also related to Chafin's mother and father. Steele noticed Chafin and said, "Raymond, how about you helping us in the election? I'll give you twenty dollars if you'll help us at Barnabus on Election Day."

Steele reached into his wallet and pulled out a crisp, new twenty-dollar bill and handed it to Chafin.

Chafin said he went home that day, and was so tickled to get that twenty-dollar bill that he could have danced in the street. "That twenty looked like what two thousand dollars might look like to me now. I was so happy that I ran home and told Dad," Chafin remembered.

"What's that you're talking about?" Chafin's father asked angrily.

Chafin explained again about the payment from Steele for working the grounds during the election.

"You take no money for working the election!" Elbert Chafin boomed from his sickbed. "No, no. By gosh, if they pay you for working an election, they've paid you for a day's work that you don't deserve. They will own you! You go down there and work for nothing, 'cause you're a Democrat. You've got a job now — driving a truck. If you work that election for nothing, later on you'll get to keep your job. And if that driver whom you replaced ever comes back, you might even get another job. Job security, son — job security!"

"Well, OK," Chafin said disappointedly, and he dutifully took the money back to Steele and volunteered his services.

Working The Polls

On Election Day, Chafin got up at 4:30 in the morning and walked from Cow Creek to Barnabus by 5 o'clock. Polls opened at the precinct at 6:30.

George Steele was waiting for Chafin when he walked onto the poll grounds. Steele carefully explained the procedure for the day and told Chafin about his duties. Then he left, leaving Chafin at the poll with the other workers.

Chafin worked all day. He would get in one car and then another. His job was to drive voters to and from the voting booth, and to smile a great deal. As he picked up a voter, he was expected to loosely explain the voting plan and hand out a placard about the size of an index card that listed the candidates who the George Steele faction supported. Along the route, he would talk about the various candidates and then make a cash offer to each one in the automobile who voted "correctly."

If the individuals in the car voted properly, he was the one who palmed a small manila envelope into each voter's hand before he took him or her home. The small packet contained a certain amount of money — normally anything from a dollar to five dollars. By accepting the ride to the voting booth — and by accepting the small, yellow envelope — the voters understood exactly whom he or she had agreed to vote for.

> In those days Mitch Robinson was good to me. He took me under his wing and taught me about politics. He also recommended me to those above him, and that certainly helped me get kicked off politically.
>
> Mitch eventually quit the state road because of politics. There were two factions at the time: the state faction and the WPA faction. Mitch ended up working for the WPA, cleaning schools and things like that. He actually made better money and was with the side he wished to be with.
>
> That left me with the state faction. They [the controlling politicians] offered me the job of foreman because Mitch had quit.

Okay, Daddy, I Won't Take It!

A poet once said that it takes the angriest thunderstorms, wind, and downpour to make the most beautiful flowers grow. So it was with 19-year-old Raymond Chafin. Not to imply that the teenager was in any way soft or ever described as being beautiful. In contrast, some would have called him a tough and overly confident punk who tried to push his way through life by using his boldness, intellect, and quick wit. He also had a tendency to be overly flirtatious with the opposite sex.

Then there were others in the area who thought Chafin was a humble and polite kid with little schooling. He was both, and which one showed itself was solely dependent upon whom he was with.

Through the process of overcoming some of life's hard knocks and weathering some angry storms, Raymond Chafin was experiencing a type of growth spurt, a time of maturing. It was the mid-1930s, and his small comfort zone of Cow Creek, West Virginia, was rapidly changing and expanding. He soon realized he had to change, too, if he was to survive.

Although his injuries from the car wreck were serious and recuperation was difficult and lengthy, Chafin had somehow miraculously survived the deadly crash. He weathered the typhoon of humiliation — by once being blackballed from the local coalmines and their company stores.

His anxiety had undoubtedly soared as he helplessly watched his father's strength deteriorate from the ravages of cancer. Meanwhile he endured the tempest of ridicule by cruel neighborhood boys for having to take a demeaning job carrying rock for the WPA, with much poorer wages and less respectability than he had earned in his position at the store.

But now, having paid these costly dues, Chafin seemed to be overcoming the odds. There was finally a calm that came over his life, and his personal waters of bitterness stilled. He was working steadily as a truck driver for the state road commission. His future was beginning to look bright. He was happy.

The break he had hoped for came after Mitch Robinson — Chafin's boss, friend, and mentor — gave up his position as county foreman for the state road.

> Ol' Mitch got mad at the politicians and quit the state road — flat. That left me with the state faction. The controlling politicians offered me the foreman's job. I headed home tickled to death. I went inside the house and told my dad.

"Well, Dad, the Democrats have asked me to be the road foreman. Mitch has quit. Whatcha think?" he asked with a grin on his face.

"No, no. You're too young, son," Elbert snapped. "Men won't want to take orders from you. You also don't have enough experience. Son, it would be a mistake! You stay on that truck and learn all you can. Wait a while. Hear me?"

"Okay, Dad, I won't take it," Chafin agreed, although his heart was crushed. "I'll listen to you, Dad."

The next day he saw Cap Snow and told him, "I have to turn down your offer. My dad says no because I'm too young. Plus, I have too many people against me — because of that car wreck — and too many people want a job. No, I'm sorry. I'll keep my truck-driving job."

Another worker, Joe Louis, who was on the WPA, was picked as the new foreman and placed over Chafin and his fellow employees on the state road.

> The state road was an altogether different set-up than Joe Louis had been used to at the WPA. One problem was that Joe wasn't a pusher. On the WPA, the men did pretty much what they wanted to. However, the state roadmen had to get it! They had to produce results.
>
> Louis didn't last too awfully long. They moved him and they left me up there for about two weeks, until they found another foreman. I stayed the whole two weeks.
>
> Cap Snow was the road superintendent at the time. He always called me "Sonny." During those weeks while the politicians searched for a new foreman, Cap caught me on the job, grabbed me by the arm, and said, "Sonny, we're not bringing Joe Louis back here. He can't get along with these men up here, and we're going to have to let him go. We were going to try to take him off the work site for a couple of weeks and train him — but that isn't going to pan out. So, I'm gonna offer you this job just one more time. If you want it, it's your job. If you don't, I'll never offer it to you again."

Before he answered Snow, young Chafin asked for a little time to go home and talk with his father again about the open position.

After work, Chafin explained to his father what had happened with Joe Louis and what Cap Snow had offered him and why.

The family patriarch thought for a minute and then said, "Well, Raymond, do you really think you can handle it?"

"I sure can," Chafin respectfully answered his beloved father. He then held his breath in anticipation of his father's response, afraid to get his hopes too high.

After taking several moments to study the situation, Elbert pointed his finger in his son's face, grinned, and announced, "Well, son, then take that darn job! But you better be good at it!"

Chafin was unable to sleep for a while that night as he thought about the opportunity that awaited him. Now, best of all, Chafin had his father's blessing, and nothing could stop him.

By morning, Chafin was rejuvenated, ready and raring to go back to the work site and accept the position. He understood the advantages and possibilities of his new position. He had stepped up the ladder, and his job security and longevity would depend solely on politics. Still, he felt it was a good move. Chafin recalled:

> I took over that job. We had eighty-five WPA men working from the city of Logan all the way up to the top of the hill at the time. I was over all of 'em! I did pretty well with the job and never had any real problems or confrontations to speak of. I got along good with all the men.

Maybe They Traded Your Paper With Mine

It was August 1935 and a new law was passed that would give a monthly income to American workers age sixty-five or older upon their retirement. Once this Social Security Act was put into effect, many hardworking older citizens felt that they could breathe a sigh of relief, knowing that a government check could afford them the luxury of not having to rise up early in the morning to go to work at an age when health and stamina can begin to diminish.

According to political godfather Chafin, many local businessmen and government workers immediately began to take advantage of the new federal program.

> Many of the old-timers retired around this time. Right away, Cap Snow retired, and a fellow by the name of I.C. Jesse took his place as state road superintendent of the West Virginia Division of Highways. Then I remember that Jesse, who had put John Asbury in as his assistant, worked for about six months before he was also eligible to retire. Before leaving, he put Asbury in as his replacement, as superintendent.

President Franklin D. Roosevelt had announced about a year earlier his intent to present a program for social security. He formed the Committee on Economic Security (CES), composed of five Cabinet-level officials, to study the entire problem of economic insecurity and to make recommendations that would serve as the basis for legislative consideration by Congress.

The CES assembled a staff of experts on loan from other federal agencies and set to work. By November 1934 the CES sponsored the first national town-hall forum on social security. The CES did a comprehensive study of economic security in America, along with an analysis of the European experience with these problems. Its report was the first analysis in many decades, and it stood as a landmark study for many years. In slightly more than six months, the CES developed a report for Congress and drafted a detailed legislative proposal.

In early January 1935, the CES presented its report to FDR, and on January 17 the president introduced the report to both houses of Congress for simultaneous consideration. Hearings were held in the House Ways and Means Committee and the Senate Finance Committee during January and February. Some provisions made it through the committees in close votes, but the bill passed both houses overwhelmingly in the floor votes. After a conference that lasted through July, the bill was passed and sent to President Roosevelt for his signature.

Roosevelt signed the Social Security Act into law on August 14, 1935. In addition to several provisions for general welfare, the act created a social insurance program designed to pay retired workers age 65 or older a fixed income after retirement.

Meanwhile, in Logan County, after both Cap Snow and I. C. Jesse had retired, John Asbury prepared to settle into his job as the newly appointed state road superintendent.

Asbury approached then-foreman Raymond Chafin and said, "Chafin, you and I can make a good go of it together and do a good job for this county. How 'bout lettin' me put you in as my assistant superintendent? The only catch is, you'll have to get the OK from the politicians."

"That's no problem," Chafin confidently answered his boss. "I'd be honored to be your assistant."

George C. Steele was the Democratic chairman at the time. He helped Chafin get his job before, so he went to him and asked about the assistant's position. He said, "Yeah, you can have the job."

> To qualify, you then had to take an examination to be a road superintendent. This wasn't a civil service exam. However, there were rules. Passing this test was one of those requirements. I only had a seventh-grade education. But John said to me, "Why don't you go on over with me and take that examination?"

"Well, yeah, I'll go to Charleston with ya," Chafin replied.

Chafin went with Asbury to the Capitol building. There were about twenty-five men sitting in the lobby ready to take that examination. The fellow who was administering the test said, "Come on in, boys! Now come on. Make it snappy!"

The two Logan countians were ushered into the examination room with the others. The overseer of the test separated Asbury and Chafin.

> Well, I didn't know what was going on, but I went on in with the others. They brought me the test papers, and I did mine. After we left, we were walking down the long hallway when John met me and whispered, "Raymond, did you take that test, too?"

"Yes," Chafin answered, snickering. "What could I do? They handed me the papers and I took it."

"Well, then what did you put down for the third answer? And what about the fifth? Did you understand the sixth question?" Asbury nervously quizzed Chafin. As they walked out of the marble building, Asbury proceeded to compare answer after answer with his friend.

"What about that last question, Raymond? What did you put?"

"I left it blank," Chafin stated, as he chuckled. "I couldn't even think of a halfway decent answer!"

Asbury then told Chafin that the test results would be mailed to them.

The two men left the Capitol full of nervous energy and relief that the testing was over. They headed back over the rough, winding mountain roads that led to Logan County.

Approximately two weeks later, Asbury went over to Chafin's home, looking forlorn, and said, "Well, I failed my examination. Flunked."

Chafin said:

> That got me to thinking that I had better go check, too. People didn't run to the post office every day like we all do nowadays. The mail might lie there two or three days, or maybe a week, before one picked it up.

51

I was boarding at Barnabus at the time. I had to stay away from my home so that my mother could get her little relief check, ya know. So when I checked at the house, Mom told me I had a letter from the State Road Commission. I anxiously opened the letter and there it was: I had made an 87 percent! I passed everything on it except measuring lumber.

When Asbury heard the news, he blurted out, "I'll be dadburned! I'll be! Here, you only went through seventh grade. And I finished high school and took some college and engineering, and I failed!"

Chafin grinned and told him, "John, maybe they accidentally traded your paper with mine!"

Asbury and Chafin snickered and laughed about that situation over the years.

Chafin added that soon after that, Asbury took the test again in Charleston. This time he passed easily. He went into office as superintendent, and Raymond Chafin became his assistant.

Here's Ol' So-And-So ...

By the late 1930s Raymond Chafin had grown in popularity and political power. After meeting Mitch Robinson and joining the state road crew, he became more and more involved in politics, always working in behalf of the state faction.

I started out as a truck driver for Mitch. I was probably making forty to fifty cents an hour at first, which was a lot of money for me at the time. From then on I worked and campaigned at every election.

Through those years, I worked as a poll worker at Barnabus. I was working at other locations, too. It was all about organization back then. I guess I knew just about everybody by that time. After I got into politics, I'd go see everyone I knew, including folks back at Earling and Micco. I had assembled pretty good workers at the precincts.

One time I was working the Barnabus precinct and George Steele came to me and said, "Raymond, you're doing a pretty good job here. How about helping us up on Island Creek, up at Earling, and up at all these other places where we need organization? You're a pretty slick ol' talker. So how 'bout lettin' me get you started out in politics? I will teach you the ropes."

Chafin agreed to the offer, and vigorous training began. Steele was determined to fashion the coarse Cow Creek boy into a polished Appalachian political figure to be reckoned with. Chafin was taught how to talk, how to walk, and what to wear when he was working a precinct or opening a rally. Steele even stressed what mannerisms to use in public speaking. Chafin listened intently to his every word, and he slowly evolved into a refined — or at least a bit more sophisticated — political figure.

The first election that Everett Workman ran in — I believe it was in 1936 — Everett was running for sheriff. The Democratic Executive Committee gave me all of Island Creek to set up. At that time, we had a school up at Sarah Ann.

We called it Crystal Block. Each school was a voting location. There were polls at Stirrat, Barnabus, Omar, Chauncey, Phico, Rossmore, Monaville, Yuma, and Cherry Tree.

I'd set things up, and I'd have different political meetings scheduled everywhere. At Sarah Ann at 6:00 or 6:30 the first rally started. My dad and George Steele taught me how to open up a rally. Now Dad was getting even sicker, and he wasn't a politician like Don Chafin and the rest of them, but he did know how to regulate and set up a meeting.

First, we'd advertise a meeting — by word of mouth. We didn't have any television in those days, and half the people didn't have a radio. Newspaper ads were too high. So, for example, we'd go up to Crystal Block and tell everyone we knew that we were gonna have a meeting at the school at 5:30, and people would come. They'd swarm around there. You might have fifty, seventy-five, or maybe one hundred people who would come out to see what candidates were goin' to say and what they were goin' to do.

I'd open up that meeting at 5:30, and I would get up and talk and tell them whom we had at the meeting that night. But most of the time we only had our faction of candidates there. We didn't have anybody else on the roster. Every once in a while we'd have politicians from another faction come and try to horn in on our meeting. In that case, I'd introduce him, but I'd point out, "Here is ol' so-and-so; now we ain't supporting this man, but he's here anyway!"

I might even mispronounce his name as I introduce him.

It seemed like everyone from the neighborhood would come to these rallies. There was certainly a lively atmosphere, with plenty of laughter, fellowship, food, and old-fashioned political speeches. Sometimes there was bluegrass or mountain music to set the festive mood for the candidates. At other times, the candidates' speeches became mudslinging fests. Deafening cheers and jeers could be heard throughout the community as the audience responded to an animated, sweat-soaked, red-faced candidate who had made a controversial point. Everyone would huddle together to get the best view of the action. Curious boys and girls might climb on their fathers' shoulders for a better view of the spectacle.

After Chafin opened up the political rally and announced the list of speakers at one location, he'd run to his car and race to the next meeting place. The meetings were scheduled back-to-back on the same night throughout the district.

He remembered those days:

I'd drive to Stirrat. I'd have about five minutes to move to each place. I'd then skip down to Chauncey, Phico, Rossmore, and Monaville. Then I'd drive on down to Yuma. I'd have four or five meetings every night and I would be worn to a frazzle by the time I finished.

Everybody got to know Raymond Chafin through these meetings. There is one thing you can say about me in those days: I was pretty well organized.

Chapter Eight
Don't Count on Votes In Island Creek

By 1936, with the help of people like Mitch Robinson, Cap Snow, and George C. Steele, Chafin was making a name for himself in the coalfields as an aggressive, diligent, and knowledgeable road builder. He was also proving himself to be a natural at the kind of skills necessary for service in Logan County's brand of governmental affairs.

Recognizing the young man's talents and admiring his innate ability to take charge, Steele, who was still head of the local Democratic Party, became Chafin's mentor, grooming the Cow Creek native for a career in county politics.

The ambitious protégé caught on fast. His position as assistant superintendent of the state road opened doors of opportunity. Just as before, when he had worked for the Junior Mercantile at Omar, the young man became well known and well liked by many people in surrounding communities. He was getting things done for people, and they took note of it: schools were being built, roads were being paved, and bridges were being constructed. At election time, voters remembered. And more often than not, they showed their appreciation by supporting the list of candidates with whom Chafin was aligned.

During that time, Chafin was getting many obscure rural roads placed into the county system. Most of these roads had been nothing more than dirt or gravel paths. However, these roadways were important to the families who had to travel in the region. By placing them in the system, the county road department would be responsible for the roads' upkeep.

> I had an uncle, Harley Curry, who lived right in the main head of this creek. He moved up there to try to make a living. He was an A-No. 1 farmer. He had ten or eleven kids and his wife was halfway throwing a fit from frustration. They had no school up there, and they were isolated from everyone.

This was a time when common people in the remote areas of the county were often unable to afford modern transportation. Few owned automobiles or trucks. Most residents of places such as Omar, Barnabus, Chauncey, Phico, and Cow Creek kept several horses for farm work that doubled as transportation when necessary.

Chafin visited Curry and said, "Harley, let me see if I can get you a school put up here."

Curry and Chafin counted the children in the community. There were eighteen, including Curry's young'uns. Chafin said that besides Harley's bunch, Uncle Plez Curry had a grandson or two up at the head of Cow Creek, and there were a few other kids there. Chafin went to George Steele and said, "George, we need a school at the head of Cow Creek!"

"Oh, what are you talkin' about?" Steele quarreled. "Lord, have mercy, Chafe. Who do you think I am?"

After several conversations, Steele finally gave in and called Frank White, president of the Logan County Board of Education, and told him to come over to Logan Storage, a business along the railroad tracks in the city of Logan. Steele owned Logan Storage at the time.

White drove to the business, where Steele and Chafin greeted him. After exchanging pleasantries, Steele said, "Frank, Chafin wants a school at the head of Cow Creek."

"There ain't no way — there's no way that I can do it," White mumbled. "How many kids are up there, anyway?"

"About eighteen or so," Chafin answered. "I have their names in my pocket, if you'd like to see. None of them have ever gone to school, and they want to go."

"Can't do it," White said quickly. "No money."

"Well, let me tell you one thing. If you don't build that school, don't be counting on any darn votes from up Island Creek at election time!" Chafin boomed.

"Now, you just wait a minute!" White shouted as his temper flared. "Who do you think you are?"

Realizing that he may have been too harsh, Chafin softened his tone. "Now, Frank, wait a minute. I may have said that wrong. But if you don't do this, it will come back to haunt ya."

White was offended by Chafin's outburst, and his chest heaved in anger. He attempted to catch his breath and calm down. Even George Steele glanced over at Chafin with an angry look that seemed to say, "Boy, you'd better watch your mouth!"

Chafin said as he recalled the incident:

> I could see that I was out of bounds. So I drew in my horns quickly. I didn't need to make an enemy of White — or Steele, for that matter!

After minutes of silence, White replied smugly, "Well, let me tell you what we'll do. My buddy Alzie Skeens has a truck. He hauls coal for all the schools. I'll get a hold of Skeens, and we'll meet up there, at Cow Creek, in a couple of hours."

Later that day White and several other officials arrived at Chafin's home. White parked his new car in front of the house, and they all stood in Chafin's yard. Skeens brought the work truck within minutes.

> We once had a school at the head of Cow Creek but it had been torn down long before this time period. Most kids went to Barnabus in the mid-1930s, if they went at all. A dilapidated school bus would run when the creek wasn't up. Kids walked out when it was up and met the bus. We had a pretty good road up to the left fork, but from the left fork on up there wasn't any road — nothin'!

There was no road up Cow Creek Hollow, so Skeens prepared to take the officials up the brush-covered indentation between the mountains in his vehicle. Chafin, White, and Clouden White, the superintendent of schools, got into the truck, and Skeens drove up the bumpy trail beyond the left fork.

Once the men arrived at Curry's farm, they all jumped off the truck. Chafin walked the BOE dignitaries to a garden on a tract of land that Curry was prepared to donate for the proposed school building. Eventually, after they looked the area over and discussed the need, the men came back down from the head of the creek. Few words were spoken as they traveled out of the hollow.

Frank White got out of the truck when they arrived at Chafin's house. After Skeens and Clouden left and headed on back to Logan, White stood for a few minutes, gazing up the hollow.

"Chafin, we're gonna try to get you the money to build your school," White said, as he continued to fix his eyes on up the mountain road. "You be at the next school board meeting."

Chafin reminisced:

> I attended that next school board meeting. I got up and told the board about the school. That night, after they all discussed the situation, all the board members voted to give us the money — $500 for lumber. They also voted that Alzie Skeens was to be paid to deliver the lumber up to the school site. It was up to us to construct a schoolhouse.
>
> Uncle Harley and the other people up there had what they called a schoolhouse raising. They built that little schoolhouse with two privies — one for boys and one for girls. The WPA actually furnished the two privies, or outdoor toilet facilities. They sent the men up there to dig the holes and set the privies in place. Now all they needed was a teacher.

Hair Tonic, Cologne, and Body Talc:
Chafin's Secret Weapons

The people of Cow Creek constructed a meager schoolhouse at the head of Cow Creek, and Chafin persuaded the WPA to furnish and install the outhouses at the site. By the end of the month the community had a little school building under roof.

Chafin flexed his political muscles to accomplish the task — nearly overstepping his boundaries. But with his questionable tactics, the people of Cow Creek were well aware that he was becoming a man who was up-and-coming, and who could "get things done."

> Then we had to have a teacher. It was at the head of Cow Creek with no roads, no nothing, and no way. The BOE picked Earl Hager's brother and sent him up to Cow Creek. He was just beginning as a schoolteacher and didn't have a school yet. He spent his first year at Cow Creek. I don't remember his first name because all they ever called him up here was "Mr. Hager." I will never forget that. He was a good teacher, too. He did a good job for us.
>
> The next year they sent Prenus Browning, son of Lon Browning, an assistant to the school superintendent. Lon's boy came in here and taught for the second year. So we now had two years of school for the children.
>
> The next year Louise Chambers came to the school. She had graduated from Concord and then went to Morris Harvey, now known as the University of Charleston, where she got her teaching degree. When she came to Cow Creek to teach, she boarded with Uncle Harley and his family on his farm by the school.

At that time, about 1937, Raymond Chafin was a stout, mature 20-year-old man who was eager to start a family of his own. Chafin went up one weekend to see Uncle Harley, and Miss Chambers was there. They spent most of the evening talking. Within a few

Tough Boys

weeks of meeting the new teacher, Chafin was taking her out on dates in his new pickup truck. A whirlwind romance ensued.

Each day after work, Chafin's ritual included cleaning up in an aluminum washtub, then liberally sprinkling heavily perfumed talc all over his body, and slicking down his coarse brown hair with hair tonic. He'd mix up a ceramic mug full of thick shave cream, and using a stubby camelhair brush, he'd lather his face. With straight razor in hand, he got rid of his 5 o'clock shadow.

Chafin put on his best "politickin'" attire and his favorite store-bought cologne and aftershave.

Leaning forward into the bathroom mirror, he examined every square inch of his reflection, straightening his collar and carefully slicking down his bristly eyebrows before stepping into the living room to pass his mother's final inspection. With Lucinda's approval, he was ready to court the new, soft-spoken schoolteacher on the creek, Miss Louise Chambers.

Nearly every night around 6:00 he'd arrive at the farm. He'd jump from his pickup, run onto the front porch, stop abruptly to re-straighten his collar, and then throw open Uncle Harley's rickety screen door. Gasping for breath because of nervousness, he'd wheeze, "Sweetie, are you ready to go-o-o?"

With a nod and a smile from Chambers, he escorted the Concord grad to his vehicle, opening her door. The two would drive off, talking and laughing.

Sometimes they would hang out around Barnabus, or they might drive down to Omar to watch a Western movie, or even travel all the way to Logan to check out the nightlife. Regardless, the evening spent together always seemed to be an enjoyable one for the new couple.

He and Chambers dated for four weeks before he asked for her hand in marriage. One night Chafin told Chambers, "If you marry me, Louise, I'll move you out of here!" Within weeks Chambers accepted Chafin's proposal.

Chafin let out a belly laugh as he talked about his proposal:

> I married her. I believe that was in 1937. So I kept my word. After I married her, I eventually moved her out of Uncle Harley's place at Cow Creek Hollow — all the way to Barnabus! There was only a mile or two between the two locations, yet I had technically fulfilled his promise.
>
> One of the many reasons I married Louise was because she was so intelligent, and she had a steady income. I wanted somebody much more educated than I was. She was extremely smart and a great reader. We saw things eye to eye politically — most of the time. She also had a good sense of humor, even though she was also quiet around the house.
>
> Louise taught school for thirty-one years. In the early days, there was no road going to the schoolhouse. So I'd go get Louise on Friday evening and always take her back by Sunday night.

When the two first married, she continued to board at Uncle Harley's during weekdays, to be near the school.

57

The little Cow Creek schoolhouse continued until the children got so dadburn big that there were none of them up there anymore, and no new families were moving in. They eventually tore that school down. That was a gloomy day for Louise and me.

Who Was Louise Chambers?

The account of Louise Chambers begins with a brutal murder. In 1926 a man named Art Chambers was killed in cold blood at Rum Creek, in hillbilly gangland style. Deputy Chambers had a reputation for being a ruthless and callous deputy for Sheriff Don Chafin, a corrupt politician in Logan County at the time. However, this day Chambers was working an extended shift for the sheriff at various polling places in the county.

Chambers was involved in an Election Day scuffle over politics — as he worked in behalf of Don Chafin's political faction at Yolyn, West Virginia. It was reported at the time that a carload of Tennis Hatfield's election workers were being driven from precinct to precinct where they were voting and re-voting for their slate of candidates. The truck, which included George Seals, eventually drove up to the Yolyn precinct, where Deputy Chambers' father was working inside the polls while he guarded the outside.

When the truck came from up the hollow and stopped in front of Chambers, several of the passengers exchanged unpleasant remarks, which were directed toward Chambers. When the deputy challenged the group, a confrontation ensued. As Chambers tried to restore peace, a man leveled a pistol at the deputy and shot him in the chest. Chambers clutched his heart and dropped backward to the ground, lying on his back at the entrance to the voting precinct in a pool of blood. Men and women stormed out of the precinct when they heard the shooting. Several men congregated around Chambers. Once the deputy's father got to the scene, he was stunned and slumped to the ground. He cradled his son's head and tried to talk to him as he covered the wound and applied pressure with his hand. It was too late. Deputy Chambers was already dead.

The fatal bullet came fom a rival party member, allegedly Seals — who was a Republican — although he was also with several other members of the Republican opposition — the Tennis and Joe D. Hatfield faction.

Tennis and Joe were the sons of Devil Anse Hatfield. Tennis had been placed in the High Sheriff's position by court action because of election abnormalities and wrongdoing in 1924.

Art Chambers had been married to the former Cynthia Raines. Cynthia and he had been in the process of getting a divorce. They had one daughter, whom they both adored — Louise. She was 8 years old when her father was murdered at Yolyn, near Rum Creek Hollow.

Louise never forgot that a Republican had gunned down her father on Election Day. In subsequent years, it was hard for her to even hear anyone speak the word "Republican" because of the memories it stirred.

Although Joe D. Hatfield was a Tennis Hatfield supporter in 1926, he became the Republican sheriff in Logan County from 1929 to 1933. According to published reports, during both Hatfield administrations the county was "polluted with slot machines, gambling halls, poolrooms, brothels, and speakeasies."

Tough Boys

The Hatfield brothers allegedly kept a large staff of deputies — sometimes called enforcers — on duty in order to collect "protection fees" from local businesses and companies. Many of the deputies were also believed to have been collaborators with Mountain State mobsters who distributed illegal moonshine to vendors around the region.

Intermarried

Raymond Chafin felt it important to explain some interfamily connections in order to make sense out of several political and family relationships and alliances.

Barnabus Curry and his family were probably the first folks to settle along Cow Creek, in the 1800s. The town of Barnabus was named after him. I suspect he owned all the land around these parts, including all the acreage up and down the creek bed. Barnabus was married at least three or four times and had around twenty children or so. He came into this region from North or South Carolina.

Nobody really knew why he came into this area, and nobody knew exactly how many times he'd been married, either. The one thing that is known is that he came here and had lots of young'uns, including Victor Curry and my grandfather, Thomas. Everyone married and intermarried around here back in those days. There wasn't anybody else here to hook up with, to tie the knot with.

In southern West Virginia, it was fairly common during the post-Civil War era on up to the turn of the century to marry within one's family. This was partly because of the limited number of people in any specific region, and in part because travel was so difficult. Roadways were treacherous along the Appalachian mountain range. Up until the later 1940s, most rural roads were little more than dirt paths carved out of the rough clay and sandstone terrain.

Towns such as Logan were especially privileged to have brick streets and sidewalks by the late 1880s and '90s. However, beyond downtown, the roads quickly disintegrated. Paths around Stollings, Whitman, Holden, Switzer, Omar, and Cow Creek were barely wide enough to accommodate more than a single Model T, spring buckboard, or log wagon at a time. If two automobiles met along a dirt road, one pulled off the roadway — into the tree line, weeds, brush, or ditch — to let the other pass by. During the winter months, high mountain travel was even worse because of rock slides, steep inclines, fallen trees, snow and mud, and huge ruts, which made passage nearly impossible.

The people of Omar and Cow Creek were hemmed in because of a lack of basic infrastructure — even up to the early 1950s. Traveling capabilities improved after modern machinery became available, coupled with a county politician's commitment to invest in the area. It took a long time to see real change happen for the people living in these secluded areas of the region.

Many years ago, before I was born, Grandpa Tommy Curry moved from the head of the creek and built a house at the foot of Cow Creek Mountain.

Curry was a long-whiskered ox driver, commonly called a "bullwhacker" in those days, and was able to make a few dollars each day helping folks get their wagons, carts,

59

and buggies up the mountain and on their way to Williamson, the Mingo County seat. He would hitch up his string of oxen, and they'd pound their hooves, grunt, and snort as they worked in unison to pull against the weight of an overloaded pack wagon or buggy.

During these early stages of the coal-mining era, Curry realized that this ox-driving venture might be a way to take advantage of the potential the coal industry promised for the region. He also filled a need for families that traveled outside Island Creek. Chafin discussed the situation:

> When travelers got to the bottom of the hill, they hollered for my other grandpa — my dad's father — Thomas "Tom" Chafin, who did the same thing for folks on the other side of the mountain.

Tom Chafin, with his own pack mules, helped travelers once they arrived by oxen to the top of the hill. On their way down the other side and up the next mountain, businesses and traveling families most likely used Tom and his four belligerent mules. He hooked his team up to anyone's wagon, and regardless of the size of the load, it seemed that his team could make it across the hill to the next peak.

According to Chafin, each of his grandfathers might make a quarter or fifty cents per wagon for their efforts.

> Grandpa Chafin's sister, my Great-Aunt Louvicey (also called Levicy or Vicey) married ol' Devil Anse Hatfield. So we have a very rich family history. I would imagine everyone's heard of Devil Anse and his feudin' years. So Devil was my uncle by marriage.
>
> Grandpa Tom Chafin married ol' man Barnabus Curry's daughter. My grandma on my mother's side was also a Chafin — but that's been a hard one for me to even chase back! I don't know where the heck she was from. Evidently, they were from across another hill or something. But when Grandpa Chafin married off his third child, a daughter, he divided his property up and gave Parlee Vance all of Littles Creek.
>
> Some time after that, Grandpa Tom Chafin's wife died unexpectedly of natural causes. By that time Tom was a full-time preacher — they actually called him "Circuit Rider." To tell ya' the truth, I don't think he liked to work too much. So he became a travelin' preacher. During his travels, he was also known to have an eye for the ladies. I guess I might as well tell it as it is!
>
> One day Barnabus Curry, Circuit Rider's father-in-law, hollered for him. When Tom came out of his cabin to see what he wanted, he found Barnabus standing on the front porch with a double-barrel shotgun at his side. Looking down toward the shotgun, Barnabus angrily roared, "Tom, looky here, you renegade! Your wife, my daughter, is now dead! Right? Look here. You know I got this coach-gun loaded, don't you? It's loaded to the barrel, son! If you marry some sweaty whore who will be mean to my grandchildren, I'll blow your head clean off! Youse understand?"
>
> My grandpa, Circuit Rider Tom, was a Chafin, so he didn't have a lick of sense either.

Circuit Rider growled and angrily responded to Barnabus, "If that's the way you feel, and you're goin' to stick that sawed off shotgun in my face, take your darn property back. I'll deed it back to ya! I don't want a darned thing you gots to offer! And I can tell you where to stick those dang shells, too!"

According to Chafin's account, the Curry family patriarch, Barnabus Curry, was actually trembling from anger as he paused to study Circuit Rider's expression and decide what his next move should be. He finally took a deep breath and tried to regain his composure. He pivoted in place and swung his shotgun ominously over his right shoulder. Letting out a low moan, he looked back at Circuit Rider and squinted one eye and pointed his finger in his face. It was at that moment that Barnabus decided to redivide his real estate assets.

"Tom, you best be glad I have decided to let you live – at least for *today*. If my grandkids weren't around, my sons and I would be burying your carcass right now. But instead, I'm goin' to give you your wish and take back all I've ever given you. I'm goin' to give your daughter all of Littles Creek," he growled.

The old man went on, forcefully bellowing out directives to the son-in-law, as his barrel chest heaved from rage. Barnabus orally gave large tracts of prime property to each of his grandkids: to Doc, the area from Littles Creek down to Barnabus; to Preacher, all of Cow Creek. And so it was.

As for Circuit Rider, he was left with nothing except a warning that if he tried to confiscate any of his children's property, he would be "pushin' up daisies at the Chafin family cemetery."

Chafin reflected on the incident.

My aunt, my dad's half-sister, eventually sold that property at Littles Creek. She got a great deal of cash, and then she bought 450 acres at West Hamlin. She had thirty-five head of prime cattle that grazed at Littles Creek. When she sold the farm, she wondered how she could move the livestock to West Hamlin, in Lincoln County. Hired hands finally rounded up the cattle and drove them, on foot, down to West Hamlin. It was an Appalachian cattle drive! The workers arrived in West Hamlin with thirty-four head; they lost one along the way.

In spite of Grandpa Barnabus Curry's threat, Circuit Rider Chafin eventually did remarry. His new wife, formerly a Browning, had four more children with him, including Elbert, Raymond Chafin's father. Unfortunately, they divorced when their children were small. After the divorce, the children were split up among family members.

"My daddy was raised by Victor and Betty Curry," Chafin concluded. "As for Circuit Rider, he lived out the rest of his days as a travelin' preacher man."

Chapter Nine
Rationing Stamps, Judge Chambers, and WWII

Chafin said that during World War II, he was called into the United States Army, exactly one year after the Japanese had attacked Pearl Harbor. He recalls:

> I was determined, like many others that I knew from Logan County, to serve my country overseas.
>
> I was ready to fight Adolf Hitler or Tojo — it made no difference to me. Unfortunately, doctors in Huntington examined me, and I failed the exam. I was turned down 'cause of that car wreck I was in as a teenager. I still had the metal plate in my head, so the doctors said that disqualified me. I came back home to my job on the state road, working as the assistant to John Asbury.
>
> During that time America was rationing nearly everything imaginable, like gasoline, sugar, and coffee. We were given stamps: for instance, "A" stamps were given for gasoline. You had a "T" stamp for trucks. The number of stamps you got was based according to what you hauled with that truck. When you signed up at the rationing board, you had to tell what you did with your truck.

Once during the war, Logan County Judge C.C. Chambers, who was a cousin to Louise, joined Bill Casto and Chafin on a business trip to Huntington. The judge had a nearly new car that he got just before the war, so he insisted upon taking it. According to Chafin:

> The judge had a "C" rationing stamp; you put the stamp on your windshield. I was driving while Bill and the judge were in the backseat going over some important papers — a land settlement deal that we had made in Huntington that day.
>
> They were both fussin' and quarrelin' in the backseat, while I steered us on home. The judge had a terrible temper. Bill and Judge Chambers were 'bout to fistfight, and I got nervous and my foot got a little too heavy on the gas pedal. First thing I knew a constable's car pulled up alongside of me. His siren was on and the lights were flashing. He motioned for me to pull the car to the curb.

"Now you've done it!" Chambers yelled at Chafin as he pulled the car off the road.

"Shush up, Judge! I'll handle this," Chafin retorted.

The constable pulled in behind Chafin, and he got out of his car and strutted up to the driver's side window.

"You goin' to a fire?" the constable asked sarcastically.

"Naw," Chafin muttered. "Don't think so."

"Well, you were sure drivin' like it, buddy! You were going above fifty-five miles an hour in a thirty-five zone. I need to see your road card and operators'."

Chafin, thinking that he could slyly finagle out of the situation, said boldly, "Judge Chambers. *JUDGE!* I need your road card since this is *your* car, Judge Chambers."

Chambers stiffened up in anger and puffed as he pulled his wallet out of his trousers and handed Chafin his car registration.

As he handed the registration to the officer, the constable bent down and looked at Chambers and then at Chafin.

"Judge, you say? Oh, uh, well … Judge Chambers, I see. Well, that's all right, fellers. You can resume on the road. I see no problem here. Let's just forget the whole matter," the constable stammered.

"H—LL NO!" Chambers shouted from the backseat. "Give him a dadburn ticket! Stick it to him!"

"What? Why you …," Chafin turned his head and angrily mumbled at the judge.

Chafin turned to the officer and said, "Well, if youse is goin' to give me a ticket, tell me where the justice of the peace is. I want to see him right now and get this thing settled."

The officer smiled as he wrote Chafin the speeding ticket and told him to follow him down the road to the justice's office about fourteen miles away. Chafin turned the car around and followed the constable, while he angrily grumbled under his breath about the upcoming fine.

Chambers laughed and taunted, "You better drive the speed limit, Mr. Speed Demon, or you'll get another fine!"

Chafin turned his head around and glared at the judge.

After driving about fifteen minutes, the constable pulled in at a secluded farmhouse along a deserted stretch of roadway. The justice of the peace, who was dressed in bib overalls and a large straw hat, was busy plowing a field behind the barn. When the cars pulled in, the farmer's wife came out to meet the constable. They talked for a minute, and then she walked alongside the barn and shouted for her husband, "Honey! You have a client. Get up 'ere. You got some people 'ere to see you!"

"You played — now you pay!" Chambers shouted, as he laughed at Chafin. "You pay your fine an' shush your grumblin'."

"No, Judge, you ain't playing fair! I was doin' fine gettin' us out of this mess, but then you told the constable to give ME a ticket. Judge, you burn me up, you old coot!"

The county J.P. eventually fined Chafin $18.60 that day. Chambers, who was starting to feel bad about the entire situation, offered to pay him back for the fine. However, Chafin refused the payment, saying he'd pay his own way.

Some weeks after the incident, Chafin went to see his longtime friend Ken Hart, who was a member of the rationing board. Chafin was trying to persuade Hart to give him more gasoline stamps for his automobile. After he finished explaining his need, Chafin playfully asked Hart what would happen to a man with a "C" stamp who got stopped for speeding?

"Well, he'd lose his stamp. Why?" Hart questioned.

"Well, you know what a stubborn and cantankerous fella' the judge is. Judge Chambers has a 'C' stamp, and we were travelin' home from Huntington some time ago and his car was stopped for speedin'. I was driving. When the officer came up to the car window, I was getting us out of the fine, but ol' Chambers pushed to get a ticket. I paid the fine, but I'd love to get him back.

"Do me a favor. Would you write C.C. Chambers and tell him that you're goin' to take his 'C' stamp away from him for reckless behavior in an automobile?" Chafin asked, chuckling. "We can have a little fun with the judge."

"Why sure, I can do that," Hart said, as they both laughed. "I'll send him a letter tomorrow."

Two or three days later, the judge's car pulled up into Chafin's driveway. Chambers swung open the car door. He jumped out with the certified letter from Hart in his hand. He stomped into Chafin's house and yelled, "Look what you've done! You got my 'C' stamp taken away!"

He continued to cuss, yell, and argue while Chafin stood at the front door watching the tantrum with a big grin on his face. "He even had my Louise ready to pull out every hair on my head — that's if'n I had hair!" Chafin said, laughing, as he told the story.

Chafin allowed Chambers to go on for a few minutes and then finally said, "If'n you had kept your big, fat, mouth shut, we could have gotten out of that speedin' ticket, you ol' codger! Now look where this has led! Who signed that letter, judge?"

"Ken Hart!" the judge hollered, as he crumpled the envelope and shook it in Chafin's face. "Chafin, you better fix this!"

"Oh, no! You're in trouble now, Judge," Chafin said, as he shook his head. "Ken Hart is a tough ol' bird! You got a letter from the worst dang Republican in the state of West Virginia. And here we are — *Democrats!* This is a real tough situation!"

Chafin finally told Chambers to calm down and come in the house. The two sat down at the kitchen table as Louise served coffee and biscuits.

"I believe I can help ya' get out of this," Chafin said, trying his best not to snicker and give away his joke. The judge finally calmed down a bit and went home, deciding to wait and see what Chafin could do about the situation.

The next day Chafin drove into town to see Ken Hart at his office. Hart greeted him and then asked, "Well, Chafe, did he get the letter?"

"Oh, yes, he got it all right!" Chafin burst out laughing as he told him about the judge's visit.

"Is he mad?" Hart asked.

"Well, let me put it this way: he was so miffed, he was shakin'," he answered, and then both men doubled over with laughter.

"Now he wants me to … uh … 'fix' it with you," he cackled.

After the meeting with Hart, Chafin decided to let the judge sweat for the rest of the week. On the following Friday, he stopped by the judge's chambers at the courthouse.

Chafin, with the most solemn look he could muster, said, "Judge, it took some doin', but I believe I gots you off the hook with the rationing board. Hart said that he's willing to let this whole thing slide — this one time. You get to keep your 'C' stamp."

"Thank you, Chafe! Thank you," Chambers said, as he reached out to shake Chafin's hand.

"You're welcome, Judge. There's just one thing…" he said.

"What's that?" the judge asked.

"Hart said that you should watch that darn lead foot of yours the next time you go Sunday drivin'!"

"Darn you, Chafin! You played H—LL!"

Chafin nearly fell over laughing as he got up and left the judge's office.

Dealing With The Rationing Board

Chafin said that the rationing board, located in downtown Logan, was extremely stringent during the '40s:

> For the war effort, we were limited on nearly everything. Anytime your tires wore thin and got too bad, you didn't just go get a new set of tires. You had to go to the rationing board and tell them your circumstances. They would hopefully allow you to recap the bad tires. Just about everything that you needed for a car or truck was rationed, except for oil. Oil wasn't rationed, but it was still hard to find.
>
> If you had a bulldozer or a gasoline shovel for your work, you had to keep a record of what the equipment used in fuel every day. The journal of gasoline usage had to be totaled and given to the board for approval. That took a lot of extra bookkeeping.
>
> To sign up for food rationing stamps, you went to the rationing board at Logan or at Omar. You told them how many you had in your family. Then you got stamps based upon your family's size and what the board thought you'd need. For almost any product that you needed or used, you had to have a stamp to buy it.

There were many things that were hard to come by even if you had sufficient stamps. It was almost impossible to get sugar during that time period, as Chafin remembered:

> That made it especially hard on the bootleggers who made the 'shine 'round these parts. But I swear they always managed to get their sugar some way. If a bootlegger knew of a store that had gotten a shipment of sugar, they might get their hands on at least twenty-five pounds worth to set up a barrel of mash.

Many times the illegal still operator was able to get raw sugar and other ingredients by bribing or threatening certain storeowners or managers. Sometimes ingredients were made available when the rumrunner agreed to a pay a percentage of the profits to a grocery vendor.

In other cases, statements concerning impending trouble were implied if supplies weren't donated.

Since the moonshine business had its underworld connections and public support, many Logan County grocery store managers or storeowners didn't want to invite the danger that denying the bootlegger could bring. Even in the 1940s, Logan County had a lawless edge that teetered on the fringe of society.

Restaurants and hospitals still got their sugar by the fifty- and one-hundred-pound bag. However, shipments to the company stores were sometimes sporadic. Once the shipment came, the demand was tremendous. The sugar went quickly when a delivery was unloaded on the dock.

Besides sugar, other essentials were hard to come by. It was nearly impossible to get a pound of coffee. When people got some, they would try to make it last by adding chicory or browned meal to the grounds. Chafin recalled:

> People did anything to make it last a little longer — including percolating it and then drying it and using it again and again.
>
> You couldn't get ground black pepper on Cow Creek, either. When we managed to have pepper in the house, Mom would warn us, "Don't dust too much of that on 'em eggs!"

Chafin explained that the rationing system worked a little bit like food stamps work today. You went to the store, opened your stamp booklet, and the clerk tore out stamps for the items you selected. The system was nationwide. It affected the poor and the rich. Everyone was restricted by the rationing system, as Chafin elaborated:

> It took so many points for coffee, lard, sugar, and meat. I have seen as many as two to three hundred people stand in line at the company store, all waiting to buy fresh meats. You were limited at that time to what you could find in the butcher shop. Cut meats and luncheon meats were especially scarce. So when anyone heard that a truckload of meat had arrived, everyone in the community grabbed their stamps and headed to town.
>
> Of course, the victory garden was popular at the time. Most folks raised their own chickens or hogs if they were able. We also helped one another back then. If someone was elderly and unable to put out a garden, we helped prepare their garden or we shared what we had.
>
> It was a difficult time, but we thought the sacrifice was worth it for our boys overseas.

One time Chafin and his road crew were busy working on the road up at Holden, West Virginia. They were changing the road at Cora that connected to lower Holden, a small community near Logan. The side road that used to go up and around a cemetery had to be rerouted, so Chafin and his crew were cutting a new roadway to redirect traffic.

While Chafin was working near the Holden company store, he saw a semi-truck pull up. The rig pulled into an extended seven-car garage with multiple doors that had once been rented to coalminers who lived in the coal camp. Two rough-looking drivers jumped out of the cab, opened up one of the wooden garage doors, and started unloading case after case of Okay Soap, a brand popular at the time.

The store general manager came down to meet the truck at the garage in order to sign for the supplies. Chafin knew him, so he yelled at the manager and asked what the truck drivers were doing.

"This is where we store supplies," the manager hollered back.

"But why not take it on up to your warehouse?" Chafin inquired.

"We have no room left over there, so we had to take over this garage and several other garages around here," he answered. "We're planning on building another warehouse, but until it's finished, this is our solution — the coal camp garages. We have several guards and night watchmen in place to protect the supplies that we stash in here. Logan County Sheriff Claude Gore has his deputies keeping a close eye on things, too."

"Well, by golly, I can't even get my dirty hands on a cake of lye soap right now," Chafin complained. "Look at all the bars you have here!"

"No problem, I'll fix ya' up," the store manager said, as he winked and smiled. "Considering what you're doing for this community, with building us a road and all, I'll be glad to get you some bar soap."

The manager went into the garage and eventually came out with a half-case of soap, two one-pound bags of coffee, and a huge bag of pure sugar.

Chafin's eyes lit up as the company store manager smiled and placed the merchandise in his arms. Considering how rare all these supplies were, Chafin felt like he had just struck gold. He took the armload back to his truck and locked the doors. He took the supplies home that evening after work.

Louise was thrilled and hugged Chafin when he placed the merchandise on the kitchen table. It had been a long time since they had supplies like that. Chafin pulled out the No. 3 washtub and soaked a long while that night. He remembered:

> It was extremely difficult to find regular cigarettes during World War II. Most folks — men and women — who smoked bought Bugler and rolled their own. There was Camel, Chesterfield, Old Gold, and Lucky Strikes — but you couldn't hardly find 'em anywhere 'cause of shortages. There were lesser-known brands, such as Wings and Sunshine, which were ten cents each. Snuff was pretty popular, too. You could buy a small can of snuff for a nickel or a dime.
>
> I'll tell ya' one thing! Men were less apt to offer you a cigarette in those days. They kept their cigarettes safe and snug in their own shirt pockets. Tobacco was way too hard to come by to give it away. It's hard to imagine now what things like that meant to us during the 1940s. Items like sugar, chocolate, coffee, ice cream, tea, and lard were worth their weight in gold back then.

My Toes Were Dangling

By 1940, Raymond Chafin was kept busy as assistant superintendent of the state road department in Logan County, playing a major role in developing the highway system, adding new rural roadways, graveling dirt roads, paving others, building bridges, creating retaining walls, and helping bring backwoods Logan County into the twentieth century.

For a year or two he was John Asbury's personal assistant. Then Black Rock Asphalt Company built a plant at West Logan. Black Rock wanted to hire John as its superintendent. Chafin remembered:

> One day John walked up to me and said, "Chafin, I'm getting that job down there at Black Rock. Don't tell anybody. Just go see the politicians and try to get my job — and get yourself a good assistant who will be loyal to ya."

Young Chafin took Asbury's advice. He approached the Democratic leadership and explained the situation. Being the logical choice, Chafin became the new superintendent when Asbury moved on to the position at West Logan, as he explained:

> I picked myself an able assistant, Raymond Bailey. He had been a mining boss and was a good politician up at Mudfork. I stayed on as Logan County superintendent until 1944.
>
> Meanwhile, George Steele had gone down to Virginia and bought himself a farm, and it appeared he was probably about to leave here and retire altogether. There were rumors that he was washed up with politics — getting tired of it.
>
> By the time 1944 [campaigning time] was coming around, Everett Workman started himself a faction of several younger candidates. Workman wanted Steele's position as Democratic Executive Committee president. Now, I had once been a bodyguard for Everett Workman. In 1936 I had even supported him politically. However, I was still for George Steele. Everett, knowing this, came up to see me one day and asked, "Chafin, are you goin' to quit George Steele and come on over with me?"
>
> "No! Uh-uh, no! George Steele has always been loyal to me. I can't do that!" I told him.
>
> "You know that might mean your job!" Workman warned.
>
> "Well, I don't think so," I answered, sharply.
>
> I figured George Steele could hold me [keep my position]. But Steele didn't like Governor Matthew Mansfield Neely — no way. Actually, they didn't get along at all, but I didn't know any of that at the time.
>
> The district engineer came here from Huntington. His name was J.N. Smith. He came up to see me, and said, "You're one of the best supervisors we've got, buddy boy! You handle your money well, and you operate everything else sound. You have the best roads. You keep the equipment up. But if you don't change hands here and go over to Everett Workman, I don't know what I'm gonna have to do, if you get my drift."
>
> I had already been fired once from Junior Mercantile, ya know. And I was married now. Louise and I were helping Mom and Dad. But I still figured, "Nobody knows as much as I know. They won't fire me!"
>
> Well, some time after that, Hokey Carper, the bookkeeper at the county road office, sent for me. I went in to the office, and Carper told me that the governor wanted to see Blutcher Sias and me at his office in Charleston.

Sias was a janitor at the road department office and a close friend of Chafin's. He was handicapped, so he walked with a crutch.

Chafin had called Governor Matthew M. Neely, who answered, "Raymond, my boy, you're doing a wonderful job over there in Logan County! I'm proud of ya. If you have time to see me, could you come over here? Oh, bring Blutcher Sias with you, too."

Chafin later told Sias, "The Governor couldn't have been nicer to me. You and I are about to get our just reward. The governor of West Virginia wants to see us. He wants to thank us for the good job we're doing!"

Neely was a Democrat from Marion County. He was elected governor in 1941.

Chafin and Sias jumped in his state car and drove to Charleston. When they arrived at the Capitol complex, he went in to see the receptionist at the governor's office. The secretary told Chafin and Sias that the governor would see them in a few minutes. The two sat in the lobby. Across the hall was a state policeman who sat outside the governor's door. After thirty minutes or so, the officer jumped up and said, "Come with me, Mr. Chafin and Mr. Sias."

Chafin recalled that the governor, smiling, met both of them at the door. He grabbed each of their hands and shook them, patted them on our backs, and said, "Come on in, boys. Sit down, gentlemen. Come in and make yourselves comfortable!"

Chafin described the governor as "a nervous kind of fella. His hands would shake uncontrollably as he talked."

"Boys, y'all are doing a good job over there in God's country!" Governor Neely said as he sat down at his oversized desk.

"Blutcher, they tell me you're a real man around that office, keeping everything clean and tidy. And you, Raymond, are one of our best superintendents. Let me tell you what I want you boys to do: I want you both to support my man, Everett Workman, over there in Logan County. Then I want you to continue to do the good job you're both doing there for this great state."

"What?" Chafin responded, in astonishment.

"Ah, boys, you know George Steele is all washed up, and I never did like him no way," the governor growled. "So what about you, Mr. Sias? Will you stand for Everett, along with me, your governor?"

"You're talkin' to a stump when you talk to me! I'm for George Steele!" Sias retorted.

The governor reared back in his leather seat, folded his arms, raised his voice, and said, "So, Mr. Raymond Chafin, what are you gonna do? Huh?"

"I'm staying with George Steele, too," Chafin answered, emphatically.

"Well, boys, you know I won't have any alternative other than to fire you both!" the governor boomed.

"Well, by golly, you've got the pencil!" Chafin responded. "Do what you want to do!"

Chafin remembered, as he retold the story, that he gave Governor Neely a "few choice words" at the time. Then he saw Blutcher start to move, and he knew Blutcher was "mean enough to take his crutch and swing it around M.M. Neely's scrawny neck!"

"Blutcher, sit still!" Chafin ordered, grabbing his friend's arm. "It ain't worth it, and he ain't worth it."

Then two intimidating state troopers walked into the room and stood behind Chafin and Sias.

Neely asked, "Boys, how did you two get over here?"

"State car," Chafin answered angrily.

"Lay the keys on my desk!" Neely commanded. "That's our vehicle."

"I ain't got no keys; they're in the car," Chafin answered, smartly.

Chafin continued:

There were two hefty state troopers — big ones, buddy! One got me under one arm, and the other one grabbed me under the other arm. My toes were dangling, barely touching the floor, as they dragged me outta there. They motioned at Blutcher and said, "Come on, shorty!"

After the two left the governor's office, one of the state troopers — the kinder of the two — walked both men out of the Capitol and onto the complex grounds and said, "Chafin, you know I know all 'bout you and the whole Chafin clan. How you ever got out of the governor's office without me having to take you to jail in cuffs I will never know! Go on back to Logan and lick your wounds and start over."

"No problem. We're going home," Chafin replied.

As they started to walk away, Sias leaned toward Chafin and whispered, "So, Chafe, where are those keys, anyway — in the car?"

"No, in my pants pocket," Chafin said, as he snickered.

"By gosh, give 'em to me!" Sias said.

Chafin gave the keys to his friend, saying, "What are goin' to do?"

"By golly, I used to play baseball. Watch me throw them in that Kanawha River!"

Sias handed his crutch to Chafin, then wound up his arm to throw the keys. Next he gave them a hard fling.

After the keys were airborne, Chafin said he immediately turned around backwards, waved his arms at the trooper, and yelled, "You fellas better go find those keys!"

Neither one of us saw where the keys landed, but if I was a bettin' man, I'd say they skipped along the Kanawha River. Regardless, we looked at each other and laughed all the way to the bus terminal. Then reality set in.

Chapter Ten

If You're With a Faction, You Can't Get Out

Although Blutcher and Chafin had had a good laugh over the keys, it didn't take long before they started thinking about their future. The two bewildered men slumped as they walked the remaining stretch of sidewalk to the bus station to catch the first transport back to Logan. The ride home was a rather quiet one — too many words had already been spoken for one day.

Chafin, as he recalled the incident, leaned back on his sofa and talked casually about the dark day:

> Blutcher Sias' wife was a member of the Democratic Executive Committee. Back in those days we only had six committee members in the county, with three districts — we had two executive committee members from Triadelphia District, two from Chapmanville, and two from Logan. His wife, from Triadelphia District, was often the deciding vote on the committee.
>
> The other committee members tried to get Blutcher and me to change our politics — with no luck. George Steele had fallen from grace politically at the time, and Everett was now supportin' Claude Gore for sheriff, or at least I believe it was Claude.
>
> It's not that I had any ill feelings against Claude, but that's just politics for ya. Sometimes your best friend might be running for office, and it might just cut your heart out when you're unable to support him. However, in Logan County — and especially with these Democratic factions — you might want to be for your friend but you just can't be. When you are with a particular bloc of candidates, you can't get out!
>
> By the time Blutcher and I got back to Logan, the governor had already ordered all our belongings piled outside the door at the state road office. It was that quick. Done.

A road department employee took Chafin to City View, where he and his wife were living at that time. Another employee drove Sias to his home at Man.

> After I was brought home, I lay around the house for a day or two. I wasn't too worried about gettin' another job because I knew nearly everybody in the county. Louise told me to lie around for a few days and rest up and not worry about it. She was still teaching school at Barnabus, so we could survive for a while on her income.

We're Still Brothers

"Politics is a whole lot like a ball game," Chafin reflected late one afternoon in 2002 as he remembered being fired by Governor M. Neely. "Let's say I'm the pitcher on one team, like for Omar Junior High, and I have a brother who pitches for another team, like maybe for Henlawson.

"When my brother's team from Henlawson comes to play Omar, it's brother ag'in brother. Now, believe me, I'd do everything I can to win that ball game — *anything*. But regardless of the game's outcome, when that sport competition's over, arm in arm we'll go — my brother and me — talking, laughing, and walking out the gate together and chatting about that tough ol' game," Chafin explained. "Politics is a whole lot the same way, just like a ball game."

Chafin said that even though members of the local Democratic Party land on different sides of the factional aisle, they are still "brothers" through and through. While the primary election campaign is under way, they'll fight tooth and nail against each other if necessary. But after Election Day, true team players will unite, hand in hand, in support of the winning candidates.

Chafin shared more of his thoughts on politics:

> That was the way it was with the Everett Workman faction. I wasn't particularly happy to be fired, and I was opposed to Everett's slate right down the line. However, after Election Day, Everett and I were friends again, and I supported the Democrats who won.
>
> Now, on the other hand, there are some politicians who get mad when situations happen like this and their side loses, or they lose their job to the other side.
>
> This type wants to fight, scratch, and never get over it when they lose an election, but they just don't understand. You see, fighting against one another is what makes good politics. That's what gets roads built and bridges constructed. When you are tryin' to outdo the other man — politically — you're going to try to do your best to build roads, schools, and anything else you can get done fer the people. Regardless of whether you are in an appointed position or an elected political office, you want people to notice that you are doing things for them. That's exactly what I have always tried to do.
>
> The more you do for people, the more support you get back. That's simple mathematics. So, this fussin' and feudin' during the campaigns is sometimes a good thing. Things get accomplished because of political rivalries; one man tries to outdo the other man and the voters are the ones who benefit. That's how the political world turns.

You Democrats Can't Keep From Fighting!

Temporarily unemployed and living on City View Hill in Logan, Chafin decided to take his wife's advice and spend time relaxing and thinking over recent events.

Louise Chafin had hoped that her husband might just be able to sort through his feelings about all the political turmoil that had led to his firing at the Capitol. However, having a lifelong reputation for being hyperactive, Chafin just couldn't allow himself to sit around and be reflective for too long. So after a couple of days or so of playing the part of househusband, he felt he had everything in perspective and was ready to start hunting for another job.

He recalled:

> I remember that I went over to see my friend John Morrison. I had once helped John get a job with the state road when he was having some problems. But he was a Republican, and his brother, Dallas, was a big, big Republican — chairman of the local Republican Party.

Morrison was no longer on the state payroll. He was working behind the front counter of a local restaurant that was owned by his brother. The restaurant, the Guyan Barbeque, was a popular eatery, and Morrison was quite successful. When Chafin walked in the door, Morrison looked up and called out, "Hey, I heard they fired ya, Raymond! Boy, it's sure a sight when a man can't be for his friends."

"Yeah, well, that's the way the ol' cookie crumbles. There's nothing I can do 'bout it," Chafin responded, chuckling, trying to conceal his anxiety. "Son, if that guy Neely runs again, I'll get even with him. You watch and see!"

Morrison grinned and replied, "I'm sure you will; I'm sure you certainly will! Let me tell you something, Chafin. I was talking to my brother this morning. Dallas told me to tell you that anytime you and your wife — and anybody else you want to bring with you — come to this restaurant, the food is on the house. It won't cost you one red penny — not one! Come in and get three meals a day, or whatever you want. It's free."

Chafin was astounded at the charitable offering, and the words touched his heart. Why Dallas and John Morrison, both diehard Republicans, would make such a generous proposal and a demonstration of kindness to a longtime grunt soldier for the opposing party was nearly incomprehensible, but nonetheless extremely appreciated.

During this conversation, T.R. Workman, vice president and general manager of West Virginia Coal and Coke Company, was sitting at a table eating, near the back of the room. At one point, Morrison pointed Workman out to Chafin and asked, "Do you know who that fellow is?"

"That's T.R. Workman," Chafin answered. "But I've never met him in person."

"He eats here an awful lot," Morrison said. "Stay here with me for a minute. When he comes up to pay his bill, I'll introduce ya."

A few minutes later, Workman walked up to the counter to pay for his lunch. John smiled and said, "T.R., I want you to meet my friend, Mr. Raymond Chafin."

"Oh-ho-ho! So you're the one who got canned, ain't ya?" Workman replied with a grin as he stared at Chafin. Word of Chafin's dismissal had traveled like wildfire.

"You ol' Democrats can't keep from fightin' amongst yourselves. You're goin' to have to join us Republicans!" Workman joshed with Chafin, patting him on the back. "At least we Republicans get along."

"Well ... I get along with my fellow Democrats — mostly," Chafin replied, as he swallowed hard.

"He's the best man in the country," Morrison added, vouching for Chafin and trying to change the subject. "He was my friend when I needed him, even though I'm Republican. I wouldn't even be standing behind this counter today if not for Mr. Raymond Chafin. Now he needs a job."

"What can you do, Chafin?" Workman inquired.

"Uh, I've been a road man for years and years, since I was seventeen or eighteen years old. I know construction."

"We're going to be doing a lot of construction at Omar," Workman said. "We're building a new plant. We're constructing railroad tracks on the side of the hill. We have several projects under way. You come up Monday morning, and I'll take you over to see Ott Holliday, my foreman, and we'll talk to you about a job then."

Chafin was thrilled as he shook Workman's hand and thanked him for the opportunity. If this worked out, he would be able to move back to the Omar area where he'd always wanted to return.

A Republican Gives Chafin a Job

You might call it serendipity. Nevertheless, that coincidental meeting with T.R. Workman at the Guyan Barbeque Restaurant made it possible for Chafin to interview for a prominent position with West Virginia Coal and Coke Company, at Omar.

The more Chafin thought about the prospects of the interview, the more he worried about the complexity of the entire situation. Would anyone remember his past?

He was scared to death. He started thinking about all the problems from years before, and it haunted me. Chafin convinced himself that when they'd go to look up his record, they would never give him a job — because he'd been blacklisted!

As he gave himself a pep talk, he traveled from City View to Omar. Upon arrival at the mine site, he took a deep breath, removed his gray fedora, and held his head high, putting on an air of confidence as he strode into the office where Workman and Holliday were waiting. He returned firm handshakes with the gentlemen after being warmly greeted. Workman offered him a chair, and he sat down and squirmed to get comfortable. Then Chafin surprised the men — and nearly surprised himself — by being bold enough to face the inevitable by bringing the dreaded issue out into the open.

"Before we start this meetin', gentlemen, there is something I want to confess. You need to know I was once blackballed from this coal company over a car wreck I was in some years ago. Let's not take up your time or mine — even though I have nothing but time — if this is going to be a problem," Chafin said.

Holliday replied, "Yeah, I remember a little bit 'bout that whole ordeal. That has no bearing on my offer, Chafin. We need you, and I'd like to have you working on our staff. But it's up to Workman because he's the boss."

The men talked for a long while about what the company needed and expected from its employees. They discussed construction projects that were under way, as well as plans for the future.

After the interview, Workman looked over at Holliday and nodded, then slowly turned toward Chafin, grinning, and said, "Raymond, as far as I'm concerned, you are now an employee of West Virginia Coal and Coke. Congratulations!"

Let's Plant Trees — Get the Gunpowder

After Chafin accepted the position, the conversation turned toward finances. Holliday, who was now his immediate supervisor, said, "Raymond, you're hired, but you and I still have to agree on your payday before you go to work. So what did you make on the road?"

"Well, is that a fair question?" Chafin responded.

Chafin had been making only around $300 a month in those days. But, he explained, he didn't want to "show all his cards" before getting an offer.

Chafin said firmly, "Uh, first you tell me what *you* are getting paid."

Workman interrupted Holliday and said, "Mr. Chafin, we're paying section bosses $12.50 a shift. If they work any overtime, they get time and a half. You work five days a week whether the mines work or not. Ott can give you the same amount that we offer a section boss. Fair enough?"

"I accept," Chafin said, thrilled with the knowledge that he would actually be better off financially than he had been as road supervisor.

***

The brisk winter morning Chafin was scheduled to start, he went to the mine site early.

Upon his arrival, Holliday instructed him, "Chafin, I want you to set some trees out along the streets of Omar, above the schoolhouse. Introduce yourself to the workers, then take the crew out there and get started."

Chafin recalled that day:

> The ground was frozen solid — about two inches deep. The crew and I took a long crowbar and punched a hole down through the frozen topsoil. It seemed like the longest day I had ever spent in my life. I had been used to getting in a car and going here and there. I had never been tied down to a job like that.
>
> The men and I stood there a few minutes and could see that we weren't getting anywhere because of the solid ground. So I asked one of the laborers, "Do we have any gunpowder? I've set trees out with dynamite before."

The employee stared at him for a second, wondering whether he was kidding, and then told Chafin that the company had plenty of explosives available in the supply house back at the tipple.

"Could you get me some powder, caps, and fuses?" Chafin asked. "We're goin' to plant us a few trees!"

After the employee returned with several crates of explosives, Chafin took the crowbar and made a deep hole, dropped gunpowder into the hole, attached a fuse, and ignited it.

Kablam-m-m! Explosion after explosion took place over the course of the day.

Chafin later recalled the incident and said that smoke and ash rolled out of those holes when the charges went off; and they planted all the trees in one day — when it had taken the men weeks to do the same type of task at other locations. He also said that people always told him "using explosives was a good way to kill the varmints in the ground that want to eat the trees."

Chafin went in to the office that evening, and Holliday asked, "How many did you get set out?" He was figuring that Chafin's crew had planted four or five trees.

"Well, we got 'em all planted — about thirty trees, give or take a couple."

"What?" Holliday nearly shouted. *"You what?* You mean to tell me you set them all out?"

"Yep — *kaboom* — I'd just soften that dirt up and shovel it out," Chafin answered, as he laughed. "I have a secret formula for plantin' trees in the wintertime: it takes plenty of gunpowder."

He began to explain exactly how the crew efficiently expedited the task with a little help from West Virginia Coal and Coke's explosive supply.

"Well, well, well, blowing holes in downtown Omar," Holliday exclaimed, as he bent over laughing. "It looks like we've got us a real construction man here — and a genuine tree farmer, too!"

So, after what had seemed like such a long time, Chafin was finally able to return to Omar to work for the company that had once fired him. Soon he and Louise moved back to Cow Creek. It was better for both of them, since it was closer to their places of employment and this was the place they had always called home.

Chafin — Making a Name for Himself

On the surface, things seemed to be going quite well. Chafin had won a certain amount of respect with his supervisor, Ott Holliday, by proving himself with his unorthodox way of planting dozens of trees.

Even though he was able to make an impression upon his employer, internally Chafin wasn't particularly thrilled with the idea of being tied down to this kind of strenuous manual labor.

He was used to overseeing mammoth operations for the state, being praised by county citizens for his ability to build rural roads and bridges. Instead, he was now taking orders from someone else and having to do the dirty work himself. He wanted to somehow break free.

Chafin had been accustomed to other perks, too. He had always enjoyed a liberal amount of freedom with his state job. He could jump in his state car and run from job to job anytime he wanted. He had been a respected troubleshooter and consultant, as well as an influential political powerhouse, and he wasn't afraid to work — but he wasn't exactly crazy about being just a common laborer again.

As state road supervisor, he had been able to take time during the day to talk politics with other politicians, merchants, and businessmen who congregated in Logan, usually at the Smokehouse Restaurant.

But now a restless Raymond Chafin was restricted — and even beginning to feel stifled. To make matters worse, he now worked for a stronghold of Republicans.

Tearing Out the Chicken Coops

"Maybe I shouldn't have been so bullheaded. Should I have supported Everett Workman and Governor Neely? Did I make a mistake?" Chafin silently asked himself during the harsh winter of 1944. "If I had been obedient to the governor, I would have received a giant promotion instead of an embarrassing firing."

No matter how often these thoughts swirled inside Chafin's head, deep down he knew he really didn't have an option: "I had to support my friend George Steele no matter what!"

Plus, the past was past. It was time to move forward.

At what was perhaps the lowest point in his new career, Chafin was under direction to destroy all the animal pens in the camps. Since that coal camp property was solely owned and operated by the land division of West Virginia Coal and Coke Company, renters had no choice but to comply with company demands.

Every fence was taken down, and whatever type of housing the renter had for animals was destroyed. The miners and their families were forced to sell or butcher their hogs, geese, and chickens.

Chafin was experiencing a political nightmare in the center of his political strength. Since the days when George Steele, along with a few others, had groomed him for a career in politics, Chafin knew the importance of "keeping the people of his precinct satisfied." It was drilled into the Barnabus resident's thinking that a supportive voter and a captured precinct were to be protected at all costs.

Chafin knew that this merciless act of tearing out pigpens and chicken coops could very well alienate the political base he had meticulously wooed and sheltered over the years. Even when he lived at City View, he was overseer of the Barnabus polls.

Chafin stated:

> These were MY people. I didn't want to do this to them. I went up to the camp with a crew, but I didn't like it! I ripped out fences for days. I went to each resident, with all the empathy I could muster, and explain, "If I don't do it, someone else will." When I talked to the people first, they would finally agree to peacefully allow me to tear them down. I think they understood I was in a terrible situation, and that I didn't really want to do it.

Eventually he completed the task in all the camps, although as Chafin had feared, people were not very happy about the situation.

Today, in the 21st century, chicken wire, poultry coops, and pigpens don't seem relevant to the world of politics. But in 1944, at the height of World War II and with citizens experiencing various forms of rationing, most depended upon their garden for vegetables and their chicken coop for fresh eggs and fryers. Families that were able to raise a hog or two had also invested a substantial amount of money into nurturing the animal — to feed their own children and sometimes those down the hollow who might be fatherless.

If they were fortunate enough to have pork to spare, they might even make a few dollars by selling it to a neighbor or trading it for some other product the family needed.

Thus, after enforcing this new policy, Chafin was undoubtedly deemed by some as a former friend who turned insensitive company man, who was willing to selfishly take food off anyone's table for a buck or two, just to keep his job. This could have spelled political doom and disaster.

However, once again, Chafin, with his gift for "smooth talking," was able to keep the political fallout under control by turning on his "good ol' boy" charm, sensitivity, and sincerity. He went on to explain:

I used whatever influence I could use to make sure that the company treated these people fairly and compassionately. After a while, Holliday put me with the carpenters and the plumbers. I liked that. We were moving around all the time. I was then able to do carpentry favors for the folks I had just aggravated. I may have pulled out their pig stalls, but I was then able to spruce up their house.

The company carpenters and plumbers maintained the coal camp communities. Because of Chafin's political ambitions and desires, every circumstance had to be looked at with reference to its value to his future. Therefore, the new job responsibilities would be more in keeping with Chafin's idea of helping the people of his precinct, which in turn would enable him to be seen in a more positive light, as he described it here:

> At that time, the company owned all of Rossmore to Stirrat. Every coal company house, from Rossmore on up the road, belonged to the coal company, except for a few private houses at Switzer and lower Switzer, and maybe at Sandy Bottom. But there were very few private homes in the region. The majority were company-owned. You can bet I kept everyone's house in tip-top shape. My future political career now depended on it!

One day, when the crew was working on a four-room house, Holliday pulled up in his company truck, jumped out, and ran across the yard. As he approached, he shouted at Chafin, who was hammering shingles on the roof, saying, "Chafin, we need a shovel operator to go down to the powerhouse and load some coal. Our shovel operator is sick and unable to work. Can you run a shovel?"

"Yeah, I can run a shovel. But I don't know if I can run that one or not," Chafin answered. "That one is so little — I'm used to bigger rigs."

"Well, go down and see if you can help us out. We have to have powerhouse coal!"

Happy to oblige, a smiling Chafin climbed down from the roof and left the rest of the gang to fill in. He recalled:

> The coal was stacked way up high behind the powerhouse. It was really a big job, but one I proved I could handle.

He learned that by accepting challenges that were thrown out to him and by successfully attempting new, difficult tasks, he was making himself more valuable to the company — and more accessible to the people of the coal camps.

According to Chafin, during this time — the first months of 1945 — there had been a local United Mine Workers of America strike, which had ended peacefully. Nevertheless, because of the work stoppage there was a severe shortage of bituminous coal. With the labor dispute settled, the company wanted to increase the coal yield to make up for loss of production. Chafin was ready to do all he could to help.

He explained:

> At that time a labor boss could belong to the UMWA. You could belong to the union and push, too. I got along with everybody, so they [the UMWA] let

me in the union. That tickled me to death, especially with regards to my political aspirations!

Being a UMWA member was something to be proud of. By faithfully upholding the union, one would automatically identify with the majority of the voters — the common man. Therefore, membership represented more than just loyalty to a labor organization for someone with political ambition — it was a status symbol, which could result in a profitable payoff at the voting booth.

Chafin recalled that although the regular shovel operator recovered from his illness and returned to his position, eventually he transferred as a full-time heavy equipment operator, adding one more notch to his career belt.

He rightfully boasted:

> Dang, in those days I could run 'bout anything — bulldozer, shovel, grader, whatever! Finally, after a while, when the shovel operator quit altogether, I took over the job permanently.

Calling For The Pastor

One cold winter evening at about this same time period, Chafin's father was not doing well. The effects of his cancer seemed to be worsening and his faithful wife, Lucinda, decided that it was time to "call in the family members, for he didn't have much time left." Within an hour, all the family had come to the house and gathered around Elbert's bedside, waiting for the inevitable. Chafin described the episode:

> Our immediate family was not particularly a church-going bunch. We did have some cousins who believed in baptizing by sprinkling; we had others that believed you had to be dunked in over your head in the creek; and some didn't think you needed any of that stuff at all. As for our house, we gave it all little thought. However, now that we thought Dad was dying, we had our neighbors send for Rev. M. K. Diamond, a spindly, gray-haired, ol' man of God who lived up the holler. Preacher Diamond was probably the only preacher-man our family knew very well. I guess we thought it only right that a preacher be with Dad at this final moment.
>
> Before Preacher Diamond could even get to the house, Dad grunted loudly, then sighed, and went limp. I was devastated, and so was the rest of the family. My brother nervously pulled Dad's sheet over his head. Apparently, he was gone.
>
> Then when the preacher, who had run all the way from his home to Dad's, finally arrived and burst in the front door, he saw all the family crying and Dad's lifeless body, and shouted, "Everybody, down on the floor and pray! I said pray! On your knees! Now!"
>
> Up until that day my brothers and I didn't put a whole lot of stock in prayin' and such; yet amidst the emotion of the moment we all dropped to our knees and tried to pray with the reverend. Without a doubt, ol' Preacher Diamond prayed the loudest, and we all tried to join in and mimic him. I've not heard prayin' like

his before or since that day. We all got serious for about 15 minutes or more. Every few seconds I peeked through one eye to see what was going on … but I kept on prayin' the best I could.

All of a sudden, as we were still on our knees and Preacher Diamond got even louder, the bed sheet jerked and quickly moved. Dad raised up, leaned his head over the bed and asked us, "What in the sam-hill are you all doing?"

Mom fainted. My heart nearly burst out of my chest! My sister screamed! The rest of my family was stunned, too. Preacher Diamond raised his hands and thanked God for a miracle. When we all settled down, we stared at Dad as if we were looking at a ghost. Dad was a little bit shook up over it all, too.

Dad felt pretty good after that. Now I'm not saying that I really know what really happened that day — but all I know is that I believe in prayer nowadays.

Preacher Diamond

Preacher Diamond didn't particularly work for a living, in a conventional sense, according to Chafin. The country preacher spent most days hanging around the front steps of the Logan County Courthouse. Chafin explained:

> When young couples came to the courthouse to be married, Preacher Diamond would be there to offer his services. He could give them a Christian marriage, instead of the couple using a judge or justice of the peace. I guess he earned two or three dollars per marriage ceremony he performed. That's mainly how he supported himself. I'd say there are still a few couples left whom this ol' preacher-man hitched. He was a good fellow and extremely good at reciting the wedding vows by memory.

Chapter Eleven
Stones Of Life

In 2002, when Chafin reminisced about his life, he talked at length about moments that he called "stepping-stones" — often only baby steps toward influence and power in the Democratic Party. Over the years, his political allies and opposition alike have called him names such as "Kingpin," "Big Wheel," "The Ol' Man," "Godfather," "Appalachian Political Boss," "Powerhouse," "The Big Man," "Cathead," and probably a few names inappropriate to print.

However, Raymond Chafin had humble beginnings, having come from the boondocks of Logan County, and he struggled as all men of his time did through the Great Depression. It may have seemed like he took one step forward only to fall back by three or four traincar lengths. Each success or gain might be followed by several failures or losses, of either a personal nature or related to his political career.

Chafin chuckled as he described many of the circumstances that happened through the years:

> This is the life of a politician. Come to think of it, this is just plain life, and I suspect that it happens to everyone. You have to expect bad with the good. Life isn't perfect. Jobs come and they go. But when you go into politics, you best hold on for the rollercoaster ride of your life! My life has had more twists and turns — ups and downs — than a ride at an amusement park.

By the spring of '45, Chafin had patiently maneuvered his way into the shovel operator's position at West Virginia Coal and Coke.

> A shovel operator's position paid the big money. There was a lot of overtime with it, and I liked that time and a half, too. I kept the job until the company really got involved in the construction business. Around that time, Workman and Holliday came to me and told me that they really wanted me to take a construction job with the company. But really, I liked the shovel. I was making good money, and I was content. I was in the union. I had all the hours I wanted to work. So I told them I wanted to keep the operator's job.

"No, we WANT you to take the construction job," Workman explained, as he clenched his jaw and gave Chafin a stern glance with his steely gray eyes.

"What will it pay me, T.R.?" Chafin asked, unable to muster much enthusiasm.

"I'll tell you what we'll do," Workman said, as he negotiated. "You'll get shovel operator wages, and if you work ten hours, we'll pay you ten. If you work any hours at all on Saturday, you're paid for a full ten-hour shift. You work on Sundays; we'll pay you the same thing. Plus, you stay in the union."

"Well, OK!" Chafin at last agreed.

With the wheels of his mind always churning ahead, he suggested, "We have a man here working for this company, Bruce Ellis, who has been foolin' with this shovel; he can run it well, too. Bruce is a good grate man, too, boys; he knows what to do. He needs to have my job here."

Workman, after analyzing Chafin's countenance and mulling over his advice, finally agreed to give Ellis a chance to be the replacement.

Chafin fondly remembered Ellis:

> Ol' Bruce was a jack-of-all-trades. Incidentally, he was Claude Ellis' daddy, and he was tough as ten-penny nails. He got along good with everybody. He was as good a dozer and shovel man as I ever did see. As a matter of fact, we actually had two good bulldozer men at the company — Bruce and a guy named Tom Farley. Tom was about the best I've seen at filling in a mine break with a bulldozer. But most fellers didn't want to fool with the ol' shovel. There were too many levers and whatnot. However, Bruce liked the shovel. He did a great job.

> By the time I began, construction had already started. I watched the crew build four tracks on each side of the hill. I also saw them build the chute and a tipple.

> I helped put in the aerial tram. Now, that was a big deal! It was up at No. 15, and they ran the tram straight up that mountainside. I was over all that — I put the forms in and checked everything out.

> Every once in a while, I'd have the engineers come out to the site to check me out. To get an engineer, all I would have to do is call him on the phone. We didn't know what two-way radios were back then. That aerial tram is still there — solid. I helped put that big plant in, too. We graded all the way to the railroad tracks. I believe we put five or six sidetracks in at the time. The construction endeavors were all major projects.

All along, while in the construction department, he was building new friendships and acquaintances. His mind continued to stay on local politics, and he never forgot the lasting benefits of remembering the simple things — a person's name, title, and political persuasion.

It's often been said that whenever someone remembers and calls a person by his name, he creates the sweetest sound that that individual will ever hear. By the time he was in his mid- to late twenties, Chafin already understood and put into practice this principle well.

Besides the political benefits of the situation, he was gaining practical construction knowledge that would help him in the future. According to Chafin, much of what he helped with still stands. You might say that it remains as a memorial to the hardworking crew, the engineers, and hillbilly ingenuity.

Three Musketeers

By the late 1940s, Raymond Chafin was a skilled craftsman and an able foreman with the company's construction division. He was also a UMWA member in good standing. He led a tightly knit crew of highly competent workers as they set out to accomplish some very difficult and often dangerous assignments.

The other men had learned to trust Chafin and his level of training, his natural abilities, and his straightforward leadership style. In time, Chafin grew even more confident in his role as boss. He felt that he and his men could tackle nearly any challenge the company could dream up.

Chafin needed all the self-assurance he could muster, for the company was notorious for coming up with imaginatively complex projects. Adding to the challenge, management's strict deadlines were often unreasonable.

Although the efforts seemed momentous at the time, Chafin felt a great deal of satisfaction in completing each job and in knowing it had been done well. The company men, such as T.R. Workman and Ott Holliday, apparently knew that he was one individual who could be counted on to get any job done — safely and efficiently.

Chafin recalled:

> Bruce Ellis had a brother working for the company, R.W. Ellis, who was a first-rate trackman. He had once worked for C&O Railroad. He was as good at laying a switch as his brother, Bruce, was on the steam shovel. There's not many trackmen in this part of the country who knew how to lay a switch. Well, for me, it was something hard. It was something that I also had to learn to do. With some difficulty, R.W. taught me how to lay a switch, but for him it came easy. We had to go by railroad regulations when we dealt with any switch coming into the tipples and the plants.
>
> At that time, steam locomotives were still used for the most part. I looked after all of this work for Ott. But the company paid me well to do it, so I didn't resent the extra work. They were good to me. At one point they even built me a house in Barnabus so that I would move back up here. When they built those big ol' company houses with eight or ten rooms for their bosses, they gave me the first one.
>
> My wife, Louise, taught school right across the road from it. So West Virginia Coal and Coke made it as convenient for her as they could so that it would also be convenient for me and we would stay satisfied.
>
> They even let me pick a good man when I needed one. Now, I never had any problems with anyone that they hired, but they let me do the picking after a while. I had good men all the days I was there.

When he and his crew got the big plant built and the railroad in, they started having trouble at the No. 5 Mine. It started drowning out.

> They had some six-inch pumps put down, and they'd pump that water straight up from the mine. Well, it got so bad that when we got close to No. 22 Holden, there was so much water in there that the pumps couldn't handle it all. So they sent me up to No. 5 to put a shaft in — 352 feet straight down! It was about a 12 X 12 or 12 X 14-foot shaft.

Chafin said they drove two enormous pipes down that shaft so that they could pump the overflow water. When they got the pump installed, it was set on the top of the ground for convenience.

When we started that pump, it took too much power to drive it all. Men had to run a power line for six or seven miles from Chauncey hollow up to that pump to gain enough power to turn that pump over.

Then the engineers were afraid one pump wouldn't handle the problem, so we put another pump in place.

According to Chafin, when they started up one pump, the lights dimmed and flickered "everywhere in the surrounding communities." When the second pump was installed, there wasn't even enough power to run both pumps. Everything came to a standstill. Blackout.

Chafin said that now they had no choice — it was time to enlarge the powerhouse.

West Virginia Coal and Coke had put its own power plant in at the site sometime in the '40s, according to Chafin, because they'd had a "falling out" with Appalachian Power Company. After building and maintaining their own power source, it took about a dozen company men to handle it. According to Chafin:

> They had their own coal, so it only made sense to produce their own power. They merged all of their mining operations and ran them off this power plant. For the time period, it was a big deal.

The company was completely self-contained and self-sufficient. It not only owned its own power source, but its own construction crews, hydraulic and machine shops, housing, general stores, water supply, and coal delivery system. Chafin remembered being in on the plans to enlarge the system:

> When we started the enlargement plans for the powerhouse, we were going to build it twenty-eight feet longer. Therefore, we had to dig down as deep [for the foundation] as we did in length. We had to go all the way down to solid rock. Bruce Ellis and I used the shovel and dozer to dig down approximately twenty-eight feet. We put the waste out of the hole into trucks and hauled it off. We didn't have clamshells or any of that newfangled stuff back then. They'd wench those trucks out of the shovel area until eventually we dug down a full twenty-eight feet.
>
> When we were nearly complete and we got ready to get out of there, we had a problem. Bruce Ellis asked me, "Now that we're down here, Chafe, what are we gonna do? How are we goin' to get ourselves out of this one?"

The two had painted their way into a corner, so to speak. The multi-ton steam shovel had accomplished its task. The hole was dug — twenty-eight feet long, twenty-eight feet deep. But now they had to figure out how to get that shovel and themselves out of the cavity.

"Boys, we're going to have to slope one edge down to get out," Chafin first suggested. Unfortunately, there was a baseball field next to the pit, so the idea of digging a forty-five-degree slope that would destroy part of the playing field was unthinkable. For

Chafin, tearing out a ball field used by community young people would be another case of political suicide. There simply had to be another way.

Eventually, Tom Farley, a master dozer operator, cut the sidewall just slightly. He also had two large wench lines ready to go from the top of the opening. After taking a deep breath, Bruce Ellis got on the massive shovel and moved his earth-moving contraption as close to the sidewall of the pit as possible.

Farley raced over to connect the huge wench-line hooks to strategic points on the shovel, and when all was in place, he waved his arms in order to notify everyone to stay away from the action. He then threw the switch that started the wenches. Within seconds, the motors chugged at full volume and let loose with unearthly groans and creaks of metal against metal. The wench lines became taut and started pulling upward, tipping the backside of the shovel while the front lifted off the ground. As the enormous machine dangled from the steel cables, Ellis grimaced and gripped onto the sides of the swinging cab, as gravity thrust him helplessly back into his metal seat.

Chafin remembered the incident:

> That shovel was brought almost straight up! The dipper swung freely behind it, and Bruce — poor Bruce — rode that shovel all the way up. I'll never know how he kept a hold of his seat as the shovel started dangling over the massive hole.

The sharp clatter produced by the stress on the shovel's joints and the ever-tightening wench wire was deafening, with the noise only adding to the anxiety of the moment. Crewmembers froze in place at the top of the hole and watched aghast as the lines stretched nearly beyond capacity, with Ellis and his shovel inching their way to the top of the deep chasm.

When Ellis finally got out of gulch, and Chafin was later towed to safety, Chafin turned and looked over at Ellis, and said, "Bruce, it ain't hot today is it, buddy?"

"No, but I was *hot* … scalding hot coming out of there!" Ellis replied, as he was barely able to collect a half-smile, while rolling his eyes and panting heavily. With his red bandana-print handkerchief, he swabbed streams of salty sweat from his forehead and neck. His once clean work shirt and pants were now mucky reddish brown from the mixture of clay and perspiration. He was a "sight for sore eyes" — but at last he was safe and secure on the edge. And most importantly, as far as the company was concerned, the shovel was still intact.

West Virginia Coal and Coke Company's equivalent of the adventurous Three Musketeers — Bruce Ellis, Tom Farley, and Raymond Chafin — had finished the prep work and saved the day. All three were out of harm's way and ready for their next escapade.

The company-owned powerhouse enlargement project was soon completed, and the water at No. 5 Coal Mine started being pumped out — with plenty of electrical power to spare.

The powerhouse ran seven days a week, and it ran like a charm.

Tough Boys

An Unexpected Visit

One hot summer evening at Barnabus, T.R. Workman made an unexpected visit to the home of Raymond and Louise Chafin. Raymond had taken a break from his yard work and was resting in a rusty metal lawn chair in the front yard. He was wearing a ribbed white T-shirt and green work pants, guzzling a bottle of ice-cold Coke. With his free hand, he waved his tattered white handkerchief, shooing away the gnats from around his face.

Inside the house Louise was busy frying pork shoulder and eggs. The aroma of the chops and buttermilk biscuits saturated the evening air outside the couple's house, signaling that it was almost dinnertime.

As Workman approached the front of Chafin's house, his black Ford coupe came to a screeching halt. With a scowl on his face, he jumped out of the driver's seat and walked straight over to Chafin.

"Chafin, you need to know that we're all going to get fired," Workman blurted out, as he waited for Chafin to say the next word.

"Well, T.R., what's the trouble?" Chafin asked, as he smirked. "What can I do?"

"We ain't got enough water to run the new powerhouse — that's the problem! Son, we've got to have water, and we gotta have it quick!"

"I dunno, T.R.," Chafin answered. "I don't rightly know what we can do. That's the kind of job that I am leery of."

"Let me tell you — we have that big tank down at the plant. We'll fill it up first — but we have so much mine water that we'll have to watch that we don't pump mine water in it," Workman instructed. "Then we're going to have to shoot that dam on the mountain ridge to get ourselves more water," he added, patting Chafin on the back as if to say, "I can count on you."

The company had one dam that held a reservoir of water for the powerhouse, but apparently this surplus wasn't enough to keep the newly enlarged powerhouse in working order.

"Meet me in the morning if'n you can. We'll take a gander at the dam before we do anything, OK?" Chafin responded, with a look of worry on his face as he escorted Workman back to his car. "T.R., Louise nearly has dinner ready. You want to eat with us?"

"Thanks, but I better head home to the little woman," he said. "She's probably got somethin' waiting for me on the table, too."

Chafin opened the front screen door and went into the house for dinner. As he ate, he told Louise about the problem. His wife was concerned about the possible ramifications of using dynamite around the reservoir, and in all honesty, Chafin was, too. After cleaning up the supper dishes, the weary couple went on to bed, but Chafin lay awake for what seemed like hours with the situation bearing heavily upon his mind.

The next day, Chafin got up early, got dressed, and headed down to the site, where he met with Henry Bare, chief engineer for the company, and five others to assess the situation.

"Ol' Man Darks, president of the company, also made a rare visit to the Omar plant. He drove in from Cincinnati. He came along with us to look at the dam," Chafin recalled.

Upon inspection, Chafin recognized that with the size of the dam, probably larger than he had remembered, there was even more to worry about with the project they were about to undertake.

"Raymond, are you afraid that if we shoot it, it will cause leaks in the dam?" Bare asked.

"Yup," Chafin said, as he shuffled his feet in place.

Holliday suggested that the men start at the back of the dam and work toward the front. He said, "When we're finally done, we can clear things up — make sure everything is stable — and we can pump the water out of the lower end of it at night."

That's exactly what we did. We started at the back of that dam, drilling down and blasting rock out of there. Somebody suggested that we build another dam. So we took the rock from the first dam, then we went up and brought in four-foot pipe, over a hundred feet long, and laid the pipe in there and started making a fill across that. It was just like what you do when you fill in a road with rock. Then we had a second dam.

Earl Fraley and Herbert Chafin were labor bosses at that time. They had taken over my former job. Anyway, Earl and Herbert were over the dam. We got a "guneyed" machine.

A "guneyed" machine was an apparatus that took mixed cement and shot it in between the rocks in order to create the dam walls and add stability.

We finished that dam. Now, it was a particularly dry summer, so the company decided we needed another dam — making a total of three dams. We had a heck of a lot of work to accomplish. We finally got it done.

Chafin credits the experience of people like Holliday and Bare for making the process of building the dams a safe one for everyone involved. Chafin recalled:

Meanwhile, we were still pumping water out of No. 5 Mine at the time, and it continued to run for a year, two, or three after that. When those two big twenty-four-inch pumps started running, there wasn't a single car or truck that would dare go through Pine Creek! There also wasn't much of a road up there back then, anyway. When those pumps started — and as long as the pumps were on — you couldn't bring your car in or out. It looked like it was really pouring rain at the head of the hollow. You'd be surprised how much water those two giant twenty-four-inch pumps can pump! Water gushed everywhere.

Chafin worked for about five years under T.R. Workman and Ott Holliday. In spite of the obviously stressful situations he became involved in while working for the coal company, those were rewarding days for him in many ways. But the following years would be equally fulfilling for the Barnabus resident — on the job and politically, too.

In those days if a man got sick and was unable to make his car payment 'cause he wasn't workin', the company would write up an order and make his car payment for him — that's if'n he was a good employee and worked every day. Buddy, they liked for ya to do your work, though.

They also tried to keep your coal camp house in A-No. 1 shape. It didn't matter to them if you lived on 700 Hill or 400 Hill. If you had something wrong with your house and went to the rental office and reported it, they sent someone out to get the work done.

Then Chafin got a promotion: Holliday came up to him one day and asked him to be his assistant. Holliday explained to Chafin that he had men who would teach him all that he would ever need to know. He said, "Actually, you don't even need to know it all. All you have to do is check on the men and make sure that they are taking care of each duty that's scheduled. Make sure they have all the materials they need to work with, and be here when I'm gone — in case a man gets hurt. You'll be over all the houses from Rossmore to Stirrat."

There were as many as one hundred men working in the tenement department. With his new job title, Chafin would be over all the carpenters, plumbers, and general laborers. After comparing mental lists of pros and cons, he decided to accept the position and immediately stepped in as Holliday's right-hand man. Chafin elaborated:

> During my time as assistant, we built a substation at the mine. Our men set the giant fan outside. We went into the mines and set casts. If there were a bad top at one of the mines, we'd take big sections of iron pipe, place them in position, and bolt them together to keep the roof from caving in. We also built giant overcasts – something like the oversized drainpipes used under the roads. Of course, I was familiar with that from my state road days.

Chafin was involved in nearly everything, from the smallest of tasks to the most significant projects for the company during his four- to five-year tenure.

But once the construction projects and tenement work began to slow down, Chafin — at the pinnacle of his leadership over a hundred-man construction team — had a difficult time staying busy. He explained that in order to appear busy — or "sort of hide and get myself out of the way" — he started working around the company garage. Before too long that would become his permanent position, but initially he had a lot to learn.

> At the time, I had been working around Fred Caldwell, shop assistant foreman, and F. Cook, one of the finest men I ever knew, at what they called the Owens Garage. Since I didn't really have a whole lot to do [in my normal capacity for the company], they kept me hoppin'. These guys were more like brothers to me than fellow employees. There was also a fellow named Barker who worked with us some. They taught me how to work on tires and repair trucks, tractor motors, shovels, even big dozer motors. They tried their best to teach me mechanics, and I tried my best to learn.
>
> We had about twenty-five or thirty trucks — we kept them all going — two dozers and a shovel.
>
> There was also a man we called "Ol' Man Sheader" — he was the shop foreman. He was really our boss, but we hardly ever saw him. The only time we

ever saw Sheader was when we needed [a special part or] something made. We'd then go see him [in a different building], and he'd make it for us on the spot.

One time during squirrel season, Chafin was "itching to head for the mountains" — specifically, the vicinity where several large beech trees grew up the hollow from his home. But he was covered up with work at the garage, making the chance to go hunting improbable.

Knowing how intensely Chafin desired to go, Fred Caldwell went into the shop one morning and said, "Raymond, you've been working a whole lot lately, and you haven't got to squirrel hunt any. I'll tell you what you can do. See those shuttle-buggy tires lying in the back of the shop? Fix those buggy tires, and by gosh, as soon as you get them fixed, you can go squirrel huntin' — and I'll mark you down for ten hours today."

"That's a go!" Chafin shouted, as he excitedly started grabbing up the small tires. Chafin stripped the tires off their rims and went straight to work, fixing every one of them and putting air back in them when he was done.

Soon a sweaty, out-of-breath but still energetic Raymond Chafin had proudly finished repairing the last tire. With a huge grin, he grabbed his lunch pail and toolbox, turned out the lights and closed the door, and headed home, where he grabbed his Winchester shotgun and started up the hollow.

In the meantime, there were problems back at work that he wasn't aware of until he went back next day. "The tires I had repaired were sent to the No. 15 and No. 19 mines," he explained.

Chafin went on to say that prior to the assignment, he had never fixed any tires himself. He had observed Cook, Caldwell, and Barker as they did, many times since he had started working in the garage. So he thought, "How hard can it be?"

The morning after Chafin's hunting expedition, the shop received a phone call that all of their buggies' tires were flat.

Caldwell panicked and asked Chafin, "My gosh, what the heck did you do? Every tire you fixed went flat. Did you put patches on 'em?"

"I sure did!" Chafin answered.

Chafin, Caldwell, and a few other men went and picked up all the tires from the mine sites and brought them back to the garage. Caldwell removed one from the rim and pulled the tube out, immediately recognizing the problem.

"When we looked, Fred noticed that I had never taken the backing off the patch. When I put all those patches on, I used some glue [we had sitting around]. That was all," Chafin confessed, as he chuckled. "An inner-tube patch has a backing you take off so that the patch will stick. But I just took the entire patch [with the backing on], slapped some glue on it and the tube, and pressed it in place. It stayed!"

"I'll be doggone," Caldwell said, as he shook his head in disbelief. "Don't you EVER let anyone know what a fool you've made of yourself!"

Caldwell and the entire crew immediately went to work fixing all the tires properly.

Chafin recalled, in an interview:

You know, that's the only time Fred ever talked mean to me. All my patches came off when that glue didn't hold. It would have been so much better if I had put the patch on right to begin with!

When the men had completed the repair job, Fred Caldwell came over and nearly whispered to Chafin, "Don't ever say nothing about this" — implying that it would never be mentioned again.

Several days after the incident, however, T.R. Workman came walking up to Chafin, grinning like a 'possum. As he got near Chafin, he threw up his hand, chuckled, and said, "Well, hello there, Mr. Smarty!"

"Hi ... uh ... Mr. Workman. What do you mean? What have I done now?" Chafin asked.

"You know what!" Workman said. "Even your ol' grandpa who drove those oxen years and years ago would have had enough dang sense to take the back off that patch before he put it on!"

He then nearly doubled over laughing, as Chafin rolled his eyes and smirked; but then Chafin began to chuckle along with him.

Caldwell and the other men had found themselves unable to keep quiet about the incident. As a matter of fact, Chafin later found out that everybody at the plant had heard about his tire patching troubles. He stated:

> I found out at that time that it's best to keep your sense of humor, especially when you don't have much of a choice. Those fellas gave me a hard way to go, but I learned to laugh with them about the tires. It was either laugh or hide my face due to embarrassment. I chose to cackle out loud.

Chapter Twelve

Raymond's Beloved Father Passes

A self-proclaimed philosopher, A. Sachs, once said, "Death is more universal than life; everyone dies, but not everyone lives."

Elbert Chafin, father of Raymond Chafin, knew how to live. He pursued happiness. Besides being respected among his peers, he was known among the neighborhood for his honesty, sense of humor, and willingness to work hard to carve out a meager living for his family. Few remember seeing Elbert publicly without that well-known "Chafin toothy smile."

He had once worked as a miner, although he never really liked being underground; he said it was too confining. He was a deliveryman at Peytona Lumber Company. He tilled the soil at his farm. Then he had a chance to work for the Junior Mercantile at Omar in a variety of capacities — butchering, cleaning, shipping and receiving, and delivering groceries and furniture. He also moonlighted as a hooch driver through most of those years.

> Dad never made any of his own corn whiskey. Nonetheless, he delivered jugs along his route. Everything was delivered by a loaded-down, horse-pulled wagon. He served customers all over these hills, and everyone knew him well. The rumrunners liked him because of his honesty. He was also close-lipped.

It was in 1935 that Elbert Chafin was diagnosed with prostate cancer. Even though many people thought of his son Raymond as being rough-edged and tough-skinned, deep down nothing could have been further from the truth. He was devastated when he heard the doctor's report. Besides being his father, Elbert was Raymond's hero and mentor. When the family received the prognosis, Chafin was mature enough to understand that everything from that day forward would be different — and he was right. Chafin stated:

> I suspect Dad could have lasted longer, and lived a healthy existence, if he had agreed to surgery when he first found out he had cancer. Instead, he wasn't thrilled about the idea of someone cutting on him. So, he refused to let a surgeon remover his prostrate [sic]. He lived many years of sufferin' for that decision.

The once hard-working, self-sufficient man the family depended upon was forced to retire from his job as the sickness zapped his strength and exiled him to a bed in the back room of the company-owned house. Chafin did all he could to support his mother and father. Being the oldest, Chafin felt it was his responsibility to "put food on their table."

Fortunately, the particular form of the disease Elbert suffered with was not the most aggressive, although its deleterious effects were evident to all. It must have been difficult for his wife and the children to watch as cancer put a stranglehold on his frail, ever-weakening body.

Raymond Chafin had to spend long periods living away from home so that his folks would be eligible for federal and state assistance. But it seemed like he was always able to find a few minutes of quality time to spend each evening at his father's bedside. There were some periods when Chafin would sit through the night with his ailing father, caring for him.

In spite of his infirmity, Elbert was able to offer his son a listening ear and solid advice. Once his dad "worried himself sick" when his boy was injured seriously in an auto accident and did his best to help him while he mended at home. He was also there to encourage this fearful young man when he was unfairly blackballed by his employer.

Elbert was supportive when this oldest son started working for the WPA, hauling huge rocks on his back. It was with his father's blessing that Raymond eventually took the state road job. Later his dad grieved with him when he was fired by Governor Neely, but also was able to rejoice with him, when he got the West Virginia Coal and Coke position. Regardless of the circumstances, Elbert always demonstrated that he was proud of his eldest son. He believed that there was little that his boy couldn't do. They had a very close relationship.

Although Elbert didn't have a formal education, it could be said that he had the homespun equivalent of a master's degree in coaching, counseling, and encouraging his son. He taught Raymond to be self-reliant and to work hard, and to never let up until a task was complete. He also taught him a great deal about the Cow Creek style of politics: always make sure a Democrat wins — *by a landslide.*

In 1948, while Raymond Chafin was still at West Virginia Coal and Coke, his father quietly passed away, his suffering finally over.

Chafin later said, "Dad was probably the only person who ever really understood me. He always said the right words to me at the right time. I still miss him."

Chafin Remembers Those Who Helped

After thirteen years of decline from cancer, Elbert passed on. The one part that young Chafin had to be thankful for was that his dad's misery was finally over.

Ironically, in many ways, due to the loss, Chafin's personal suffering had just begun. For the first time he had to face challenges and trials alone, without having the security of knowing he could go to this man — who was not only his father but his mentor and best friend — for his "concrete advice."

It was just about this time that Chafin's wife, Louise, gave birth to their daughter, Margaret — on October 30, 1949. Little Margaret, a tinier than normal newborn with dark eyes and fair skin, would never know her Grandpa Chafin except through the colorful stories that her father would tell her about the good ol' days at the company store.

Maybe, in one sense, Margaret filled the cavernous hole in Chafin's heart. Chafin remembered:

> The first time I looked at Margaret I was speechless. She was so beautiful. Up until that day I never could imagine myself as a dad. I was too selfish for somethin' like a child of my own. But once I saw her in her crib, I was completely taken with her. I was immediately ready to be "Daddy" to her.
>
> I loved to just sit and stare at her and watch her spontaneous movements when she was a newborn. She was so tiny and helpless, and she would grasp

hold of my index finger with her small hand. She had a strong grip, as I can still remember.

If I couldn't see her little chest stir slightly when she breathed, I would yell for Louise. Louise would run into the bedroom and inspect her. Then, once everything checked out OK, she would calm me down and tell me, "Raymond, settle down. She'll be fine. See, she's still sucking on her bottle. She is just so small you can't always perceive her breathing."

I had a lot to learn as a parent, but one thing came naturally — love. After little Margaret was born, I took out insurance on Louise, Margaret, and me through the company. My dad didn't have any health insurance to rely on when he needed it most. Louise and I didn't have any money to speak of, so we couldn't help him much. This is why I had to thank Dr. W.W. Brewer, who owned the Logan General Hospital at that time.

Chafin was referring to the time when he had to take his father over to Logan General for treatment, and Dr. Brewer said, "Raymond, why don't you just leave your dad here for a week or so?"

"Well, we can't pay for it," Chafin whispered, blushing from embarrassment. "I just don't have the means, Doc."

"Raymond, as long as I own Logan General Hospital, your dad will never have to pay for anything," Dr. Brewer responded. "That goes for your mother and the rest of your family. None of you will ever have to pay a dime."

Dr. Brewer was a first cousin to Elbert Chafin. So Chafin's dad stayed at the hospital that week, and he was in and out of the hospital every few weeks thereafter. The local ambulance, then owned by Harris Funeral Home, would pick Elbert up at the house and then take him back home as needed.

We didn't have the ambulance system that we have now. I can only guess that Dr. Brewer must have paid Harris Funeral Home, because we were never billed for any of those ambulance runs. At one point they were coming for Dad every week — sometimes twice a week — and hauling him there for treatments and then home.

Matter of fact, Harris Funeral Home ambulance drivers got so chummy with Dad that they would occasionally drive him on up to the top of the hill, just so he could look around from inside the ambulance. That's how much friendship we had with the hospital and the funeral home.

The Harris family and the Chafins go way back. Anytime I ever ran for an office, they were always for me. I owe a lot to them. I have always appreciated them.

The company store doctors — Dr. Starcher, Dr. Moore, and Dr. Logan — would come to the house to see my dad because they liked him. He had built himself a friendship with them when he worked for Junior Mercantile. He'd take them medicinal herbs from the farm. Dad helped the doctors find good moonshine, too. You gots to remember — yous didn't have these liquor stores back then.

In those days, Prohibition was still in force. At the stroke of midnight on January 16, 1920, the Eighteenth Amendment — called Prohibition — was put into effect. All legal importing, exporting, transporting, selling, and manufacturing of intoxicating liquor had been ordered to end. It wasn't until 1933 that Prohibition was lifted.

However, the amendment didn't stop the flow of liquor completely in Logan County. White Lightning — Appalachian moonshine – was the powerful drink of choice for many citizens during the late 1920s and '30s. Underground operations hired men like Elbert Chafin to provide a system of distribution for the illegal brew. Every time Chafin spoke of his father delivering 'shine,' he clearly pointed out that Elbert never owned a still or played any part in producing the product. He only transported it for others. He added:

> I like to think back about Dad and how good he was to people. And people were so darn good to him — like Dr. Brewer and those other doctors — when he needed them the most. They doctored Dad for free and helped us all out. They were our friends.

After his death, Elbert Chafin's wake, an all-night vigil over the corpse, was held at his Cow Creek home, as was the custom of the time. It must have seemed like "most of the Creek" and hundreds of Elbert's relatives came to the wake. Elbert's remains lay in state in the center of the living room, and fresh flowers surrounded the rough wood casket. Neighbors and acquaintances casually stopped by and left whenever they felt like it throughout the night, while a handful of family members staying for the duration. The observance was often called "staying up with the dead" in those days.

Neighbors brought in ham, fried chicken, hot vegetables, casseroles, covered dishes, breads, and desserts with them. The house was crowded with people visiting, reminiscing, crying, laughing, singing, eating, and paying their respects to the elder Chafin.

Harris Funeral Home, on Main Street in Logan, was in charge of the funeral arrangements. They prepared the body and oversaw the proceedings. The next morning, they drove the casket to the cemetery for burial.

Chapter Thirteen

Chafin Leaves WV Coal and Coke

By 1950, Chafin had held a variety of positions with West Virginia Coal and Coke. However, things were slowing down at the plant, and he had been working in the garage with Fred Caldwell and others.

One day, Workman asked Chafin to come to his office after clock-out. When Chafin appeared hours later, Workman said, "Boy, you sure have done a good job here over the years. We have just about all our work done, and everything is in good shape. I want you to know how much I appreciate all the things that you've done."

Chafin stood at Workman's desk, eyeing him suspiciously, and responded, "So, uh, what do you want now?"

All sorts of questions raced through Chafin's head as he looked intently into the eyes of his boss. Chafin had come to learn that whenever Workman appeared with that rather pathetic, forlorn, basset-hound look on his face, he was about to be asked to take on a near-impossible challenge. Having deduced that this day was no different, he braced himself for the worst. Could i be that there was a water shortage again, or would Workman ask him to build another dam, perhaps?

Alas, this situation turned out to be a bit different from those in the past. "Well, I want you to go back to the state road," Workman explained. "Things have sort of gone downhill since you left them, as ya' know."

The suggestion was followed by momentary silence. Neither man said a word while Workman's statements echoed in their minds. Somewhat shaken and confused, Chafin finally broke the ice, answering softly, "T.R., here you are a Republican, and you know that they ain't goin' to hire me back on the state road. Now, I sure like to hear you say that a Democrat did a good job at something, but, sheesh, I can't really afford to go back there now."

"I have a way to get you back on, Raymond," Workman said, as he motioned for Chafin to sit down in the tufted leather chair across from his desk. "They really do need ya on the state road. If you'll go back to the state road, I'll see that you don't lose a thing with West Virginia Coal and Coke."

Since Workman declared without hesitation that he had a plan of action for making the transition, Chafin considered the offer serious enough to ask for a few days to think about it and talk things over with his wife.

Chafin had been approached a few times by certain politicians, even before Workman had said anything. He had always brushed off the notion. However, for some strange reason, he entertained the idea this time.

After checking out the position and the implications of such a move, he took into consideration how easy it had been to be fired by Governor Neely some years before — over differences in politics. Even though a new governor had taken office in 1949, Governor Okey Leonidas Patteson, a Democrat from Fayette County, the thoughts of going back made Chafin a bit nervous.

"Go on down and talk to the local politicians," Workman pressed. "I believe if you go, you will be pleasantly surprised how much they want you back."

Thinking back, Workman was surely the worst Republican that I've ever seen! But, sure enough, I did go see the politicians. We talked for a while, and we negotiated. I finally agreed to go back to the state road.

The experience that I had gotten from my various duties with West Virginia Coal and Coke fell perfectly in line with the state road. I was a better man for working in Omar. I had also kept my position with the Island Creek voters during that time period.

Chafin had matured since he last held that position with the state. Not only was he older, but he also had learned so much more about construction work, carpentry, and, yes, even politics. Hopefully, he wouldn't let himself get caught in a "Governor Neely" type of situation again. This time he was determined to keep his job — no matter what!

He was also ready to make a name for himself in the county. After all, he now knew even more about how to get things done for the people and how to make political alliances that would help his position in the party — or so, he thought.

It's Politics Again

Chafin says there are certain truths all politically minded folks should know. For example, when you accept a job that's controlled by politicians, you can never feel completely at ease. One's position is only as stable as his relationship with whomever is in office — and totally dependent upon how much the particular political faction in charge likes you at any given moment in time. If you somehow rock the boat, you might as well figure it's time to start checking out the "Help Wanted" section in the classifieds.

Chafin's job at West Virginia Coal and Coke had basically dried up and T.R. Workman had worked out a perfect solution for Chafin, somehow propping open the door of opportunity for him at the state road department.

It was late 1950, and Chafin still lived at Cow Creek on a small farm with his wife, Louise, and daughter, Margaret. They rented the farmland from West Virginia Coal and Coke.

Ray Watts and a few other politicians came up to my house and we talked at length about how I was taking back the state road position. The money was right and I was ready to begin.

Things were already a bit "sticky" politically at the time. Ray Watts, one of the main local leaders partially responsible for approving Chafin's re-hiring, was not a part of Chafin's faction. Thus, from the beginning of his new position with the state road, the goings stayed interesting, if not complicated.

The bad thing at the time was that Ray Watts was running against Floyd Murphy. Floyd was one of my boys from the Creek — and as popular as could be! He'd been on the county court and a magistrate, called a justice of the peace or J.P. back then. Ray Watts was pretty well known, too. But he didn't have the vote gettin' power that Murphy had. They were both running for sheriff on the Democratic ticket.

Therefore, if Chafin were going to continue to dabble in politics, he would have to maneuver cautiously in order to maintain his position with the road department. He would soon find out that this situation with Watts versus Murphy would be a difficult one to work under. But he was determined to keep his job this time.

I had accepted the state road position. The offices and garage were located at Stollings then. Plans for a boulevard [in Logan] were just beginning when I went in. Not all the people along Main Street were pleased about this boulevard. It would be taking away their backyards that went directly to the river.

Some of the local businessmen were convinced that it would kill downtown and that shoppers would just drive on by the city. Black Bottom merchants were especially upset. In their thinking, this new state road would make it easy for shoppers to bypass their stores altogether. They liked things as they had always been. I'm tellin' ya that it took a lot of salesmanship and fancy talkin' to overcome these kinds of problems. Some folks just can't accept change.

So once the people got to where they accepted the plan, I got in there and helped get the rock needed for the job from R.W. Buskirk, from over in Buskirk Addition.

We had to talk to him about his house. He didn't want to sell. So I went over with some engineers, and we went through the process of looking around to see if we could move his home and still get our project done. I knew the property pretty well 'cause I had picked apples there when I was just a kid. There was a great deal of property that we would have to remove in order to get the rock.

Instead of buying the house, the state paid Mr. Buskirk a certain amount [for his trouble], and then moved the structure back a ways on his property to allow the excavation work. He also had three or four more houses that he used as rental property, and we moved them, too. Buskirk then sold us his right-of-way. We had all the rock we needed — once we dug it out.

Then we had a problem when we started taking out land for the road. Some of it was with C&O Railroad property. We would have to go up behind the C&O Railroad property and remove dirt. Then other problems came.

There was other property that was leased by Monitor Coal and Coke Company. The company mined coal underneath the ground — actually under the place where we were going to take the rock out.

So we had to go to C&O and see about the right-of-way, and then we had to go to the coal company. We finally got everything accomplished. Colonel Browning, of Monitor Coal and Coke, and his crew were not too hard to get along with concerning this problem because they wanted the boulevard, too.

C&O, on the other hand, couldn't have cared less whether we had a boulevard or not. They were only interested in their rail lines. Obviously, they've never been interested in roads because they wanted people to use their passenger trains. They wanted business to rely on their rail system for hauling merchandise in and out of the county. However, we finally got C&O to agree — but it sure wasn't easy!

At last everything was in place. R.W. Buskirk gave Chafin and his crew the much-needed rock for the mammoth project. Monitor Coal gave the state complete right-of-way. C&O reluctantly agreed to give rights to the state, too.

So the first order of business was the building of a temporary bridge in order to make construction traffic possible. The boulevard project was no longer just a dream. It was now a reality.

City of Logan Boulevard Is Dedicated

A number of obstacles had been overcome, and now — in the early 1950s — Raymond Chafin, the new head of Logan County's division of the West Virginia State Road Department, and his men were moving along with the Logan Boulevard project. A temporary bridge across the Guyandotte River was erected to make traffic flow more easily around the construction. Everything appeared to be going smoothly, and the work was moving along quickly.

Chafin picked up the story there:

> Then we ended up with one more problem at the end of the project, as far as I was concerned. We ran up to the end of where we wanted to go with this boulevard, and it looked like we would have to take out the temporary bridge we'd built. But I wanted to keep that darn bridge *right thar*.
>
> On the day we planned the dedication for Logan Boulevard, the road commissioner came down to Logan for the festivities. It was one of those cold, rainy days. It was just awful outdoors.

"Just awful" it was. The wind gusts had picked up and rain seemed to be coming down in buckets as the local dignitaries scrambled to take shelter under the canvas canopy where the dedication was to take place. The din made by the hard rain thumping against the canvas made it nearly impossible to hear one another. In spite of it all, the small crowd, with rainhats on and umbrellas in hand, seemed exuberant and the city leaders elated. No one, however, was more energized than Raymond Chafin. This was his chance to be seen as the "big wheel" behind the successful completion of the boulevard.

The structure was a marvelous site, adding four-lane convenience to the city of Logan.

> Few people came to the dedication because of the weather, but I introduced the road commissioner anyway. When the dedication was over, I talked to the commissioner and said, "Sir, it's a pity that we can't leave this bridge in."

"Sorry, it's an over-water bridge, and it was designed to be temporary, so we'll have to take it out. The federal government won't allow it to stay in, anyway, Chafin," the road commissioner, who was now shivering from the downpour, responded as he abruptly turned, shuffled his papers together, and grabbed his worn briefcase. He stepped down from the podium, intending to immediately jump into his state car to head back to Charleston. It seemed obvious that he was trying to ignore Chafin as he followed him each step of the way.

"Well, hold on, sir. If we can't have that temporary bridge, is there any way for us to get a new bridge?" Chafin questioned. "These ol' bridges around here are ready to fall in. Seriously. That temporary bridge was one of the ways that our citizens could get to Logan's hospital, Buskirk Addition, and even to Island Creek."

"Well, Chafin," the exasperated commissioner answered, "we'll send engineers over here, and they'll survey and see what we can do. But for now, let's drop it, okay?"

"We need that bridge, sir!" Chafin pushed, as he smiled and grabbed the commissioner's hand and shook it firmly. "Thank you in advance."

"Well, you'll get your bridge, Chafin! You'll get your darn bridge!" he wearily agreed, as he chuckled and sat down in the driver's seat.

"Take care, Chafe," he said. "See you after the bridge is built!" He then threw up his hand, waved, and drove off.

Raymond Chafin grinned from ear to ear as the commissioner's car splattered water all the way up on the canopy and over everyone standing near the curb, including him. After pausing to replay the conversation with the commissioner in his head, Chafin grabbed up his notebook and opened his umbrella. He began to whistle merrily as he high-stepped on down to the Smoke House Restaurant to celebrate his victorious maneuver with his political buddies.

As the commissioner had promised, state engineers came in a few weeks to survey and make plans for a brand-new bridge. Soon the bridge that Raymond Chafin had pleaded for became a reality. That same bridge currently crosses the Guyandotte River, connecting the city of Logan to Buskirk Addition, near Hospital Drive.

The completion of the first leg of Logan Boulevard totally changed traffic accessibility to downtown Logan. Up until that point, there was basically one narrow way in and out of the Logan County seat. Now, businesses flourished and residents seemed pleased. For the first time in history, people could easily drive to and from the city without being caught in endless traffic jams.

Chapter Fourteen

Meeting Robert C. Byrd

The first time Chafin ever saw Robert C. Byrd, it was probably early 1952. He was driving along an unpaved offshoot of Route 10 near Harts Creek, West Virginia, daydreaming, with his windows rolled down because it was a beautifully sunny day. He was enjoying the cool breeze coming down through the hollow.

As he snapped back to reality, he noticed alongside the road was an odd-looking fellow standing beside his automobile, combing his hair.

> He had this big, fat bass fiddle tied down with twine to the roof of his jalopy. It took up the whole top. I slowed my state car down to a crawl as I approached him, and I thought, "Ah, looky. What do we have here? A hawk-nosed city slicker in these parts?"
>
> When I drove up to him, I stopped my car, jumped out, and greeted him anyway. I remember that he had this ugly, rusty ol' Chevrolet. When I looked a little closer, I saw that he had a smaller fiddle lying on the front seat, too. When I started talking to him, he told me his name — Bob Byrd — and that he was running for United States Congress. He wasn't a city boy as I thought. He had a thick West Virginia accent.

The two shook hands, and after he began to chat, Byrd told Chafin about his background. That's when it dawned on Chafin that he had seen Byrd before, in Charleston, walking hastily between corridors at the Capitol building. He was a state senator from Raleigh County.

"Now that you know me, what do you do for a livin', Mr. Chafin?" Byrd asked Chafin, as he looked him directly in the eye.

"Well, I'm the state road superintendent in these parts — for Logan County that is," he answered. "As a matter of fact, I was checkin' out this poor excuse for a road when I first saw ya out here. It's nice to meet ya, Mr. Byrd."

"No, it's my pleasure," he said, as he reached out for Chafin's hand again. "I suspect that you carry a lot of weight around here since you're the superintendent. You obviously influence others. This is an interesting meeting, indeed."

"I do keep my hand in politics pretty good," Chafin said, his cheek quivering as he tried to keep from laughing out loud. He recognized a good politician when he met one — they were easy to spot — and he knew that this guy was turning on that country-boy charm. Nevertheless, there was something about this fiddle player that Chafin instantly liked. He seemed down to earth when Chafin talked to him. He also appeared to be very intelligent and knowledgeable about the area and the state.

Then Byrd asked Chafin if it would be possible to visit his state road office and play a song or two on his violin for the employees.

> When he asked me, he promised he'd play his fiddle and meet the guys — without trying to win them over with any politics and salesmanship. So I told

him, "Sure, come on over whenever you'd like. My boys will love it. However, the best time to catch 'em all is in the mornings."

Actually, looking back, I guess I was more curious about that fiddle than anything else. I wondered if this peculiar politician could play that contraption.

The two continued to talk about county and state politics for several minutes before Chafin broke away and went on up the road on business. Chafin smiled as he recalled the meeting:

Bright and early the next day, before 6 in the morning, that same ol' ugly Chevy was parked outside the state road garage when I pulled up for work.

Robert Byrd was already waiting outside his car, wearing a wrinkled white shirt and a loosened red tie. His hair was heavily slicked down with hair tonic, and his worn fiddle was jammed under his chin. As the guys came in to work, he started playing one tune after another. He played that foot-stompin' mountain style of fiddling' — none of that sophisticated stuff or those teary-eyed slow numbers. He was good! Several of the men even danced a jig as they strolled up to the office to clock in.

When it finally was time to break it off and start working, all the men were smiling, and they lined up single file and shook hands with this flamboyant candidate.

He made quite an impression that day, without giving a long-winded speech or making any grand promises. He just played and then greeted the fellas. He showed them that he was one of them. I'll never forget that first meetin'. I doubt that any of the workers ever forgot, either.

The Grand Fight

Chafin talked about a particularly stressful time during his political career:

Grover Combs was the sheriff of Logan County at the time. He had taken office in 1949. He was a rather tall individual with a pug nose, plump jowls, and wire-rimmed glasses. As a young man he had moved to the county from Kentucky, settling in Triadelphia District. Combs first worked in the mines and then later entered local politics with an enthusiasm and eagerness seldom seen at the time. He had served as a city councilman and as mayor of Man, West Virginia, for approximately eighteen years before being elected sheriff. Even though he had no formal education, he was described by local political powerbroker Bus Perry as a good politician and a methodical thinker, always looking to the future. Toward the end of Combs' term, he pressured and eventually persuaded Ray Watts to run for sheriff against Floyd "Crook" Murphy, an admired justice of the peace.

I guess this was a time of learning for me. I was asked to run the entire 1952 campaign for Watts and his political machine.

I used my new friend, Robert Byrd, who was running for United States Congress in the 6th District, for campaigning at various rallies 'round the county.

Byrd could attract a sizable crowd, that's for darn sure. He would jump up on a porch step or wooden crate and start playin' that fiddle of his — maybe playin' "Turkey in the Straw" or something like that. Soon all eyes were on him. He was also a pretty good speaker when folks allowed him to talk.

They loved that violin of his, and they'd yell out song requests, like "Orange Blossom Special" or "The Old Gray Mare." He'd play the requests, too.

Besides Watts, Floyd "Crook" Murphy was also liked and well known in this area. He had been a tipple boss at Micco and later a justice of the peace. Now he was running for the sheriff's position against a tough candidate, Watts. Floyd knew a great deal of people around Logan precincts, and he made sure that he cultivated close friendships throughout the county. His father had been a well-liked deputy, too.

Floyd also had a brother, Wirt Murphy, who was a likeable fella. He was the general manager of the liquor stores in those days. He was a natural-born politician and helped "Crook" with his campaign. Floyd also had two sisters with influential husbands. One sister's husband was Willis Cook, who lived down around Peach Creek. His other sister's husband was the manager of the Peach Creek Store, which was owned by Don Chafin. Don worked five or six hundred men at the coalmine in that area at the time. That's a lot of possible votes.

As J.P. in Logan District, Floyd had accommodated a lot of people while in office. He was the opponent that Watts most needed to worry about.

With all these contacts, this gave Floyd Murphy a great big boost. So I had my hands full, all right! There were a lot of folks 'round here who said Watts didn't have a chance against ol' Crook.

Ray Watts was the Logan County commissioner from Triadelphia District. Grover Combs supported Ray partly 'cause he was from the Man area, too. Ray was fairly popular because at that time the county court and the state worked together to provide a check-weighman in our county. A weighman traveled 'round the mines and checked the scales. This was especially important 'cause many of the miners were paid so much per ton of coal mined at that time. So the scales had to be exactly right, down to the last ounce. Payroll depended on it.

A weighman, a United Mine Workers of America man, and a company man stood together when the railcars were weighed and when scales were checked. The check-weighman was to make sure a coalminer wasn't cheated. And he made sure that the company got a square deal, too.

Ray was known as a fair weighman. So he was pretty popular with the UMWA members.

Murphy was awfully popular, but Watts was well liked, too. Maybe the only advantage Ray Watts had going for him was that he had an organized political faction behind him, because he was also the Democratic county chairman. Once Sheriff Combs talked him into runnin', he hired me to be at the faction helm 'cause he knew 'bout my influence on Island Creek and my contacts through the

West Virginia State Road Department. Little did I know the type of hornet's nest I was putting myself into.

I knew I would have to take sides. Ray had control of the county court and the executive committee at the time. So he was the one who approved me when I was hired for the state road. So he had quite a bit of leverage over me.

We had a heck of a fight. Crook Murphy and Ray Watts were battling each other and working against one another across the county. There were factional fights on nearly every other position, too.

It was nearly an everyday occurrence to see fistfights and verbal exchanges erupting on Stratton Street, the main street of Logan, between respective bloc supporters. The Murphy followers were passionate about their candidates. The Watts' folks were equally loyal to their man and his slate.

Chafin talked about the time period:

I was in the middle of a screwed up mess. I was personally using every trick I had up my sleeves in order to keep Ray and our group united and strong. I was constantly working with and training precinct captains and inside workers as we prepared for the election. Even though times were tough, we had collected a good amount of money for the cause.

Meanwhile, Chauncey Browning had gotten into the West Virginia attorney general's race. Chauncey was related to me. His mother and my mother were first cousins. He had been the prosecuting attorney in Logan. He was now on the ballot for the attorney general's office. His opponent was W.C. Haythe.

William "Bill" Marland was the actual attorney general, and he and Chauncey were running together in the campaign. Bill Marland decided to run for governor. Therefore, he supported Chauncey, a longtime friend, and campaigned that he would take his seat.

Because the UMWA also supported Marland, the famous union leader, John L. Lewis, came to Charleston for an important meeting that I attended at the municipal auditorium.

A generously proportioned man with thick, bushy eyebrows and a rough and gruff voice, Lewis gave a stirring speech in behalf of William Marland that night. However, in spite of the fervent speech, the UMWA membership was hopelessly split on that race. Many officials, miners, and even coal operators supported Congressman Dr. H.H. Hedrick for the governor's race.

Our faction was definitely for Bill Marland for governor; Robert C. Byrd for congressman; Chauncey Browning for attorney general; Harley Kilgore, United States Senate; Glenn Jackson, state senator, 7th District; Claude Joyce, prosecuting attorney; and C.C. Chambers, judge.

According to Chafin, one of the most interesting characters on his slate was Judge C.C. Chambers. "He was always a stubborn ol' coot," he said.

Chambers, a high-strung, hot-tempered fellow, was first nominated as judge in 1936 and was supported by George C. Steele and his powerful political faction. It was a hard-fought campaign against incumbent Judge Bland, and by the night of the primary election the Logan County Courthouse was jammed with people as votes were counted. According to published accounts from that era, several overzealous supporters on both factional sides were packing loaded weapons. There was a series of tense moments in Logan that evening when many in attendance expected the worst. Considering the level of anxiety and anger among those in the courthouse lobby, everyone believed a spray of gunfire could occur at any moment. Therefore, many of the curious onlookers huddled near the doorways while they waited for precinct totals. In spite of numerous fistfights, shoving, and several drawn pistols, unbelievably no one was violently injured, and by night's close, Chambers was victorious.

It was now sixteen years later and the county Democrats in this campaign were in a terribly torn state again, especially when it came to Bill Marland's candidacy. Because of the UMWA controversy, Floyd Murphy stayed completely clear of the governor's race and remained neutral for fear of offending any voters or politicians. He focused on his own campaign and the local races.

My man, Ray Watts, was a bit of a nervous type. He was a little bit timid of the governor's race, too. However, some of the local politicians and coal operators got to him where it counts — in his billfold. They met with him and gave him a wad of money under the condition that he supports H.H. Hedrick for governor on his slate. Watts quickly took the money and double-crossed our faction.

Watts then drove over to Chafin's house around 9 o'clock on the night before the primary election. Louise had had a hard day at school and was already in bed when he arrived. Chafin was lounging in his recliner in his undershirt, listening to the radio. Watts opened the screen door, greeted Chafin, and casually said, "How are you doing, campaign manager?"

"Fine, Ray. What's up?"

"Chafe, I'll just spit it out. We've made a switch or two on the slate. We are now supporting Hedrick, for starters."

"What do you mean ... switch?" a puzzled Chafin asked, as he stood up.

"Several of us met, and we've decided that we're moving our entire support over to Hedrick's campaign. We've switched," Watts said, as he raised his voice. "Marland can't win, Chafe. We all know that."

"Who switched? I haven't switched, Ray!" Chafin said angrily. "You might switch. But I'm not switchin'. We have worked for Marland all this time. I gave my word."

"Well, it's already done, sir. So what are you goin' to do with your Bob Byrd, the congressman?" Watts said as he smiled deviously. "We are now for Hedrick and Dale G. Casto. How about that, Chafe?"

Trying to keep from shouting, Chafin, with teeth clenched, responded, "Hey! Uncle Ed McDonald, Red Bivens, two or three others, and I are for Bob Byrd. If it weren't too late, I'd throw my whole support to Floyd Murphy and whip your ol' hind end tomorrow! You dirty —."

"What are you goin' to do with me tomorrow... well, why not do something to me today?" Ray Watts asked sarcastically, as he grinned and rubbed his forehead.

"Since I started with ya, I gots to be fer ya' now, Watts. I know it's too late 'cause I got everything set up. But this is wrong, wrong, wrong!"

Maybe it was an intentional mistake, but even though Watts stated that he made a switch of candidates at the last minute, Robert Byrd's name remained on the final slate. However, Hedrick's name replaced Marland's for governor.

By the next day, the various poll grounds in the county were alive with activity. A stout young man named Claude "Big Daddy" Ellis and others like him had their hands full as precinct workers. Across the county, the normal Election Day antics were under way — including swapping corn whiskey and dollars for votes.

When the polls closed and the totals came in, William "Bill" Marland swept the county for governor. In spite of the switchover by Ray Watts and his comrades, "Marland tore up the county and walked away with the governor's seat," according to Chafin.

Ray Watts became the new sheriff of Logan County, with 9,576 votes. However, Floyd "Crook" Murphy still made a respectable showing with 8,406 votes.

In the congressional race for the 6th District, Robert C. Byrd received an astounding 6,944 Logan County votes and took first place. The second largest vote getter was Dale Casto with 2,545 votes; Ned Ragland received 1,959 votes; and the remaining votes were divided among Garland Wilkinson, Lewis A. Hatcher, and John M. Eckard.

Claude Joyce won the prosecuting attorney's race with 8,180 votes, compared to 6,587 votes cast for Curtis B. Trent Jr.

Chauncey Browning easily clenched the attorney general's spot when he walked away with 12,042 county votes. The remaining 1,399 votes went to W.C. Haythe.

"Even though it was a terrible double cross, and Ray Watts' and my friendship became strained from that day forward, I proved to most of my peers that I could get things done efficiently. They knew that I could wage an effective campaign," Chafin explained. "They also knew I could stick with what I thought was right, regardless."

Afterward, in spite of all that I did for his campaign, Ray and several others gave me a real hard time in the Democratic Party, but they couldn't do too much to me 'cause I supported Gov. Bill Marland through it all.

Actually, some of the Democrats held it against me 'cause I didn't switch over when most of the others did. However, because of Chauncey Browning, I now had the new governor's ear. I became quite popular with him. So I was pretty safe in the county, even if I had to tussle a bit with the local Democrats.

Governor Bill Marland didn't pay any attention to the Logan County Democratic Executive Committee after he took office. Also, he had no use for Ray Watts.

He listened to me. In spite of the jealousy among the committee members, I enjoyed that time period. I was able to get much done for our county, as in roads, bridges, repaving, and puttin' ol' roads into the state road system.

People saw specifically what I was accomplishing for 'em. Believe me, results are more important than windy speeches anyway. Results speak a whole lot louder.

Logan Boulevard Extension Is Planned

By 1954, after the permanent bridge was built across the Guyandotte River at the point where Logan Boulevard begins to hug the back side of downtown, Raymond Chafin and some of his associates started talking about extending the boulevard all the way to Cherry Tree, a well-populated community outside the Logan city limits. After discussing their ideas with the West Virginia Road Commission, Chafin was even more enthusiastic about the possibilities when the road commissioner surprised him by agreeing with his liberal proposal.

Chafin took little time between projects. He had a vision for the area, and for some unexplainable reason, he couldn't rest until he saw a project come to its closing stages. That's not to imply that his motivation was completely altruistic. He was well aware that he was also on a political mission. He had been taught "mountain politics" by the best — by formidable men such as George C. Steele, T.R. Workman, and even his father, Elbert Chafin. Road projects like this create jobs and more than enough publicity on local radio stations and in the newspaper. Jobs and publicity equal votes and power — tremendous political advantage that can be later used for his best interests and the interests of the Democratic Party.

Logan had two radio stations, WLOG and WVOW, at the time. WLOG had been around since the early days of radio. WVOW had opened its doors in 1952. There was one predominant county newspaper, The Logan Banner.

Chafin saw his picture and name in print many times, and he was most thankful for the notoriety. He also heard his name broadcast from atop Ward Rock Mountain, where the steel radio towers jutted toward the sky, overlooking Logan in the narrow valley below. The radio publicity was a sweet, sweet sound to his ears.

"Votes, votes, votes," is how Chafin translated the various press releases. "The more I accomplish as the state road supervisor, the more political influence I can muster in behalf of the region." He went to on to say more about his various projects:

> We wanted that thoroughfare to go all the way from Logan to Cherry Tree — then on to Holden Road. So we got the state money to build the road, and we had to get the right-of-way. There were several houses and stores standing in our way at the time. It took us a while, but we eventually bought up the right-of-way and started building from the new bridge in Logan toward Cherry Tree.
>
> When we got that portion finished, I started thinking that all this isn't going to help Holden much. At that time we probably already had more right-of-way at Holden than we did coming out of Island Creek. So then we started talking about buying and even building us another bridge over the railroad — the one that now comes out at Corridor G.
>
> We eventually got the money and finished the road where it goes up by the church, Central Baptist, and we even got all the right-of-way where U.S. Route 119 now comes out at Holden. I was with the state road during that entire time

we were getting that job done. We had more right-of-way than road. Little did I know that I was unintentionally planning for the county's future.

During my time with the Department of Highways, I was able to get many, many county roads put into the system. There's nothing that will make ya feel any better than when you can take an ol' muddy path or abandoned logging road — maybe the only way to several mountain homes — and have it put into the roadway system. Then we could grate, gravel, and start pouring the blacktop to it. That makes people happy — and very thankful, ya know.

Looking Backwards

Even though the Cow Creek politician was especially pleased over what he had accomplished along with his crew at the state road in the 1950s, he says that the high point of the project, and a great deal of inner satisfaction, came forty-some years later in the 1990s.

Many, many years after the boulevard was complete, I stood with Senator Robert C. Byrd a few years ago, on the day they dedicated the finished road — called Corridor G — which ran from Chapmanville to Logan, and on to Williamson, West Virginia. Senator Byrd, the West Virginia Road Commission, and a few others had asked me to be a part of the ceremony. As far as I can remember, Alvis Porter, Glen Adkins, and I were the only county politicians present for the ceremony.

Senator Byrd, with a sorrowful look on his face, leaned over and said to me, "Chafe, it's sort of funny to me that we didn't have very many people here today."

To tell ya the truth, I think thirty people would have killed the whole darn crowd [meaning that there were fewer than thirty total in attendance].

Chafin said he believed that the lack of response from the public at the time was a sad thing to see. Nevertheless, after the dedication, Senator Byrd took a few moments to reminisce with his old friend Chafin. He said that he appreciated what Chafin had accomplished while working for the road department many years before. He also recognized that the Corridor G project was just another extension of Chafin's original dream of helping the people of Logan County and making Logan more accessible for business.

Chafin elaborated more about the modern highway system:

When I first heard about the completion project and I saw the plans on the drawing board on how they planned to connect Logan and Chapmanville, I tried to envision it and picture it out in my mind. I could never really get it pictured the way it actually looks.

But, ah, when I attended the ceremony, it's then that I realized that this was a wonderful thing! The way it connected into what we had already done years ago — coming across to the hospital and up the river — was really something. Nobody ever dreamed back then, when we finished the Logan Boulevard, that someone would tie it all together with a four-lane highway system. It seems like the good Lord, or something, helped us all along. And with thanks to Senator Byrd, it became a reality.

Chafin pointed out that when he looks back, he still finds it remarkable and "mind-boggling" to see how his small vision back in the 1950s blossomed into the development of the stretch of four-lane highway now called the Robert C. Byrd Freeway.

Chafin stated, "It perfectly connects into the Logan Boulevard project at the Route 44 intersection. Robert C. Byrd made it all happen."

Now the area alongside the new stretch of highway near Logan is under private development, with the more recent formation of a Wal-Mart Supercenter, Lowe's, Dollar Tree, Radio Shack, and several other stores, restaurants, a bank, etc., at a facility called the Fountain Place Mall. Chafin said, "People still don't totally realize what this project has meant for all of us — we are about to boom again!"

As Raymond Chafin stood at the dedication ceremony site on that warm, windy afternoon, with politicians Alvis Porter, Glen "Houn' Dog" Adkins, and his dear friend and statesman, Senator Bob Byrd, it was all he could do to choke back tears of joy over what had been accomplished for little Logan County over the course of his lifetime.

Actually, when you think about it, you might say that much of it started with a little boy, a plug horse, and a rented wagon — delivering groceries at the company store at Omar.

"Being With the State Road, I Supported the State"

Since he was working for the state, Chafin was expected to support the state politically in the early 1950s.

> I stayed true blue to Governor Okey Patteson [1949-1953] and Bill Marland [1953-1957], and even a Republican, young Cecil H. Underwood, [1957-1961].
> I could get things done pretty well, and the governors seemed to say things like, "Listen to that Raymond Chafin over in Logan County 'cause he stays with us, and he's a man we can trust."

During the various elections of the early to mid-1950s, Chafin was definitely a state man, and he supported exactly whom the governor supported. It's been said that in the time period there was little room to think independently when you were on the state payroll.

Chafin boasted:

> That's why I pretty well got anything that I wanted done. We had good men over in Charleston, for the most part, at that time. That's when I really started working on the roads in a big way. I seldom was turned down on a job I wanted to do. We stripped out the old roads through most of Logan, taking out the ol' brick streets, replacing the red bricks with concrete. We thought that would patch Logan up and fix it, but it didn't seem to fix the streets completely. We

still had plenty to do to get downtown Logan straightened up — it became an ongoing job.

All during my time at West Virginia Coal and Coke, and then while I was with the West Virginia State Road, I kept myself in politics, sort of as a lobbyist. The mine had me running over to the Legislature and talking to senators and delegates over some of their main concerns. Then, after taking my state road job back, I was still in the thick of local and state politics — and I continued lobbying for what we needed here in Logan County.

I also remember when the big controversy around these parts was establishing a coal pipeline and doing away with the railroads altogether. There was talk that this pipeline would shut Peach Creek train yard down. Well, I didn't think that was a good idea, and it wasn't good for local jobs. Sure, the pipeline would have run the coal from state to state. But in the meantime, we would lose good jobs, people — and voters. So I fought that pipeline with everything I had in Charleston. Not many would stand up agin the pipeline at that time, or they plumb didn't know anything about it. Well, I didn't know much 'bout it either, but I knew I wasn't fer it!

To this day, I think that's why railroaders consider me their friend.

Chapter Fifteen

Moving to Sharples, West Virginia

Chafin stayed with the state road and was happy until 1955 or so.

Governor William Casey Marland, a friend of Chafin, was in office at the time. The climate around the state was subtly changing. People were apparently looking for change. Within a few years, a young energetic Republican, Cecil H. Underwood, would take the governor's office.

Chafin reminisced:

> When I left the state road department, we were still working on the road from the hospital up to Holden, on the Logan Boulevard. It wasn't quite finished at the time, but I started that whole ball rolling.
>
> From there, I went to Sharples, West Virginia, and began to work for Boone County Coal Corporation. I had an offer that was hard to refuse. I was their new strip superintendent, and the money was darn good. I moved to Sharples with my wife, Louise. She started teaching school over there. That was also the year that Margaret, my daughter, started the first grade.

After some time, an old West Virginia Coal and Coke fellow, Frank Wilson, came to Sharples to ask Chafin for a job. He had been working at a Paris, Kentucky, mine at the time, and the coal had run out.

"Frank, I've known you for a long time," Chafin said, "and I'd like to hire ya as a foreman. I guess you'd know the work. But I'd like to make you a better deal if you'd consider it. I have a lot of responsibilities here, and I have two phones in this office — and they drive me crazy sometimes when both phones go to ringing. This superintendent's job isn't what I really like here. Plus, I can actually make more money operating some of this mine machinery.

"We need operators here. How about allowing me to give you my job, and I'll go back to operating for you?"

"You really wanna do that?" Wilson said, as he looked at Chafin in disbelief.

"Sure do," Chafin answered.

So the two of them went and talked to Ed Greenwall, the chief engineer and vice president. By the time Chafin finished talking, Frank Wilson was superintendent and Chafin was back in the United Mine Workers as an equipment operator.

Chafin said that he could run just about anything they had at the Boone County mine site. According to Chafin, the largest dozer they had at the time was a D-8. They also had a seven-yard dragline with a 170-foot boom that he helped put together. It had been shipped to the site in five railroad cars.

"That was just about as big a piece of machinery that you saw around these parts in that time period," he added.

Seeking the Don Chafin Blessing

By the late 1940s and early '50s, politicians had talked to Raymond Chafin many times about running for office. "I didn't take it too serious at the time," Chafin recalled.

Then, one time nine or ten political figures came to Chafin's house at Sharples and urged him to run for justice of the peace. Besides that group, two dear colleagues, Lester "Bus" Perry and Arnold Harkins, also thought Chafin could be victorious.

Perry, in particular, was a giant of a man when it came to county politics. He had been a schoolteacher at Dehue and a former member of the West Virginia House of Delegates. In 1941 he was involved in a payroll-padding scandal in Charleston, and indictments were rendered against Perry, Chairman of the Rules Committee at the time, and the Speaker of the House. Perry spent time in prison for his involvement and misconduct. He paid his debt to society and was once again involved in county politics by this time.

Perry had been close to members of Ray Watts' bloc, Chafin's main political opponent, but he had been known to support Chafin and a few of the other names that were designated as being with his faction, too. Watts was a powerful politician who had held a variety of influential positions in the county. He was also said to have been a cunning and often devious political fighter who had been able to amass a group of loyal and commanding candidates over the years. The Watts' faction had great success in various elections and often gave Chafin and his faction fits in the primaries.

Because of this "closeness with Watts" in the early days, Chafin kept a close eye on Perry at all times. Chafin was terribly suspicious of his actions. However, as their relationship grew, Perry became one of Chafin's closest associates and most trusted friends.

"Ol' Bus was probably the smartest politician I ever knew," Chafin said.

After several meetings with the group of men, Chafin got serious about the possibility of forming a justice of the peace campaign. Before he would make that decision, he wanted to seek the approval of a formerly very influential political figure, as he said here:

> I was serious enough about running that I went to Huntington, West Virginia, to see Don Chafin, my dad's cousin, who had once been a controversial politician in Logan. Arnold Harkins went with me because Arnold actually knew Don better than I did.

Before Louise and he made a final decision about running for office, Chafin visited Don in hopes that Don would give his blessing and his support for his candidacy.

> At that time, Don Chafin had a whole lot of remaining support from the old-timers in Logan County. However, Don and I had personally disagreed a time or two over the years, because once or twice he was for one candidate and I, working for the state, had to support another candidate.
>
> Mind you, this was the same darn Don Chafin that had once been Logan County's sheriff and had dealt with all that union trouble up on Blair Mountain — now called the Blair Mountain Mine War.

Tough Boys

With his headquarters in the city of Logan, Sheriff Don Chafin had once nearly controlled all of the county's populace — using excessive force and ruthless tactics to remain in power. From 1910 until the UMWA finally accomplished unionizing the district, he was in charge of a disreputable group of deputies — made up of mostly kinfolk, in-laws, and outlaws. The Logan County Coal Operators Association subsidized the department. Don and his henchmen — also known as "Don's thugs" — made sure that any union sympathizer and supporter was forcibly removed from the county. At the time, it was also rumored that several overzealous union organizers didn't live long once deputies got hold of them to be taken to the county's edge. Horror stories of legendary proportions remain of "union troublemakers" allegedly being thrown into the Logan powerhouse furnace alive by Don's henchmen. Other stories involve drive-by killings and makeshift burials beneath a mountain cliff, brush pile or soft creek bank. However, the sheriff and his band were never arrested or charged with such activities.

At other pivotal moments in the union struggle, Don Chafin's deputies were stationed atop the county courthouse with machine guns pointed and ready for impending violence from UMWA supporters.

It's been said that one or two deputies carrying tommy guns were posted at each of the coal camps around the area. Some of the hired ruffians worked undercover in order to obtain suspected union organizational information. This was a time of great misery and oppression for coalminers and their families in Logan. However, amazingly — in spite of the brutality, scandal, and corruption — there were many county citizens who remained loyal to Don Chafin.

Raymond Chafin continued:

> By the early 1950s, Don was quite aged, and he had a penthouse in Huntington at a prominent hotel. When Arnold and I arrived, he welcomed us and asked us to stay the night. We did. We talked politics nearly all night long, and we went to bed at 3 or 4 o'clock in the morning. Even then, I couldn't sleep as I thought of all we'd discussed.
>
> The next morning Don, Arnold, and I went out to a restaurant to have breakfast. Once we started eating, Don looked over the table at me and said, "Raymond, I hope you'll take my advice. You know, the union is now awful, awful strong. I don't know what they'll do to you, being that your name is Chafin. If I was you — as young as you are — I don't believe I'd want to take the chance at this time, Raymond. Let this ol' stuff about me die down a little bit, son, 'cause someone who wants to beat you is liable to bring my name into it, and then you'd be in a heap of trouble. Logan's still a tough place, ya know. Wait another term or two...
>
> "So, Raymond, what do you think of my advice?"
>
> "Well, I thought enough of you to ask your advice in the first place," I responded. "I guess I got enough spunk 'bout me that I'll take that advice and wait another year or two, like you said."

The Curse

Wait he did. It was a few years later that Chafin again considered jumping into the political arena as a candidate. By the time he was 39 years old, he felt that he had built up enough political clout to step into a campaign. He felt that he could now overcome the "Don Chafin curse," since he had proved to be a reliable politician who had helped many citizens in the county.

> I was working for Boone County Coal Corporation, at Sharples, when I got the hankering' to try again. It was mid-1955, and I was considering running in '56. So I went back to see Don Chafin to talk about running one more time. This time he said, "If you want to try it, Raymond, try it."

Chafin said that he told Don, "This time I'm going to run agin your ol' friend Otto Manns. How about that?"

Don paused for a minute, looked him over warily, and mumbled, "Whew, son, sounds tough, doesn't it?"

"Well, maybe we like them tough!" Chafin responded quickly.

"Well, you're a Chafin, aren't you?" Don chuckled.

"Sometimes I think I'm full stock, maybe too much Chafin for my own daggone good," he retorted, jokingly.

"Ya wanna try it, then try it," Don replied. "But Otto is going to ask me to be for him, ya know. What about that? What am I gonna do?"

"Well, sometimes it works two ways. If you come out in support of Otto, they'll say he is a Don Chafin thug. If you're for me, they'll say I'm a little Chafin thug. My question for you, Don, is this: Will you stay out of this altogether?"

Don smirked and answered, "Claude Gore has a boy, Ludrus, and he's a runnin'. What if I was to decide that I'm going to be for Ludy Gore?"

"Fine! You be for Ludy!" Chafin said. He shook Don's hand and nodded, and the political aspect of the conversation ended.

> That split the vote three ways — a perfect situation for me. Don knew that was perfect political circumstances, too. So, I came back home and filed. I ran in 1956, which was the first time I ever tried for a political position. I ran for Democratic Executive Committee. The committee was a great thing at that time.
>
> We had a total of six committee members in this county at the time, with three districts — two from each district. You had to be a big, robust politician to have a chance of winnin' a position on the committee. This group nearly ruled everythin' that went on politically in the county and controlled all the county jobs. All county officeholders listened to the committee, and state leaders first approached the members when they wanted to accomplish a task within the county's borders. So, for the most part, the committee controlled all election of officers.

On April 6, 1956, Chafin's official announcement was published in *The Logan Banner*, Logan County's daily newspaper. It read:

Raymond Chafin In Committee Race
To the people of Logan District:

I, Raymond Chafin, wish to announce my candidacy for member of the Democratic Executive Committee for Logan District.

A lifelong Democrat, I was born and reared at Barnabus, W.Va. I am now a resident of Sharples and am employed by the Boone County Coal Corp. My wife, the former Louise Chambers, is a schoolteacher in the public schools of Logan County. We have one daughter.

I am a former superintendent of roads for Logan County. I resigned that position in July 1955. I think that those people who knew and worked with me during my time with the State Road Commission will readily approve of me for public office.

I want to state at this time that I hold no animosity toward any other candidates for the office I seek. Rather, I wish them well in their efforts.

To my friends and supporters I would like to say — I appreciate from the bottom of my heart their efforts in my behalf.

Should you the public see fit to elect me a member of the Democratic Executive Committee from Logan District, I pledge myself to always hold the welfare of the people above the wants and desires of a few.

Sincerely,
RAYMOND CHAFIN
(Paid for by candidate)

Jack Ferrell's wife, Faye Ferrell, had already filed. She was eventually aligned with Chafin. She was described as a young, attractive woman and "a good talker — not a lazy bone in her!"

Faye Ferrell hit every house, introduced herself, then reached them a campaign card and asked for their vote. When she reached them her card, she reached 'em my card, too. Then she'd tell them to vote for me for committee, too.

When I went house to house, I handed out my card and hers, too. I also asked people to vote fer her. Everyone in the county was talking about the committee fight that was brewing. I was in the thick of it and lovin' it.

The stage was set.

Claude Ellis, Franklin D. Roosevelt, Jr., and Raymond Chafin stand together in the Logan Courthouse during the height of the John F. Kennedy presidential campaign in 1960. — *Photo Courtesy of The Logan Banner*

Claude "Big Daddy" Ellis, Alex DeFobio and two additional campaign workers meet in the Kennedy for President Headquarters in downtown Logan, WV. — *Photo Courtesy of The Logan Banner*

1A

Three politicians meet in room 220 at the Aracoma Hotel in early 1960; the center figure is believed to be Raymond Chafin. At this time period, the Chafin faction was supporting Hubert Humphrey for president. That, however, was soon to change. — *Photo Courtesy of The Logan Banner*

Ray Watts, was often at odds with Raymond Chafin, and was a member of the Claude Ellis faction in '60.

Senator John F. Kennedy and Senator Jennings Randolph meet with West Virginia coalminers, while campaigning in the Mountain State. — *Photo Courtesy John F. Kennedy Presidential Library*

Claude Ellis, far left, poses with others at a moonshine bust in Logan County in the late 1950s. In this raid, which happened while he worked for the liquor commission, did little to curb the problem of illegal corn-whiskey stills in the county. — *Photo Courtesy The Logan Banner*

Litz McGuire

Bill Abraham

Judge C.C. Chambers

Lester "Bus" Perry

WV Governor Wally Barron

WV Governor M. Neely

3A

Claude Ellis walks down Stratton Street in downtown Logan in the 1970s. At this time, he was the owner of The Smokehouse Restaurant and a political leader in southern West Virginia. — *Photo Courtesy The Logan Banner*

Claude Ellis, Robert Kennedy, John W. Davis, Jr., Raamie Barker, and Lester "Bus" Perry pose for the camera shortly after Bobby Kennedy spoke to the crowd in downtown Logan. — *Photo Courtesy The Logan Banner*

Attorney Dan Dahill stood outside the Logan County Family Court Building in September 2003. A respected citizen, Dahill continues to practice law on a limited basis. — *Photo Courtesy of Martha Sparks*

5A

Raymond Chafin reminisced about his life at his home on Cow Creek in Spring 2002. — *Photo Courtesy of Martha Sparks*

In 2003, Claude Ellis recalled his days as a precinct commando and faction leader in Logan County.
— *Photo Courtesy of Martha Sparks*

7A

JFK and Teddy Kennedy speak briefly as they campaign at a southern West Virginia rally. Far right, FDR, Jr. shakes hands with well wishers. — *Photo Courtesy of John F. Kennedy Presidential Library*

Senator Robert C. Byrd, and his wife, Erma O. Byrd, meet with Claude Ellis and Tom Godby to discuss factional politics. — *Photo Courtesy of Claude Ellis Collection*

8A

Kenny O'Donnell, who is allegedly the primary campaign worker who delivered election money into the hands of Claude Ellis and his Logan County faction of candidates. — *Courtesy John F. Kennedy Presidential Library*

Bobby Kennedy meets with Alex DeFobio and Claude Ellis while campaigning in Logan County for his brother, Senator John F. Kennedy, in 1960. — *Photo Courtesy of The Logan Banner*

Senator John Kennedy meets with reporters at the Smokehouse Restaurant in Logan, while Raymond Chafin waited for Kennedy at the nearby Aracoma Hotel. Among the attendees, Clifford Ellis (brother of Claude) stands directly left of JFK, along with, far left, Al Otten of the Wall Street Journal; Rowland Evans of the New York Herald-Tribune is on the far right. — *Photo Courtesy of The Logan Banner*

WESTERN UNION

TELEGRAM

CLASS OF SERVICE
This is a fast message unless its deferred character is indicated by the proper symbol.

W. P. MARSHALL, PRESIDENT

1201

SYMBOLS
DL=Day Letter
NL=Night Letter
LT=International Letter Telegram

The filing time shown in the date line on domestic telegrams is STANDARD TIME at point of origin. Time of receipt is STANDARD TIME at point of destination

CTB016   1960 JAN 21 AM 11 2:

CT WA052 PD=FAX WASHINGTON DC 21 1024AME=

CLAUDE ELLIS=

        LOGAN WVIR=

MY BROTHER TED TOLD ME YOU WERE A GREAT HELP TO HIM
WHEN HE VISITED WEST VIRGINIA ON MY BEHALF. MANY THANKS=

    JACK KENNEDY.

TELEPHONE No. 2-4280
TELEPHONED TO
TIME 1130A
BY
ATTEMPTS TO DELIVER

THE COMPANY WILL APPRECIATE SUGGESTIONS FROM ITS PATRONS CONCERNING ITS SERVICE

Raymond still enjoys reminiscing about past elections and political upsets. As he points out, "I don't like to lose — nobody does; and I am certainly not going to hold back when I set up a precinct or plan strategies for one of my boys on the slate. When I get my eye on a candidate, I can usually help him or her to be victorious." — *Photo Courtesy of Martha Sparks*

Panoramic snapshot of the City of Logan, Logan County, taken in the 1930s. — *Claude Ellis Collection*

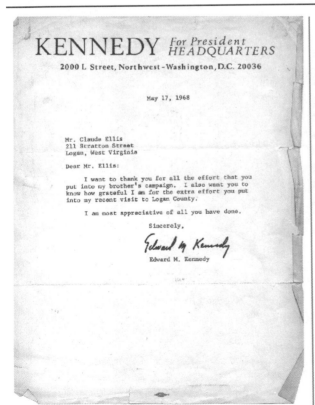

Raymond Chafin and Lillie Bowen marry in September 2003, at the Logan County Family Court in Logan. — *Claude Ellis Collection*

KENNEDY *For President* HEADQUARTERS

2000 L Street, Northwest - Washington, D.C. 20036

May 17, 1968

Mr. Claude Ellis
211 Stratton Street
Logan, West Virginia

Dear Mr. Ellis:

I want to thank you for all the effort that you put into my brother's campaign. I also want you to know how grateful I am for the extra effort you put into my recent visit to Logan County.

I am most appreciative of all you have done.

Sincerely,

Edward M. Kennedy

Edward M. Kennedy

Rosemary and Claude Ellis. — *Claude Ellis Collection*

Chapter Sixteen

Geets Spends Time Behind Bars

Claude "Big Daddy" Ellis, Chafin's main factional opponent, was a member of the West Virginia Young Democrats in 1956 and was considered an up-and-coming political figure in the county.

Claude, who is now 77-years-old and still resides in the City of Logan, recalled working during the controversial 1956 primary election, saying:

> I remember working the lower Mt. Gay precinct, and I had made a trip over to Mingo County to get a load of moonshine. When I returned, a friend of mine helped me switch the white lightnin' into little half-pint drugstore bottles. In most instances, we gave away a half-pint and a five-dollar bill per voter at that precinct. We had plenty of bottles and bills to do the job with, too.

> During this general time period, two federal boys came in on the upper precinct over at Coal Branch and caught one of our election workers, a black fellow, who had some of our shipment of moonshine. His name was Harry "Geets" Johnson. The agents — revenuers — tried to grab him by his arms and whisk him off to jail. He struggled and fought with 'em. He bit one of their noses off — completely! When I heard about the incident, I took my remaining whiskey on up the creek and had it dumped. I surely didn't want to deal with the feds.

> I believe Geets spent some time in the federal penitentiary for biting off the tip of the guy's nose during the scuffle. But that's just one example of the way politics was played back then — money, liquor, and fistfights. It was happening everywhere. It wasn't just Logan County. It was happening all around us — in Lincoln, Boone, and especially Mingo County, too.

***

Raymond Chafin also discussed the election outcome:

> When Election Day was over. Faye and I won! Faye Ferrell beat Mrs. Charlie W. Bias, and I beat Otto Manns, as well as Ludrus "Ludy" Gore, who only received 880 votes in spite of Don Chafin's support.

> I beat Manns. I received a whopping 2,319 votes cast, whereas Otto received 1,112. Roy Baisden, of Verdunville, received 696 votes; Gene Gallo, of Holden, had 665 or so. Glen Bias got 497 votes, and Todd Willis, of Stollings, got 403. The rest of the district's votes were divided among Alton Isaacs, Rufus "Shotgun" Lester, Larry Spriggs, and Don Hensley. It was definitely a tough election.

> Faye was the top vote getter with 2,410 votes. She beat Mrs. Bias, who had 1,608 votes cast for her in the district. Mrs. John Asbury had 1,331 votes.

Mrs. Claudia Gore garnered 798 votes. Irene Beres got 604 votes for committee. And finally, Ola Jackson received 240.

Uncle Ed McDonald, who was president of the Logan County Court, won the highly publicized sheriff's race in the May primary. A Crooked Creek native, he ran a successful campaign against former sheriff Grover Combs (1949-1953). In unofficial tallies, McDonald received 6,478 votes, and Combs received 4,521 votes. Chafin added:

> Since it was my first experience running for an office, I learned a lot about campaigns and pólitics in '56. However, over the coming months, I found out there was much more I would learn.
> Ol' Litz McGuire, who was often called "Cuz" by his friends, was running for sheriff, unopposed on the GOP ticket. He received something like 2,700 votes when everything was said and done. He was unable to prevail as sheriff at the general election, but he would later end up having a long political career in the city of Logan as mayor.
> I guess he was the friendliest fellow I ever met — at least publicly. He never missed a chance to talk to someone who was visiting Logan and walking along the streets; and he knew nearly everyone who lived in the city limits. He was popular, and I always wished I had thick white hair like his. Instead, I had nothing on top, except peach fuzz.

Among the others on the Republican ticket, Garland Scaggs was running for county commission, Early Ball for assessor, William McKnight for county clerk, Averill Hunter for circuit clerk, and D.E. Hensley, Kate McDonald, Harvey Napier, and N.D. Waugh for House of Delegates. Justice of the peace candidates were Nollie Justus, Jack H. Smith, Steve Justice, and K.M. Morgan. Constable candidates included Fletcher White, Woody Armstrong, Archie Browning, William Surgoine, A.M. "Arch" Peyton, Clifford M. Spurlock, and Everett Adams.

Chafin: Politickin' Isn't Pretty

Chafin talked about his philosophy of politics:

> Politics is a lot like an ol' car. After a while, you get tired of an ol' automobile, because it might seem to run a little sluggish, and you want to trade it in on something else. You want to try another one — with more options and less rust. I guess that's what happened with my opponent at the time. The public just got tired of him. He was a little worn out, if you know what I mean. I was new and rarin' to go.

Chafin had just been elected for the first time, and he was determined to make great strides early in his first term so that he would make a name as a go-getter.

> When we had one of our first Democratic Executive Committee meetings, everybody wanted to put Glenn Jackson in as chairman. He was the state senator

at the time. We voted, and we tied 3-3-3 — that's how we ended up. To break the tie, I decided to listen to some of the political bosses who were wispering to me behind the scenes. I figured that the best thing to do was to put Glenn in since he was the state senator and all. So we appointed Glenn, but we could never quite get him to come down to earth with us — with politics or anything else. Jack Ferrell, who was a good friend of mine and Faye Ferrell's husband, came to me and said, "Chafe, let's take Glenn out. I believe we got the votes to boot him out of the position and put in somebody else."

"Let me go see if we can get him to leave on his own," Chafin suggested as he answered Ferrell. So he went to visit Jackson at his home and explained to him that everyone wanted him to step down, but if he balked, he would be voted out.

"Well, Chafe, my boy, I don't believe you gots da' votes," Jackson snarled, as he sat up straight in his living-room chair.

"I got the votes. I just don't want to embarrass you, Glenn. Don't make me do it."

"I don't believe ya!" he replied angrily. "Ya ain't got the votes, Chafe!"

Chafin finally stopped trying to negotiate, got up, dusted off his hat, and left Jackson's house without another word. When the committee met the next time, Chafin's prediction came true. Jackson was voted off the committee as the first order of business.

Paul Creason, who was a politician from Whitman Creek, was voted in that night. He was a deputy sheriff, and he knew a lot of people. Chafin recalled:

> Paul stayed in three, four, or maybe even five months, but he never could get things off the ground politically. So they [the committee] came to me and asked me if I would take the chairmanship.
>
> "We have to check the law," I remember saying at the time. I didn't rightfully know if I could be the chairman while being a committeeman. I also wondered if it was possible, would the choice be based on how many votes a committee member had?
>
> At the time, it turned out that the law stated that I could be the chairman. However, if I needed to vote on something that specifically concerned the chairmanship, I would have to step down, step aside, and let the vice chairman vote in my place.
>
> So I made pretty darned sure that we had a vice chairman who would vote based upon what I wanted to do!
>
> Winning in the election and then being named Democratic chairman had knocked ol' Ray Watts out of the box, so to speak. His power greatly diminished after that. Not that I'm gloatin' — not at all — but Ray had been a sharp thorn in my side for some time after that 1952 election. Now I was takin' control and bustin' his hide.
>
> I spent the next thirteen or fourteen years on the Democratic Executive Committee — most of those years as chairman — and served with some mighty fine people, and a few tough nuts, too. But ask anybody — I got things done!

Louise Packs Up to Leave

Raymond Chafin worked at Boone County Coal Corporation from 1955 until spring 1958. During all that time, he and his family lived in Sharples, near the Logan and Boone County boundary. Technically, he still lived on Logan's side of the line. However, he was a long way from Barnabus.

Little Margaret, his daughter, was doing well in grade school. She was a bright, happy student and was seemingly well adjusted. She had dark brown hair, usually tied up in ponytails, wide-set eyes, and fair skin. She was her father's pride and joy.

He would often scoop her up in his arms and take her with him when he traveled to talk with politicians at the Logan County Courthouse or when he met dignitaries at Taplin Airport — a grassy stretch of ground between two mountain ranges.

In many ways, Chafin and Margaret were inseparable. She was Daddy's girl, and life couldn't have been better for the two of them — except that Chafin was just a little homesick for "the Creek."

However, it was altogether different for Louise. She wasn't happy at all. She liked her work as a teacher, but the area caused her to be more and more depressed. Louise had not been content since Chafin moved them over to Sharples. She loved and missed Cow Creek and her neighbors and kinfolk, probably even more than her husband did. She yearned to head back to the village — to her simple little dwelling along the creek bank.

One day, at the supper table, after enduring all she could, Louise aberrantly blurted out, "Raymond, I don't necessarily mind the people of Coal River, and I like teaching over here pretty well at times. But I don't want to live here. Period. It ain't home. The people at Cow Creek are a little bit different than they are here.

"Before the last day of school is out, I will have a moving van waiting in front of the house, Margaret and I are packing it all up and going back home. You stay here or do whatever you want to do, but I'm moving!"

Chafin sat stunned at her words. He commented on his wife's out-of-character remarks:

> She was a Chambers through and through, and they don't usually talk a whole lot anyway. I never heard a peep after that.

After her outburst, the two resumed their meal as if nothing had been said. By the next morning, Chafin went back to his normal routine, working as a machine operator at the Boone mine. As the days passed, he nearly forgot about what his wife had said. But as months flew by, the last day of school finally came, and Chafin paid little attention to the day.

> After work, I had a brief meeting to attend. Around 4:00 p.m., I finally headed for the house. When I came around the corner and could see my house, I saw DeHaven's moving van sitting outside and several good-sized men loading up all my furniture.

118

When Chafin pulled into the driveway, he jumped out of his car and ran up the long driveway to Louise. Breathing hard from the run, he gave his wife an angry and puzzled look, and gasped, "Hey, Louise, what in the sam-hill is going on here? What's happening … uh … Louise?"

"Raymond, don't look so dang surprised, bucko. Didn't I tell you that on the last day of school I was moving back to the Creek? You can go or stay here. It's your call, but Margaret and I are headed back home."

She then pointed her finger angrily into Chafin's face and growled, "And those men over there better not take a stitch of my furniture back off that truck, either! I'm warnin' you, mister."

There must have been five seconds of hesitation as a startled Chafin assessed the situation and evaluated his wife's expression. Then he nervously doubled over laughing, uncontrollably shaking from the hilarity and anxiety of the moment. Once he gained his composure, snickering between words, he said, "Well, I'm … I'm going … going back to Cow Creek with ya, I guess! I'll help these boys pack it all up, okay, Louise?"

"Whatever floats your boat," Louise grumbled as she pivoted and went back into the house to pack up the remainder of the furniture and whatnots. Chafin rolled his eyes, shoved his hands in his pockets, and followed her to the front porch.

The Chafins moved back to Cow Creek that night. It might be that Chafin found a new respect for his wife that day. As Chafin stated, "She had a lot of spunk — of course, she was a Chambers. I should have known that all the time."

Although local political opponents sometimes shuddered at the thoughts of having a confrontation with Chairman Chafin, Louise had no problem expressing herself to her husband when she felt strongly about something.

He decided to continue to drive over to the Boone County job every day until he could find another position closer to home. But the drive was extremely difficult, so he knew he wouldn't keep working at Boone for too long.

Chapter Seventeen
Chafin Negotiates Over Drinks

"Well, I could have had a state job after I moved back to Barnabus, on Cow Creek, but state jobs weren't exactly paying much at the time. Soon Ken Hart called me. I had known Ken from years before, but he now worked for Massey Coal Company," Chafin said.

A.T. Massey had originally established Massey Coal in 1920 as a coal brokerage company. However, in 1949, the company plunged into the mining business by buying its first West Virginia mine. West Virginia Coal and Coke was eventually one of its prize acquisitions. Along with the purchase, the company-owned coal camp and company store system were dismantled and most of the rental property was turned over to a land company. Some territory was eventually placed in the hands of realtors, and many area families were given the opportunity to own their own home and property for the first time.

Chafin gazed at his living room ceiling as he reminisced:

> It was 1958, and as it turned out, Massey's mining operation at Omar desperately needed a good construction man. Ken Hart told me about the position, and he told me the pay scale for the job. It sounded like Massey was mighty stingy to me! Regardless, I asked if I could meet with him or his assistant on that upcoming Saturday.
>
> He agreed. So I was to meet with one of Ken's assistants, Russ Squibb, over the weekend. I was supposed to join him at 10 o'clock in the morning, ready to tour the operation.
>
> I got there at 10 o'clock on the nose, and there was this long, black Chrysler waiting on me. Charlie Jones, the construction superintendent over the mining operation, was in the driver's seat, and Russ Squibb, standing outside the car, greeted me with a hearty handshake. He and I got in the backseat. Mr. Jones pulled away from the offices and drove us up Pine Creek to show me a small bridge that they had recently built. There, men had awkwardly cemented two pieces of structure together and called it an over-water bridge.

"Well, what numbskull put this in?" Chafin blurted out sarcastically to Jones. "By golly, every time a cow pees in the creek, this thing will flood you out! I was raised up on this creek, and I know it can get pretty big."

Chafin didn't know that Russ Squibb had been the one who directed the construction of that particular bridge. Jones chuckled, glanced over at Squibb and winked, and kept on driving.

He drove on up to where Massey hoped to put a shaft in, and the two began to describe in detail what all they had planned for the site.

"Wow, look at the mess this is in," Chafin remarked to the men concerning the piles of steel that were laying haphazardly all around the site. "Well, in spite of this clutter, I've heard y'all already have a real good man — Walter Johnson — working here for you. I don't see why you'd even need me here."

"Well, Walter can't work for me or Squibb, either one," Jones lamented. "He has trouble taking orders — at least from us. But you — you're the diplomat, Chafe. You may be able to get somethin' out of him."

Johnson was a foreman who'd had a lifelong reputation for butting heads with authority, but at the same time, he was an extremely skilled construction man. Raymond Chafin remembered working with Johnson many years before, and he understood exactly what the Massey duo were talking about. However, Chafin also recalled that he'd seen supervisors — with a little encouragement, some diplomacy, and a rather strong hand — overcome Walter's contrariness. But that was in the past. He realized that things could be altogether different now, were he to assume the leadership role.

Chafin continued:

> We drove on back to Omar and stopped first at Squibb's house. He lived right across from where the rent office and post office used to be in Omar.

Russ Squibb got out of the car, shook hands with Chafin through the window, and went on into his house, leaving Charlie Jones to talk privately with Chafin. Jones asked Chafin to move up to the passenger seat in front. He drove back to the mine site. Once there, the superintendent led his prospect upstairs to Massey's district offices. "We talked and talked, and we had a drink or two — or three," Chafin remembered.

Finally, the conversation rolled around to a job offer. Chafin said that he didn't know what to think about the proposal. He actually came out and said, "Mr. Jones, y'all don't want to pay a man nothin'! There, I said it!"

"You haven't talked to the right person — me — about the money yet. If you talked payroll before, you talked to Ken Hart," Jones responded as he poured another drink. "You need to talk with me now. What is it we need to give you to get you to come here? What are you getting over at Sharples?"

"Wait a minute!" Chafin said. "I didn't ask you what Massey Coal is paying you — and I know you wouldn't tell me if I asked. When I went over to Sharples, I went over as superintendent. Now I'm just their operator, but a dang good one. But what I make there is just as private to me as your pay stub is to you. That's not a fair question."

"I'll pay you $1,200 a month flat!" Jones offered, as he slapped the table. "You want the job, Chafin?"

"Nope — no can do," Chafin responded confidently, even though $1,200 was considerably more than he was making in Boone County.

"You mean to tell me that little coal company is paying you..." Jones started to say.

"Uh-uh-uh! I said I wasn't gonna tell you my pay, didn't I?" Chafin interrupted, as he poured Jones and himself another drink.

"Son, you are getting to come back home in this deal. No more driving across country to work," Jones fired back, "except occasionally for our other mine sites."

"Are you a darned politician, too?" Chafin asked, as he laughed out loud. "There are other good-paying mines all over this corner of the country. When I find me one that will pay me the right money, I'll run to and from work every day, no matter where it's at, even if it takes all night and all day to do it. Plus, y'all have coalmines everywhere. I'd still be on the road this late if I worked for y'all."

"OK, listen to this: I'll pay you $825 a month — and every time you have to go to one of our other sites and stay as long as 36 hours extra, I'll give ya an extra $600 bonus. I have already talked to Morgan Massey about this. What do you say?" Jones fired back at him.

"$975 a month and a $625 bonus!" Chafin countered, leaning back in the office chair.

"Let's shake on it!" a weary Jones pleaded. "When do you want to go to work?" he asked, as he broke out into a big smile. "You're a daggone lawyer, politician, and arbitrator all rolled into one, Raymond Chafin!"

They shook hands firmly — as they chuckled, rolled up their sleeves, and had another shot of whiskey. Jones teased Chafin, who now appeared flushed and unsteady, about how he had probably offended Squibb over his comments about various projects earlier in the day during the tour of Pine Creek.

"When you made fun of his bridge, I almost laughed out loud," Jones cackled.

Chafin doubled over, laughing uncontrollably, as he clasped his hand over his mouth in embarrassment. "Oops, sorry 'bout that!" Chafin said, rather jovially, obviously feeling the effects of the alcohol.

The co-workers shared another drink before calling it a night and going home. A clerk ran up from the office and took both men home.

Working for Massey

So in the later part of 1958, Raymond Chafin left Sharples Coal and began working for Massey Coal Company. He went to work immediately after being hired by Charlie Jones as his personal assistant. In no time, it became the talk of the town: Raymond Chafin had come back to Omar!

First, Chafin was responsible for building a mining shaft and a mine portal that went down a good three hundred and fifty feet. He described the process:

> First, it was time to dig the hole. I actually did that myself. I did all types of construction and auger work. Then my crew had to put the cage in. They also had hired me to build a road up Pine Creek, so they could take the men up there. They decided to move the portal about a mile up Pine Creek, up to about Three-mile or Four-mile.
>
> I put the cage in — a double-decker. It was like an elevator. Ten or twelve men could get in that cage, and they were shafted up and down, in and out of the mine. It's the way the men entered into the dark mine, and it was their only way out. I put that whole thing in with the help of Walter Woods. Yep, I never had a minute's worth of problems out of ol' Walt. We made a pretty good team together. You just have to treat a man with due respect, that's all.

Chafin said that once the portal-and-cage project was finished, it had to be inspected by the state and federal government, so "everything had to be just right."

Tough Boys

I worked until about 1959 or so, doing all this extra construction work in the Omar area. I also made bonuses on a regular basis. Bare in mind, Massey Coal owned no houses at the time. All of their coal-camp houses had been turned over to private ownership by then. My work was for the Massey mining needs.

All through this time I was also involved — very deeply involved — in county politics as chairman of the Democratic Executive Committee. During my years as an employee for the mining operator, my political clout, so to speak, proved to be a benefit for Massey Coal. It was an exciting time for me and for Logan County.

They treated me well at that operation. Even though Omar work had slowed down by this time, I had been getting plenty of work at three other operations for the company, plus I received my regular salary. I was also given a brand new company station wagon every other year, and I had three company credit cards in my pocket to use [at my discretion].

Once Charlie Jones called me up and said, "Chafin, I'd like for all of our bosses to take their vacations. Do me a favor. I know your wife will soon get out of school [being a teacher, for summer vacation]. You have that brand new station wagon, and you have credit cards. Go to the office and tell the cashier to give you three thousand dollars. You, Louise, and Margaret take your vacation — and when you get back, you take care of everything while the miners are off on their vacation. I will leave you in full charge."

So I had a three thousand dollar bonus, three credit cards, and a new car. All the bosses were taking their vacation at the same time. When we returned, the miners would then go on vacation, but we had to produce while they were gone.

That was some deal! For two solid weeks, Louise, Margaret, and I stayed at the best motels in Florida. I bought Louise and Margaret things, and I bought myself things. We went to the best shows and did all we wanted to do! We had a grand ol' time! I think I came back with less than eight hundred dollars to my name.

When I returned, I did what was asked. Several of us took charge of the mine while the miners were gone — and we produced! Massey Coal at Omar was a good place to be working at that time.

123

Chapter Eighteen
On to Gilbert, West Virginia

A.T. Massey Coal Company had opened up a strip mine at Gilbert, West Virginia. Over time, the company had some problems there, and it had run off some of the best men, the ones who really knew what they were doing. Now it needed good people. Meanwhile, Charlie Jones had gotten into a certain amount of trouble at Omar, so he was transferred to Gilbert as general manager.

Chafin remembered:

> I was asked by Charlie to work for Massey's Gilbert operation for a couple of weeks while he got the place on its feet. So I did.

An odd thing happened around the same time. Jones had mentioned to Chafin that he had sold the coalmine he personally owned at Big Creek, which Morgan Massey had helped him buy sometime earlier. He had also sold all of his stock in the company. When Jones told this to Chafin, he looked at Jones with a puzzled expression but decided to ask no questions. This is about when he had started driving over to Gilbert every morning for work.

> Not long after I started helping out, one day Charlie and I were eating sandwiches at a restaurant, and he told me, "Raymond, E. Morgan Massey will be here in a few minutes. I guess his plane has already landed, someone has already picked him up, and he's on his way."

Chafin's mind began clicking, wondering why Morgan, the wealthy son of A.T. Massey, would be joining them for lunch at a small, run-down café in the middle of rural Gilbert.

"Something's up. Hmm, this must be important," Chafin thought, as he shrugged his shoulders and took another bite of his egg-and-tomato sandwich.

Within fifteen minutes, a well-dressed, handsome young man walked into the eatery. According to Chafin, Morgan Massey was a "practical man — the kind of man who would sit down and talk to you anywhere at anytime... a real gentleman."

"So, boys, what's the occasion?" Chafin asked Jones and Massey, suspecting that something unusual was about to take place.

"Not much, actually. Well, Chafin," Massey said, "Charlie Jones needs some real help over here — for maybe another two or three weeks or so. We need you to build us some roads and take care of some of our problems. Can we count on you to pick up the slack?"

"Well, uh, sure … I can do that," Chafin muttered as they shook hands. Chafin was a bit confused and apprehensive. He still felt as though there was more that he didn't know. Nevertheless, he kept his thoughts to himself.

They enjoyed the rest of their meal together and discussed Massey's vision for the Gilbert operation and for all of West Virginia. He thanked Chafin for helping the company with his "politickin'" at the county health department and the state Legislature.

"We appreciate your assistance as our strong voice over at the county courthouse and at the State Capitol, too," Massey said. "We always need a good lobbyist in our behalf."

Jones Chooses to Retire

About a week later, Chafin walked into the office at Gilbert, and Jones said, "Chafin, come here. I need to tell you something: I'm leavin'."

"Aw, Charlie, don't tell me they fired you. I'm next then!" Chafin said, astonished. "Where you going?"

"No, Chafin. I figure they want to keep you — here at Gilbert. I'm retiring," Jones explained. "I've sold out to them, including my coalmines and stock. They aren't puttin' this ol' bug on me no more! I'm going back to Omar," Jones said as he smiled and patted Chafin on the back.

"They ran one of my best friends off from here at Gilbert. He was a dang good engineer. I figure that if I stay, I'll be finished, too," he said. "However, Morgan and the ol' man Massey want to see you, Chafe. I wouldn't be surprised if they want to make you the general manager over here. They are bringing in their plane to pick us both up at Taplin Airport. We're going to Richmond, Virginia."

"Charlie, I suspect that if I stay here, I'll be a goner, too. As far as the general manager's job, nobody they've ever had up here has lasted too awfully long. But Charlie, they may be calling us up to the headquarters to fire us both. So I wonder if I ought to go ahead and resign right now."

"Naw, Chafe, at least hear them out."

Jones and Chafin drove to the airstrip that afternoon, after Chafin called Louise to explain the peculiar situation. The small, single-prop corporate plane finally came into the small runway between the mountain peaks. Both men walked across the swinging bridge — the only access to the grassy runway — in order to board the plane.

Nervous, Chafin began to chatter. "Charlie, holy cow! I got myself fired one time in a situation something like this. But it's a whole lot farther to get home from Richmond, Virginia, to Cow Creek, than from Charleston to Cow Creek! Hot dog, Charlie, I ain't sure 'bout this at all! If they fire us, will they send us back thumbin'?"

"Dang, Chafe, it ain't like that!" Jones said and laughed. "Goodness! Just hold on for the ride. You'll find out when we get over there."

When they arrived at Richmond, they were taken over to the Massey corporate offices. They were led into a large conference room. A highly polished walnut table, which could easily a couple dozen people, was the center focus in the room. Jones and Chafin quietly went in and sat down and stared around the room at all the ornate decorations and original paintings. A gentleman in a three-piece suit walked into the room and said, "Mr. A.T. Massey will be here in a few minutes, gentlemen. Make yourself at home."

Jones and Chafin looked at each other in amazement. They both felt completely out of their comfort zone, something like what Jethro Bodine would have felt visiting the Taj Mahal.

Several other employees — all women — walked through the door over the next few minutes and seemed to be waiting with the two Logan County men. After about thirty minutes, the door flew open and everyone jumped to attention.

"Sit down, men! Sit down, please!" A.T. Massey growled, as he rushed into the room and took his seat at the front of the long table.

"Let's get this show on the road. I've lost a great deal of money over at Gilbert, boys! That's a cancer on this company."

Massey looked over at Jones, and snarled; "I can see that you've helped us some, Mr. Jones, in your short time there, but surely not enough."

The way the meeting seemed to be going, Chafin was sure that he was about to become unemployed. Massey continued to snarl about the many disappointments at the operation. Finally he paused and looked toward Chafin — eyeing him up and down.

"Well, Charlie, I understand you want to retire from the company and you've brought us a man — this fellow here — that you'd like to take your place. Is that right?" Massey said, without taking his eyes off Chafin.

"Yessir, Mr. Massey," Jones stuttered. "I think he can do the job — much better than me."

Chafin blushed and sat flabbergasted at the words being said.

"Well, Charlie, first things first. We bought back your stock and that old coal mine of yours, but as long as there is a Massey Coal, if you ever need a job or even if you want your old job back, we have a place for you right here," Mr. Massey said, as he broke into a broad smile. He then stood up to shake Jones' hand. "Charlie, we appreciate what you've done. Overall, you've done a lot of good for us. I may grumble sometimes, but you have made us proud.

"Now, with that out of the way, I suppose this fellow, Raymond Chafin, is the man that you want to take over Gilbert?" he asked, as he sat back down and pointed casually toward Chafin.

"Well, yes, but he hasn't said that he'll take the job, sir. Actually, I didn't even talk to him about it much yet. I figured you would," Jones added.

"No, I'll leave it to you. You need to fill him in now," Massey said. "I need to walk down the hall and take care of a few things while you fellows chat."

As Massey gave the men a few moments to privately discuss the situation, Jones filled Chafin in on the opportunity and then whispered, "Whatever you do, make sure you get a contract when you take this job."

When the meeting resumed, A.T. Massey shook everyone's hands again and left. Morgan Massey was called into the room, designated by his father to finalize the offer.

"What are we going to have to pay you?" Morgan Massey asked, as he got right to the point. "What is it that you want, Mr. Chafin?"

"Well, I'm pretty well happy with all that I've been making at Omar, along with the bonuses when I work at other operations. To tell ya the truth, I'm a little bit worried about getting fired at Gilbert. You have gone through quite a few men," Chafin said. "Before I would be shipped to Gilbert to get fired, I would rather resign."

"No, it's not going to be like that. We need you over there. You are the only one we've ever had who knows about building roads and organizing mammoth projects. You also know a great deal about our plant — and can solve our water problems over there. We don't want to lose you. Raymond, you won't have to go to these other mines anymore either to earn extra pay. How about $1,600 a month?"

"It's all right with me," Chafin answered. "The money's fine, and I've always been satisfied with the way I've been treated. However, if you want me at Gilbert, I'd like an agreement that if anything happens that doesn't quite suit youins', that you can't just kick my rump out without paying me at least a certain amount of income. I know how easy you can run me off if you want to run me off."

"Will he still get his new station wagon every other year?" Jones interrupted.

"Yes," Massey answered smugly. "Plus an ol' pickup truck to drive to and from work since I understand you live about thirty miles away from Gilbert. You can still keep your credit cards and anything else you already have, too.

"I will agree to writing up an agreement with you that protects you — and me. However, will you still help us with local politics?" Massey said, as he looked steadily at Chafin.

"Yes, we can do that," Massey said, as he stood up and smiled. "Welcome aboard, Mr. Chafin. We feel sure you'll do well at Gilbert."

He then looked to Jones and added, "Charlie, best of luck in the future. I hope you have a wonderful retirement. Call us if you need anything."

Morgan Massey, Chafin, and Jones all shook hands. The meeting ended, and Morgan escorted them out of the meeting room.

Within days after they returned to Logan, Chafin met over a three-day period with an A.T. Massey lawyer who was in charge of creating the employment contract.

> The finished contract said that if I quit I would get half-pay for five full years. If Massey fired me, I would get two-thirds pay for that same five years. There was no way I could go wrong with this kind of agreement.

Once the contract was signed, Chafin became the general manager of the entire Gilbert operation, because of Charlie Jones' recommendation. He was also given a great deal of liberty as he watched after the company's political interests in the county – and the interests of his faction.

Storm's A-brewing

During a routine visit to Gilbert by Morgan Massey, Raymond Chafin mentioned to the coal baron that the upcoming primary in 1960 would be a landmark election for southern West Virginia and that he [Chafin] would have to give all of his energy to the candidates of his faction.

Chafin recalled:

> I told Morgan Massey that Okey Justice wanted to run for county sheriff, but I hadn't decided what I wanted to do. Ray Watts was running, and he still had his own faction. Ray hadn't done me right by double-crossing me two elections before. So I was lookin' forward to takin' him on this time 'round.

Actually, there was a history of "bad blood" between Watts and Chafin. It may have begun when Chafin, and others on the Logan County Democratic Executive Committee, ousted Watts as county chairman in 1956. However, they had squabbles even before that when Watts "sold out Governor Bill Marland in the 1952 primary for quick cash."

Again, in 1958, County Commissioner Watts promised to support Okey Hager for a commissioner seat. Instead, at the last minute, he switched to Okey Justice. Therefore, Hager lost his election bid. Watts had a tendency "to often flip-flop when he made a better deal with the opposing side."

It was 1959, and preparation was being made for the upcoming election in the spring of 1960. Crooked Creek native E.A. "Uncle Ed" McDonald was the sheriff. According to later comments from Bus Perry, no one ever knew of any graft or corrupt activity that "Uncle Ed" participated in. Many described him as a Christian gentleman. But the sheriff position in that period lasted one term, so Uncle Ed was reluctantly stepping down from the position.

Some time before, Ray Watts had promised that he was going to support Okey Justice for sheriff. Then his brother-in-law, County Commissioner R.J. Cook, decided he wanted to run for the office. Watts, who had served as sheriff from 1953 to 1957, changed his mind about both and decided he wanted the sheriff position for himself, so he told his brother-in-law to keep his commissioner seat. He then told Okey Justice about his plans as well.

R.J. Cook, an extremely well liked politician, decided to run for sheriff anyway, even though Watts wanted the candidacy. A few days after Cook announced his intentions, he allegedly committed suicide. It was said that this was most uncharacteristic of R.J. and for several months afterward there was much debate and gossip concerning the tragic death. According to published records, his brother-in-law, Ray, was with him at the time he took his own life. Chafin elaborated about the incident:

> Some tried to even accuse someone of causing Cook's death. But I don't think anyone killed him. I believe R.J. just got terribly disappointed when he saw how the campaign was going — he was deeply overwhelmed and depressed.
>
> That threw a wrench in the cog. Hager and Justice had both been double-crossed at one time or another by ol' Watts.
>
> I saw that it was time to do something — quickly — so I went to Ray. I scheduled a meeting with Watts, and I said, "Ray, it's not in the cards for you to run for sheriff. You promised everyone in the world at one time or 'nother, and you ought to support them. You promised Okey Justice and then double-crossed him. You promised Okey Hager once, and you did him in, too. You went to your own family, R.J., and you decided you were going to run over top of him as well. C'mon, Ray, give it up."

"Chafe, there ain't nothing you can do about this," Watts said, as he laughed scornfully. "Before it's over, I'll even take the committee chair away from you."

"Take 'er, *big boy!*" Chafin growled, as he pivoted on his heel and walked away. The two parted, and Chafin went to work on creating a faction that would hopefully overpower Watts and his list of candidates.

By the next committee meeting, Commissioner Watts demanded a new vote on the Democratic Executive chairman's seat. He was ready to make good on his threat and maneuver Chafin out of the picture.

He was mighty powerful, and he tried to change the committee on me, but I had committee members — Elizabeth "Libby" Hager, the wife of Red Hager, Faye Ferrell, Jack Ferrell's wife; and myself. Both ladies were on my side. So I had the committee tied, and Watts — no matter what he tried — couldn't change a daggone thing.

When he tried to throw me out, I didn't get mad. I got busy — extremely busy! I organized. I picked up some good politicians to help me prepare, such as Arnold Harkins, Bus Perry, and Elvie Curry. They agreed with me politically, and promised to support me if I could get Okey Justice as a candidate for sheriff.

Okey Hager and the Justice family down in Chapmanville District had been at each other's throats for a long, long time. Okey Justice had beat ol' Okey Hager in the Ray Watts' double cross for the commissioner's seat. It had caused more hard feelings between those two than you could ever imagine. I had a hard time getting them together.

I made several trips down to Okey's home. I went late at night, mind you.

Justice had been elected to the county court and had served there several months before he was handpicked by Uncle Ed to fill the seat of sheriff after McDonald's term ended. However, now that Ray Watts was entering the ring, Justice was hesitant to throw his hat in the ring.

I had a hard time getting him to run 'cause he didn't think he could win over Ray Watts. He had also once been a chief deputy under Ray, and he hated to run against his ol' boss.

I finally worked that deal out, and then I went back to Ray and said, "Ray, I gots me a man that will beat ya! Best thing you can do is stay out of this election altogether. Don't embarrass yourself and your family."

"Who?" Watts asked, as he chuckled. "Who do you think can beat me, Chafe?"

"Okey Justice, that's who!"

"Okey Justice?" Ray said, as he bent over laughing, obviously amused. "You'll never get him to run against me!"

"It's a done deal, Ray; Okey is geared up and ready to whip your hind-end. Get ready for the campaign of your life, big boy."

Within several days, Justice filed for the election and his campaign began.

"Judge C.C. Chambers decided to run again for judge, and he also joined with me — especially after he heard Okey Justice was with us," Chafin remembered, explaining that Chambers was a cousin to his wife, Louise.

"Watts had Claude Joyce, the prosecuting attorney, running for judge. So there was a big fight waitin' to happen there, too.

"Judge Chambers never got along with the Damrons. However, we needed someone for prosecuting attorney, so I decided to contact Oval Damron.

"With that, I now had to go see Judge Chambers at his office and sell him on Damron. I told him that Claude Joyce, the former prosecuting attorney, was going to give him fits."

"I can beat him — easy!" Chambers grumbled, as he shuffled papers on his desk.

"No, you can't — not without my help!" Chafin barked. "You both have sent a lot of folks up the river. Face it. There are a lot of families that are going to remember that, judge. I believe he may even have a little bit of a lead on ya right now. You aren't the most loved of candidates with that cantankerous personality of yours."

"I'll beat him, Chafe!"

"Now, I have to put someone in for assistant prosecuting attorney. I've got an idea for the right man, but don't you go through that ceiling, judge!"

"Who is he?" Chambers asked, as he snarled and squinted one eye.

"Oval D. Damron," Chafin said.

"Oh, no! No, no, no!" Chambers boomed. "No, sirree."

"Now hush. You let me handle this," Chafin said, and then explained to the judge that he was going to have to let the petty past stay in the past.

"I left his office late that evening," Chafin remembered. "I went straight home to sleep on it. The next day I went back to town. I called Bill Damron, Oval's father, and Oval, and scheduled a meeting at their downtown office. When I got to their place, I told Bill, 'Lock the door. Tell the secretary that you won't be taking any calls. I gots to talk to you!'"

When Chafin explained what he envisioned for the faction, Oval said, "Nope, not me. Sorry. Dad and the judge have been at it too long. I won't be doing that. I'm not getting in the middle of the fight between those two."

"I already went to see the judge," Chafin said, as he poured himself a cup of black coffee from the coffee pot in the room. "I can get the judge to accept it. He took the information \. uh ... pretty well."

"Yeah, yeah, yeah, he can run," Bill said. "I'll finance whatever he will have to have, too."

"I need to talk it over with my wife, Birdy, before I get into this mess," Oval said. "I need to do some heavy thinking about it, Chafe."

"I gotta know in the morning," he said, as he smiled and shook their hands.

By the next day, Chafin returned to his office to see what his decision would be. Oval said, "Well, if Dad and you agree, I will go ahead and run."

He filed. Oval Damron would have his hands full, facing Ray Watts' man, Bill Lockhart, for prosecuting attorney. After Chafin chose a House of Delegates candidate, he had his slate filled and ready. The faction was in its infancy, but it was ready to grow in power — and to do it quickly.

A few days later, Claude "Big Daddy" Ellis, who was the powerful leader of the Logan County Committee to Elect John Kennedy and the overseer of the Ray Watts' political faction, saw Chafin walking down Stratton Street in Logan and hollered, "Hey, chief! You got you a good one started, don't ya?"

"Well, big'n, I guess us two Island Creekers are going to have us some fun!"

"Yes," he said, as he chuckled. "You can't beat Watts for sheriff."

"Wait and see, big'n!" Chafin said.

"I hate to see you go down in defeat when you ought to be up at the top!" Ellis said, as he playfully smirked.

"You worry about yours. I'll worry 'bout mine," Chafin responded dryly.

Republican Cecil Underwood was governor. However, both Chafe and Ellis chose Wally Barron for the governor's race.

"Other than the governor's race, y'all keep your list of candidates. We will beat you with ours. Fair enough?" Chafin laughed, as he patted Ellis on the back.

"Uh-huh," Ellis grunted, as he sarcastically rolled his eyes.

However, within a few weeks there was bitterness between the two political factions as each hammered away against the other.

> Claude Ellis was the toughest son of a gun I ever ran up against. He would do just 'bout anything to win. Looking back, he had some darn good candidates, too. Of course, I guess I'd do just 'bout anything to win, too.

As Logan County Democratic chairman, Chafin felt that he was king of the political hill — and it was said that he ruled his kingdom with an iron fist. Logan was, and still is, a one-party county — predominantly Democratic. However, his opponent was Claude Ellis — a powerful politician in his own right, head of the Young Democrats, and considered by many the fastest-rising political star in Logan at the time. Ellis had been well trained, and he was ready to wage an effective campaign for his own candidates.

Chafin, a man with only a seventh-grade education, felt that he was ready for anything — including the Kennedys.

Chapter Nineteen

Humphrey Campaigns in Logan

Around late fall 1959, one of Hubert Humphrey's campaign workers contacted Raymond Chafin's political faction. After a lengthy discussion, the representative donated twenty-five hundred dollars in cash to their faction — handing it directly to Chafin. Quickly, Chafin handed it over to his faction treasurer, Jack Ferrell. Most of the Democratic elite in Charleston already backed Humphrey, and after the donation, Chafin and his minions took a special liking to Humphrey, too.

Months later, as Democratic chairman, Chafin organized a giant "Meet Your Candidates" breakfast — eggs, bacon, gravy, and biscuits for three hundred — above the old WVOW radio location, in their large dining hall. Wendy's restaurant, near William "Bill" Abraham Memorial Bridge, now stands approximately where the radio building once stood.

The breakfast was also set up to welcome Hubert Humphrey and his wife, Muriel Buck Humphrey, to downtown Logan. It was April 11, 1960, at the height of the presidential campaign, with the primary election only a few weeks away. Along with Humphrey and his wife, a number of local candidates spoke that day to the packed hall of county dignitaries and guests.

Chafin clasped his hands together as he reminisced about the historical day:

> Humphrey and his people came in on his campaign bus. The whole breakfast didn't cost us over four hundred dollars to put together. It was really something. Most of my fellas — mostly incumbents — spoke that day.
>
> It was still a little bit too early to give our public support on the presidential campaign, so I mainly used the occasion to watch and see how the people reacted to my candidates, including ol' Humphrey. After meeting him myself, when I received the money, I certainly felt pretty good about supporting him. Even though I hadn't said a lot at this time, everyone knew that my faction and I supported Humphrey.

The street outside the facility was wild and alive with folks from all corners of the county — men, women, and children — who were unable to attend the breakfast because of the limited seating. Many pushed and shoved one another in order to get a better look through the glass front doors of the building.

The constant sound of people clamoring, chattering, and complaining made a distinctly unfamiliar buzz above the common, small-town sounds of dogs barking, trucks passing by, trains chugging through downtown, and car-horns blaring.

Everyone hoped to catch a glimpse of the presidential candidate from Minnesota. It was nearly a party atmosphere when he finally came outside after the breakfast was over and the speeches were finished. He spent time shaking hands, kissing babies, and briefly talking to several individuals about unemployment, poverty, and the general needs of Appalachia. Chafin recalled:

After that Democratic breakfast, I started working hard for Humphrey. After spending some time with him, I found him to be a good man, and in ways he was even smoother than Senator Kennedy.

But around the state, things started getting bigger and bigger for John F. Kennedy. The people whom I was with — our faction — were all for Humphrey. Most were Masons or Shriners, who didn't take kindly to Catholics in the first place, and they certainly didn't think this Kennedy could win even if they did support him. They just simply weren't for JFK.

Humphrey had come in here, and he had given us some money — handing it directly into my palm. I went down to Aracoma Hotel, in the center of Logan, to set up a headquarters — at ten dollars a day.

Jack Ferrell, Red Hager, and some of us were struggling to pay for the hotel room — well, that was until I spoke to Morgan Massey.

I was general manager at Massey Coal at Gilbert at the time. We were running their tipple over. We were actually running so much coal that the tipple couldn't keep up with us and it couldn't take it all in. I was really doing A.T. Massey a good job. So not too long after this time period, Morgan Massey flew back in. We were standing together at the top of the hill [at Gilbert].

Chafin said, "Morgan, we need a new courthouse and a lot of other things in Logan. Hubert Humphrey has promised me that he'll help us. I need to get back over to Logan and help him with his campaign. Wally Barron is also running for governor, and I'd like to be for him. Judge C.C. Chambers is running again — I've got to be for him, too. I need to be in the city."

Massey responded, "Raymond, I have never told you what to do politically. You're settin' on those eggs — not me. But you take all the time you want. Whatever you need along the way, we can take care of it."

"That's OK with me!" Chafin said, grinning.

"Just make sure you have a man here at Gilbert to keep things going. Maybe you could stop over here two or three times a week to make sure everything is going well. We gotta have coal," Massey said.

"I'll take care of all that," Chafin said. "The coal will continue — it sure will."

"We'll also take care of you and all your expenses while you're in Logan — hotel expense and meals. You make sure things go in our favor," Massey said.

So Democratic Chairman Chafin spent the next few weeks in Logan working for the faction and the Humphrey campaign. He ate and "politicked" daily at the Smoke House and continued to strategize with all the local politicians who were a part of his group.

Nevertheless, as the days went by, Chafin said that Kennedy was becoming the buzz around town and across the state – and the JFK campaign was gaining momentum.

Every time I turned around, that's all I heard on the street — Kennedy, Kennedy, Kennedy. I could see the problem. Even brother Teddy was in Logan rallying support for his brother. We were going downhill, as far as the presidential race was concerned. So I called my boys in at the hotel headquarters and told them, "Now, fellers, we're going to get beat if we don't do somethin' about this presidential thing."

The other politicians on the team just scoffed at Chafin, believing that he was exaggerating. So Chafin cut his conversation short and took everyone down to the Smokehouse for dinner.

Chafin worried about his original decision to support Hubert Humphrey.

"Maybe the guys were right ..." he thought to himself. "Maybe I am making a mountain out of a molehill. Humphrey had originally taken the lead. There is still time for him to regain his position."

He continued to campaign and talk to voters about Humphrey's vision for southern West Virginia.

> At that time I knew Humphrey much better than I knew this Kennedy fellow. Besides, I wouldn't dare be seen getting on a platform with Kennedy early on. If I had done that, Judge C.C. Chambers would have been agin it. He would have blown a gasket. Okey Justice and Okey Hager would have been agin it and agin me, too. The prosecuting attorney would have been agin it! They didn't want to get over there with Kennedy. They definitely weren't for him. They thought Humphrey was going to sweep the whole thing — and I did, too — at least, at first! Now I wasn't so sure.

Things Really Begin to Heat Up

"The election kept getting hotter and hotter, and then Morgan Massey unexpectedly flew back into Taplin Airport," Chafin remembered. He was told to pick A.T. Massey's son up at Chauncey Hollow because he wanted to chat with him about politics.

When they met, Morgan Massey stated, "Raymond, this fellow Humphrey looks like he's down the drain."

"By golly, he is," Chafin said, as he shook his head in disbelief. "But what the heck am I supposed to do about it? I don't have one single man who would be with me if I were to come out for Kennedy. Every one of these guys who is with me is a Mason. Every last one of them is agin Kennedy."

"By golly, *you* work it out!" Massey said roughly, as he folded his arms and kicked the dust. After a few minutes, the conversation ended. Even though Morgan Massey didn't say the specific words "you'd better support Kennedy," Chafin felt that he understood the underlying meaning behind Massey's unplanned visit. But by this time, Chafin had started to look toward Humphrey's strongest opponent as the only winning choice anyway. Now he was left with the challenge of "working it out" among his strong-willed buddies.

After meeting with Massey, Chafin darted back to Logan and found several members of his faction at the Smokehouse. He said, "Boys, I got to see you all tonight at 11 o'clock. It's mighty important — so go tell the others to be at the Aracoma, at the crow's nest."

When they all met late that night, they greeted one another and shook hands. Chafin eventually sat down, took a deep breath, and appealed, "Fellas, I have you all here for a reason. I don't know what the heck I'm going to do. We're in a heap of trouble 'cause Kennedy is gainin', gainin', gainin'."

Perry interjected, "Shoot, Chafe! He isn't gaining that much. We still have the Freewill Baptists and the Church of Christ voters who aren't goin' to switch over, right?"

Harkins said, "No, Bus, he's gaining."

"For gosh sakes, there's no need for the likes of Kennedy in this county," Elvie Curry remarked. "Don't tell us, Raymond, that you're thinkin'..."

"I don't know what to do, boys," Chafin fired back, as he smacked the armchair. "But rest assured, we're in deep trouble in the direction we're now going, with Humphrey."

The conversation continued and tempers flared as Chafin talked about what he was hearing on the streets of Logan, Man, Chapmanville, and around Omar. He said that people are impressed with the handsome and charismatic JFK and "the Humphrey ship is tumbling — sinking fast."

"Bus, darn your little soul, you're the smartest one here," Chafin said, as he singled him out. "You got to work it all out!"

Chafin scolded Bus Perry for not having a handle on the problem. He finally stood up. "You figure this dang thing out. I'm tired of worrying' 'bout it!"

"I'll tell you one thing fer darn sure: you get in a fight over this thing, they'll kill you, Raymond Chafin," Perry warned him, talking about other faction members in the county. "They'll have you killed, sure as I'm sittin' here."

The meeting ended and the anger eventually cooled. Raymond went on:

> Within a week or so, Morgan Massey came in again — for what he called a "delayed Christmas dinner" at the field house at Holden. Yep, a delayed Christmas dinner, he called it. He had every employee there — from Logan to McDowell County. I wasn't going to go, but he called the sheriff, Uncle Ed McDonald, and had two deputies come over and get me and take me over to the dinner. He had a big rib roast and everything you could have imagined there — probably a thousand dollars worth of food.
>
> When I got there, he motioned at me, and he and I walked out to the center of that gymnasium floor. Everybody could see me with him. I had no idea what he wanted with me — in the middle of the room.

"Do you know what I'm doing right now?" Massey smiled, as he put his arm around Chafin's shoulder.

"Well, not really," Chafin said, as he shuffled his feet.

"I'm aligning myself up with you. By golly, everyone in the room now knows that I am with you. Look at them looking at us, Chafe. From here on out, whatever you want, they'll do it for you," Massey said through his clenched teeth, as he grinned uncharacteristically for the benefit of the captive audience.

"Boy, you are surely puttin' me on the spot," Chafin said, as he blushed slightly. "This is a ticklish spot for me."

"Have you worked your way out of your ... uh ... problems yet, Chafe?" Massey inquired.

"Nope, I don't know what I'm goin' to do 'bout that," Chafin said. "I gots a problem fer sure."

"Well, I will have the best man in the country come in and see you," Massey added. "He's a problem solver of sorts. His name is Jim McCahey. He is one of the biggest coal buyers in the entire world. He's from Chicago, and he is a strong Kennedy man. He can help you with everything you might need."

Massey patted Chafin on the back and escorted him back to a seat at his own table. The other employees in the room seemed to look at the Cow Creek native with a new sense of curiosity. Among the men and women in the room, Chafin's status had been greatly elevated.

Even though the rest of the night was uneventful and Chafin finished the dinner, that night after he went home he couldn't sleep. How was he going to make C.C. Chambers, Okey Justice, and the rest of his easily angered candidates see that Humphrey was a corpse — political dead weight — who would certainly slow down the momentum of their political machine, and that it was time to consider a change — a dramatic change?

Chafin said that it's funny now how certain recollections will stand out above others. For example, he said that while the faction was firmly for Humphrey, Bus Perry's oldest son, who was going to college, had a different opinion.

Chafin recalled:

> On one of his visits home, Bus' son told his dad and me that we were barking up a tree — and that there's nothing up that sapling to begin with.

"Kennedy's going to win this presidential thing," he said.

"What?" Chafin scoffed, trying to hide his concern.

Bus Perry jumped off the couch and said, "Son, you're not for him, are you?"

"Well, no, Dad, I've always done what you ask," he said, "but I don't believe Humphrey can pull this thing off."

"Bus, something's got to happen here," Chafin whispered after his son left the room. "I hear the same thing your son is saying everywhere. Listen, I'm supposed to meet with a man named Jim McCahey. He is supposedly the richest coal buyer in the world, as I hear it. Bus, he buys all of Massey's coal, and I'm goin' to have to work somewhere when this election is over. What the heck can I do?"

Perry stared at Chafin with a look of unbelief for a few minutes and said, "Chafin, we already have Humphrey's money, right? You know that. Is Kennedy offering you money, too?"

"No, no," Chafin answered, brushing off the question. "I'm just worried, OK? I am just fretting for nothin', that's all. Never mind. Forget the whole thing."

***

The first great match up for JFK against contender Humphrey was the Wisconsin primary, being held in April 1960. Strategically preparing for the political battle, the glamorous Kennedy family stormed the Wisconsin borders with a vengeance, with the first wave being John's sisters — Eunice, Pat, and Jean — holding tea parties and coffee klatches at targeted homes around the state. JFK's brothers, Bobby and Teddy, traveled out across the counties shaking hands, kissing babies, meeting with newspaper reporters and speaking with regional television anchormen. It was a media blitz that rolled across the state as Humhrey, with less charismatic resources, struggled to counteract the Kennedy barrage.

Eventually, through this family-campaigning enterprise, Kennedy won the primary with 56 percent of the vote. However, final tallies showed that he had an extremely poor showing in Protestant regions of the state. Although JFK was clearly victorious — an important step toward the Democratic nomination — the win was not substantial enough to close down the Humphrey race.

Chapter Twenty
McCahey Arrives at Taplin Airport

A few days later, Jim McCahey flew into Taplin Airport, near Logan, and met with Claude Ellis, another local political boss. Ellis, who had aligned himself with the powerful former county sheriff, Ray Watts, was already for John Kennedy. He headed the Kennedy campaign in Logan County. After exchanging pleasantries, McCahey asked Ellis what type of man this Raymond Chafin was.

"Well, he's one tough son of a gun!" Ellis said, smirking. "He's also a crackpot. I wouldn't worry too much 'bout him."

"What do you think it'll take to bring him along to our side?" McCahey asked.

"Money," Ellis said dryly. "Money and job security. He has to work."

They continued to talk about Chafin, the area, and the local campaigns — including the popularity of political slates in southern West Virginia.

Several Democratic factions existed at every election. County voters usually chose one group or another and stayed true to the politicians who made up that particular faction. Bus Perry wrote in 1970 that a slate is the "most coveted place for a candidate to have his or her name."

A slate, a faction's list of candidates, was printed on index-style cards. The cards were distributed to voters, often just before they entered the voting booth, to help them in their choice so that they stayed true to their group of political allies.

A politician usually paid a hefty fee, a "contribution," so to speak, to be included on a certain political slate with other like-minded candidates. Sometimes shenanigans – or double crosses — happened when a faction secretly, or not so secretly, dropped a candidate off its slate at the last minute in spite of his contribution. The money was seldom returned. So money was no guarantee of slate placement. However, it greatly improved the odds.

To maximize their efforts, sometimes candidates bought their way onto more than one slate.

People were apt to vote in blocs back then, too — meaning that a particular family, or an extended family, would often decide who they were going to support, candidate by candidate. That family would also influence neighbors and friends. So the support from a prominent family in a neighborhood could fan out and mean a significant vote share at the polls.

Armed with this information about mountain politics, McCahey called and met with Chafin that same day.

"Who exactly are you, buddy?" Chafin asked him as he shook his hand for the first time. They met at an out-of-the-way location, at Island Creek Coal Company.

"Well, I'm James B. McCahey Jr. My friends call me Jim. I'm the guy who buys all the coal that A.T. Massey, your employer, wants to sell," he answered, as he chuckled.

"Well, that explains some things," Chafin said, as he shrugged his shoulders. They continued to talk about local politics and Humphrey's chances as a presidential candidate. McCahey also mentioned Ellis' name as they spoke.

"You already talked to "Big Daddy" Ellis? Well, looky what we have here. You want my support, but you're not exactly for my man for sheriff? Isn't that interesting?" Chafin snapped as he clenched his jaw concerning McCahey's conversation with his main opponent and rival faction leader. Even though Claude Ellis was a personal friend to Chafin, during political seasons they usually became strong adversaries. This election was no different.

"Raymond, I assure you that we will be for every man you're with, and we can help you a great deal in the county — but ONLY if you're for John Kennedy.

"By the way, you work for Massey, right? I don't want to put any undue pressure on you; however, think about this one thing, sir: I already told you I am a coal buyer, and I buy nearly all of Massey's coal," McCahey said, as he grinned, explicitly stressing that he had great influence with Chafin's employer. "I hope you understand that. I know that people can easily get blackballed in the industry around this area. I think that's a sad thing to see happen, don't you, Mr. Chafin?"

Chafin listened and weighed each word that the Chicago native said, and wondered what McCahey might be implying with the statements. Was McCahey offering financial help if Chafin supported JFK? Was he trying to intimidate him when he emphasized that he was Massey's largest client? Did McCahey somehow know that Chafin had been blackballed as a young man?

This highly successful coal-buying tycoon also talked about Jack Kennedy's background and his style of politics. The get-together soon ended and they scheduled another visit to be held later that night, before McCahey flew out of West Virginia.

At 4 o'clock in the morning, Chafin again met secretly with him. He chose the unusual hour so that no one would see them together. For Chafin to be talking with a known Kennedy man in broad daylight might be dangerous, especially if certain Logan politicians found out.

"What do you want to do, Mr. Chafin?" he asked, as he continued talking about what Kennedy could mean for West Virginia and the county.

"Uh, well, it looks like I'm going' to have to be for Kennedy, but I don't really know how I can help him. You know I am going to be in a dangerous situation. I could wind up six feet under. Plus, I already have Humphrey's money, and we already spent several hundred dollars of it."

"By golly, send it back to him. And for gosh sakes, be sure you DO send it back," McCahey retorted. He then asked "what it would take" to get Kennedy positioned on one of Chafin's slates, meaning how much cash.

Chafin paused for a minute and tried to figure out in his head what he would need for his election necessities.

"Hum … well, about thirty-five?" Chafin mumbled to the coal buyer, meaning thirty-five hundred dollars. As the words came out of his mouth, Chafin's eyes nervously twitched back and forth as he waited for a response. He later recounted that he didn't necessarily need that much at the time, but he could always use more. Chafin explained his thoughts:

> I might have asked for a few hundred more, but I tried to keep the figure reachable. Since I was negotiating, I thought I would up the figure from what we had first received from Humphrey's people. I thought I could stretch it to thirty-five hundred.

"That shouldn't be a problem. Thirty-five it is," McCahey said, as he reached out his hand to shake on the deal. "In the meantime, you get things lined up here in Logan. Pull your team together."

"Yup, and you can personally let John F. Kennedy know that Raymond Chafin has just come on board his political ship!" Chafin arrogantly responded.

"I'll do that, Mr. Chafin. I'll do just that."

McCahey also said he would take care of the responsibility and expense of having a new batch of slates printed. He said that he would have them printed in New York with John Kennedy's name already listed on it.

"Oh, by the way, no double crosses. Do you understand me?" McCahey stated sternly.

Chafin nodded and chuckled, although a cold shiver went up his spine.

They shook hands a final time before McCahey left for his private plane, which was gassed up and waiting for him at the grassy airfield on Route 10, a mile or so past Rum Creek.

Chafin and Perry Pick Up "Literature"

Four or five days before the election, Chafin said he received a telephone call from a gentleman who said that he was to meet an airplane at Taplin airfield. The caller said that a plane was bringing some important campaign literature to help with the Kennedy presidential campaign.

After the phone call, Chafin told Perry, "I need to just lean back and rest. Let's take your Cadillac up to the airport and get that literature."

There was a cloudburst that evening. When the two got to Taplin Airport, they waited approximately thirty minutes until they saw the small plane slice through the thick fog, crossing the mountain as it searched for the landing strip. When they saw it coming in, they jumped out of the car and ran for the swinging bridge that connected to the runway. Perry slipped as he dashed across the wet planks on the swinging footpath. When they reached the other side, they stood and waved their arms toward the plane.

> It was rainin', and the tiny plane circled the runway before it landed. We were soaked and I could hardly see through my glasses 'cause of the constant drizzle. The pilot landed the small aircraft and two fellas jumped out of the plane, holding two sealed bags. When they got up to us, they handed the sopping-wet bags over to Bus and me.

There were three men on the plane — the pilot; Robert McDonough, a well-known printer and industrialist from Parkersburg, who had been coordinating John Kennedy's campaign in the Mountain State; and a campaign worker.

When Chafin asked what type of literature was in the bags, McDonough shrugged his shoulders and said quietly, "Well, Chafe, all I know is that it's supposed to be from headquarters. It should help you do the job right."

140

I then signed a paper saying that these fellas had delivered the bags to me. I handed the confirmation to Bus. I turned 'round and leaned over. Bus placed the document on my back and signed as my witness. He handed the document to Mr. McDonough. Then the men all boarded the plane and prepared to leave.

Bus and I ran back across the bridge and threw the bags in the backseat of the Cadillac, and we took off. We came back to the Aracoma Hotel, and we headed up to my private room with the bags, where Elvie met us in the lobby. Bus, Elvie, and I went on in the room.

The three men talked for a few minutes. Then Elvie Curry asked if either of them had seen any of the literature yet. Chafin grabbed one of the heavy bags and broke the tight seal. He looked inside to see what had been delivered, expecting things such as campaign brochures, posters, badges, and bumper stickers.

"Gosh-dawg!! There's ... m ... money! Money!" Chafin stuttered, as he stood startled in the center of the room. After a few minutes he dumped both bags out on the full-size bed. Temporarily speechless, Perry's and Curry's eyes were fixed on the pile of legal currency. When the entire amount was counted, there was a little bit more than thirty-five thousand dollars.

It immediately hit Chafin what had happened.

When I told McCahey that we needed "thirty-five," he must have mistakenly thought that I meant thirty-five thousand. I told the boys what happened. I'd never seen so much money in my born days — and I had no idea where it came from.

There were fives, tens, and twenties — all wrapped up. The money was in crisp, new bills. The bags were soaking wet, and when we counted it all, there was even some green ink left on the sheets of the bed.

Perry, beginning to panic, said, "I've already been in the penitentiary once! I'm not going back! I haven't seen anything — nothing! I don't want anything to do with this!"

"I'll see ya, buddy," Curry said, as he started toward the door with Perry.

"Hold it, boys," Chafin shouted. "Now just wait a minute. We all are stickin' together. We are all in this."

After they talked some more, they all started to worry that a huge mistake may have happened and that this could backfire in their faces if Chafin didn't report the snafu. Perry reminded Chafin that lots of folks have been killed for a lot less that thirty-five thousand in Logan.

Chafin placed a call to Jim McCahey and told him about the plane arrival and the two bags with their surprising contents. "Jim, I believe there may be a mistake — a big ol' mistake here," Chafin stammered.

"No, Raymond," McCahey said, chuckling. "I don't know where the money came from, but you have a job to do there. We know you'll be able to take care of things with those two bags of ... uh ... literature, right?"

"You mean to say ... are you saying ... ? Yes, sir. Thanks for your time, Mr. McCahey," Chafin said, as he got off the phone, slid down in his chair, and involuntarily stared at the pile of cash lying on the bed. Meanwhile, Curry and Perry looked at their boss and waited for his thirty-five thousand dollar explanation.

Chafin turned to Curry and Perry with a glazed look on his face and said, "I reckon this is our campaign donation. Now, boys, we can't take this down to the bank, and we surely can't take this to the sheriff's office either. I'm afraid to take it home — for fear of being robbed."

"Let's take it up to Mommy's," Curry said, speaking of Cindy Curry — Elvie's mother and Chafin's aunt. "Nobody would think of any money being at Mom's."

Cindy Curry was a kind, elderly woman with her long gray hair always worn bobby-pinned into a tight bun. Usually attired in a flowered zip-up housedress, worn black leather shoes, anklets, and a food-stained apron, Miss Curry lived alone in her little frame house. She was an honest well-respected woman in the community — who adored her son, Elvie, more than life itself.

"OK, that's a deal — to Aunt Cindy Curry's house. That's a good idea," Chafin answered, as he tried to regain his composure.

After repacking the money into the sacks, Chafin and Curry lugged the loot out to Chafin's car and drove to Miss Curry's small home place, up Island Creek, while Perry stayed behind in the hotel room waiting. Curry opened his mother's front door and the two men dragged the bags into the living room.

"Mommy, we got some campaign literature here that we need to leave. We don't want anybody to get it."

"Put it under the bed, honey," she said, as she continued to rock in her favorite chair and labor over a difficult crossword puzzle from the *TV Guide*.

Chafin and Curry looked at each other, smiled and nodded, as if to say, "This is the only place where these bags will be completely safe."

They took the plump bags into her bedroom and pushed the money all the way to the wall underneath her bed.

"Thanks, Mom," Curry said, as he bent over to hug her goodbye. His mother smiled and kissed her son's cheek and then continued her puzzle.

The two politicians went back into town and hooked back up with Perry, who was waiting, along with Arnold Harkins, at the hotel — Room 220.

No one slept that night.

Chapter Twenty-One
Chafin Tells Friends About Change

After his final meeting and agreement with Jim McCahey, Chafin said he immediately sent the Humphrey cash back to his campaign people, as McCahey told him to do. Then he scheduled a meeting with Arnold Harkins, Elvie Curry, and Bus Perry, explaining the entire situation and how he had sent the money back to Humphrey's folks. He also told about his meeting with Jim McCahey.

"Why in the sam-hill would you send twenty-five hundred dollars back?" Harkins sternly asked. "I ain't doing this! What are you going to do with Judge Chambers, Okey Justice, Okey Hager, and the rest of our people [in the faction]? They won't like this one dern bit, Chafe."

"I know. I don't know what I'm goin' to do yet. I don't rightly know how I'm goin' to deal with all of that. But we're getting thirty-five thousand in return," Chafin explained, as he grinned. "That's a heck of a lot more than what we WERE gettin'!

"So in the meantime, don't go 'round saying too much about the presidential campaign," Chafin said. He then explained that most people in the county already believed their faction was for Humphrey because of the campaign signs. So until he got everything worked out, he suggested that everyone lie low and allow him time to scheme.

"All right," Harkins finally said, as he looked over at the others in the room. They were speechless as they tried to figure out what was happening to their faction and how Raymond Chafin could turn events around like he had, without their knowledge.

Chafin later met with several of the candidates — Judge Chambers, Okey Justice, Glenn Jackson, and Oval Damron — about their respective campaigns. He met with each one alone at his upstairs hotel headquarters.

Chafin gave a fiery rundown of what he was hearing on the streets and finally told them that their presidential candidate was losing too much ground to ever recover in Logan County. He then suggested that each one should continue his own campaign, but "don't speak about the presidential race — stay completely out of it so that it won't affect your candidacy.

"The signs are up; that's enough," he said. "Leave it be!"

According to Chafin, after he argued with the others, they still didn't necessarily like what he was implying about Humphrey's loss of support, but all decided to keep quiet about their feelings in case he was right. However, with only about a week before the primary, none of them ever dreamed that Chafin had completely flip-flopped and was now a Kennedy man.

Okey Justice, Judge Chambers, and Oval Damron didn't know a thing in the world about what we were scheming. We immediately set up precincts that we knew we could handle.

Meeting Senator John F. Kennedy

Chafin said that the first time he met John F. Kennedy was when he had come to Charleston shortly after announcing his candidacy. Chafin remembered the circumstances, saying that he and Glenn R. Jackson drove down to meet the new presidential candidate:

> I had gone to Charleston with "Big Shot" — Glenn Jackson. Kennedy was staying at the Daniel Boone Hotel, but really not that many folks went to meet him at the time. When we arrived on the floor, Glenn immediately went into a special room to talk to John. While I waited, I saw Jackie Kennedy sitting at a desk, alone, in the hallway. There weren't too many people paying attention to her at the time. I guess the ones who showed up wanted to look at him.
>
> So I had a chance to walk over, sit down next to her, and talk. She was really nice to me, and she asked me, "Do you think he can win here?"

"Yessum, it's possible," Chafin mumbled, smiling and blushing as he looked toward her. He vividly remembered the day:

> But I recall that I couldn't be for Kennedy at the time because this was early on in the campaign. I was already committed to Humphrey — bought and paid for — during that period of time.
>
> Ah, but she was a gorgeous woman, and she'd stand right up and talk to ya'. She knew how to work that thing — especially for someone like me. She looked like the kind of woman that you couldn't make mad. She had that kind of personality. Wide-set dark eyes, and slim . . . she was a real looker.
>
> I guess Jackie and I talked for twenty minutes or better. At the end of our conversation, I got to meet him — Senator John F. Kennedy. It was funny to me that he already knew about the Chafin name when I entered the room. I guess it's a name that's gone all over the United States, and around the world, because of Don Chafin and the Blair Mountain War.

The first thing JFK said to Chafin was, "Mr. Chafin, are you one of the originals? I've heard of the name Chafin before."

"Well, my dad was original," Chafin said, as he shook hands with the young senator from Massachusetts. "I guess I am, too. Yup, I suspect I'm an original, all righty."

"Will your kin be for me?' Kennedy said, as he smiled, still holding firmly to Chafin's hand.

"Well, I don't know about that yet. With all due respects, I gots to see about that, Mr. Kennedy."

Chafin said the whole meeting lasted about fifteen minutes and that Kennedy was charming and made a good first impression. However, regardless of Kennedy's charisma, Chafin had to keep telling himself that he was already committed to Humphrey.

Chafin remembered:

I think he personally liked me at that very first visit. We sort of hit it off and I felt like I could just be myself around him. He was smart and personable. I talked about factions and how elections tend to work here in the Mountain State — vote buying and power politics. He listened intently and he didn't even seem shocked about what I was tellin' him. I would guess his papa, Joe, the bootlegger, already taught him the ropes.

After the meeting, Jackson and Chafin rode back to Logan together. At one point along the way, Jackson patted Chafin on the shoulder and said, "Cathead, you lucky dawg, you made a hit with ol' Jackie. I saw you guys together. Y'all were just a talkin' and a laughin' it up."

"Yeah, buddy, she's a smart one," Chafin said with a smirk, as he daydreamed about their chance meeting. "Now, I'll tell you one thing: John Kennedy was okay; but she could easily get me to support *her* if *she* was running for president, or anything else for that matter. I will tell you that much! She knows how to treat a man!"

They looked at each other and then burst out laughing.

***

A month or so before the election, Chafin said that most of the Kennedy family came to Logan. Logan was buzzing over the "Massachusetts clan" who had nearly taken over the backwoods county.

The Kennedy boys came here, and they had these big meetings. They really made their own way into Logan County, as far as campaigning goes. Besides what a faction could do for JFK in Logan, the Kennedy family knew how to make a lot of things happen for themselves.

Rose Kennedy, John's mother, came into Logan and stayed at the Aracoma Hotel. Her daughters came in, too.

Young Teddy Kennedy was already in southern West Virginia when they arrived. He spent several grueling months campaigning in the area, coming in and out of the state on a regular basis, making contacts, courting coal executives and local politicians as he prepped the area for his brother's arrival.

Chafin talked about the visiting Kennedy family:

They all ate at the Smokehouse Restaurant, along with the rest of town. When they would finish eating, Rose and the clan would just get up and walk out. There was a fellow who walked behind 'em who would go up to the counter and take care of their bill. I guess that was his sole job — paying for things they picked up or ordered.

At the time, a lot of customers in the restaurant would stare at Rose and the Kennedy girls, thinking that they were getting up and walking out without paying their bill.

Don't let anybody tell ya different — that ol' woman, Rose, was a smart ol' cookie. Once she invited me up to her room at the Aracoma 'cause she wanted to talk to me 'bout the campaign. She and her daughters had double rooms with a door between 'em. They slipped me up the elevator just before they were fixin' to go out to Coal Branch for a big meeting. First, Rose wanted to tell me about her campaign idea. Rose wanted to have small social parties. She wanted to start planning tea parties at different homes in the area.

According to Chafin, Rose was always thinking about how she could reach out to the common people.

"We want to plan tea parties. Now, how would I go about making that happen?" Rose said with a thick Massachusetts accent.

"Mrs. Kennedy, the women down here don't drink no tea!" Chafin said, with a devilish grin. "They drink coffee, beer, and whiskey!"

She laughed boisterously and said, "Well, we'll have ... coffee, then, Mr. Chafin."

Chafin recalled other memories of Rose:

She didn't seem to care about money. She told several of her helpers to get plenty of coffee, pastries, and good, thick teacups and saucers. Mamma was spendin' the money this time 'round. Money was no object.

Kennedy campaign workers started jumping on the phones and calling precinct captains and coordinating with the Women's Club for Kennedy, an organization that "Big Daddy" Ellis had organized in Logan. They arranged for Rose and her daughters to have a coffee party at different houses in each precinct. They began by asking if there were people in the region who would like to have coffee with the future president's mother.

You couldn't squirm or wiggle your way into the house after they arrived with their coffee 'cause everyone in the community showed up. Just think what that did for JFK's campaign, and she only had to drink coffee for a few minutes at each place. They were slick campaigners!

Rose and her entourage didn't go to Midelburg, the most affluent housing development in the county. She'd schedule her parties in coal-camp communities in remote areas. It was said at the time that it was as if a spell had been cast on the women in the community. Many of the coalminer's wives had never had anyone pay such attention to them before, especially someone of such stature.

Rose would sit down with miners' wives and their kids. She'd go into their homes with daughters Eunice, Jean, and Patricia. Rose would introduce herself and her family. Then she'd pour coffee and have ol' fashioned girl chat. She seemed to get along with everyone she met. Of course she had a plan behind it all — it was all for votes for her son.

Rose Kennedy had married Joseph P. Kennedy after he graduated from Harvard in October 1914. Together, they assembled a strong and wealthy Irish Catholic home. With

Joseph's unrelenting search for political power and wealth, it has been said that he used all means, legal and illegal, to amass his fortune and influence. His worth was estimated to be around $350 million in 1957, according to *Fortune* magazine.

By the late '50s, the Kennedy daughters were all married. Eunice, "the tall, freckle-faced Kennedy," had married R. Sargent "Sarge" Shriver, in May 1953, when she was 31. Coming from a well-known Maryland Roman Catholic family, he had attended Yale, where he was a baseball standout, and later served in the Navy during Word War II. Sister Pat gravitated toward the bright lights of fame and Hollywood, marrying Peter Lawford, a British-born movie actor, in April 1954, who was best known as a member of Frank Sinatra's Rat Pack. In May 1956, 28-year-old Jean married Stephen "Steve" Smith, a brash businessman.

The culture and surroundings that Rose and her daughters found in southern West Virginia must have seemed like something from a strange foreign land — or another universe — when compared with their customary luxurious lifestyle in Hyannis Port or their winter abode in Palm Beach. Yet, to Logan County residents, they were polite, personable, and most importantly, down-to-earth.

Chafin remembers that once, hours after a huge rally for JFK in the streets of Logan, he was invited to John Kennedy's room. Rose, Eunice, Jean, and Pat were out campaigning, and the hotel hallways were unusually vacant.

Chafin reluctantly went up to the room and knocked on the door. Kennedy himself answered, grinning, and graciously inviting Chafin in. When Chafin walked into the modest suite, JFK walked him over to a window looking down over a busy street, two floors below. He then glanced over at Chafin, smiled, and said, "Come and look. Mr. Chafin, take a long look below at the people. These are your people. If you'll be for me, you'll never regret it. I'll help these people — I can help them greatly. I can help you, too.

"I understand you are trying to get a new courthouse in Logan, and you're trying to get new roads in here. You want and need other things, too, like new industry and diversification. I'll help you do it all," he said confidently, as they both gazed out the window.

Chafin asked Kennedy several questions about how he planned to help Logan. Kennedy answered each question without hesitation.

"There's one additional thing I want you to think about, Mr. Kennedy," Chafin said, as he built up his nerve. "It's these dang commodities — American cheese, yellow meal, and that powdered milk — it ain't no count! Adults can't eat 'em. Kids don't want 'em. Now if you could do something about that …"

Kennedy looked at Chafin as if he had temporarily lost his mind. They had been talking about infrastructure and economics. Now Chafin tried to change the subject to substandard cheese and dry milk. Kennedy seemingly ignored the comment and continued to talk about the poverty level in Appalachia.

After they both spoke candidly, Chafin and John Kennedy shook hands, and Chafin indicated that he would head on home and think about everything that had been said.

"I will, too, Raymond," Kennedy said, and chuckled. "Commodities, you say? I will have to think on that one. Remember, I can help you and these people — I can help a great deal."

Chafin reminisced about the life-changing moment, and said:

It was an odd night. Just before Jack Kennedy spoke at the rally earlier in the day, Claude Ellis had asked me to introduce him, being that I was the Democrat Executive Chairman. I declined the offer since it would have stirred up a hornet's nest among my slate. Then, the same exact night, I'm in his room — face-to-face — discussing what he could do for *me*. Incidentally, Kennedy had the best handshake of any man I have ever met. He had a man's man of a handshake. I have tried to imitate that shake in my own career. He didn't squeeze your hand too hard. It wasn't too soft, either. He would look you square in the eye as he spoke. It was certainly hard to refuse him with that toothy grin of his.

I couldn't talk my wife and Margaret out of it. They loved Kennedy, even when they knew I was a Humphrey man. While in Logan County, Kennedy came to Omar, at Bill and Niddie Abraham's grocery store parking lot. Snap. Snap. Snap. The local newspaper took pictures of Louise and Margaret in the crowd as they went to the rally. It made the newspaper! Now my political people were saying, "Aha! Look at that! There is Raymond Chafin's family at the Kennedy get-together."

Even my guys — my closest buddies — wondered what was going on. I wasn't at the rally, though, and I couldn't control those two. Louise and Margaret had minds of their own — those two always did.

Chafin's daughter, Margaret, was 11 years old at the time. She was definitely Daddy's girl. However, she already had strong Democratic opinions of her own and sided with her mother when it came to the election.

Even before I made the contact with McCahey, JFK's people were spending nearly all of their time in the state.

I never did have any association with John Kennedy's little brothers — Bobby and Ted. Claude Ellis, leader of the other faction, associated with Teddy and Robert all the time. But I liked the Big Cheese. I didn't really want to fool with the little fellas at the time. I think ol' Claude always expected to be appointed federal marshal, or something like that, if Kennedy won the presidency. He definitely tried to cozy up with the whole family.

Claude and I laughed about it after the election. Nevertheless, I was big enough to thank Claude when it was all over with. He was really the one who put the Kennedy gang on me in the first place! Claude was trying to beat me 'cause he was the campaign manager for Ray Watts, who was running for county sheriff.

Claude already felt like Kennedy was going to win, but he had another motive for getting me connected with the Kennedy family. He's the crafty one, ya know. He wanted me to make all of my side mad at me by being for Kennedy. He could have cared less if I was really for Kennedy, except that if I joined up with the senator, my side would be fightin' and flubbin' up the whole election for our boys on the slate.

Sure, I grabbed up ol' Kennedy, but nobody actually told me I had to do it. He was hot as a jalapeno pepper, and people were moving away from Humphrey. I knew what I had to do.

I was told that Claude Ellis and Ray Watts went up to New York — or some-dang-where — to get their money from the Kennedy supporters. I doubt that Claude and Ray got anything compared to what I got 'cause I had the power — the MACHINE — the coal operators. They — the Kennedy people — were certainly playin' the union, too.

I heard Claude and Ray were at that giant campaign headquarters, waiting with others for their name to be called over the loud speaker to receive their allotment of money for the Kennedy campaign. All of a sudden, while Claude sat in the waiting room beside Watts, the intercom barked, "RAYMOND CHAFIN!"

Ellis looked over at Watts, snarled, and growled, "Doggone, that son of a gun. Is that worm here, too? What's going on?"

Chafin said that Ellis and Watts were both "fit to be tied."

Chafin laughed and then expounded about the incident:

I wasn't there. Nope, not at all! They had made a blunder and called my name over the intercom, being that my name was probably right above Claude's name on their money list.

Chafin said he was told that Ellis and Watts received money for their faction that day — even though it was possibly thousands less than Chafin had in his two cloth bags.

However, Claude Ellis tells a bit of a different story. Ellis claims not only that he received more cash than Chafin, but that the figure totaled somewhere around fifty- to sixty- thousand dollars, a considerable amount of county precinct money to work with at the time. Ellis also says he has no recollection of the New York incident.

***

Maybe a week or so before the election, Margaret and Louise drove to Charleston to see JFK again. When they got to the airstrip and maneuvered toward the front of the crowd, as he came off his plane, John Kennedy spotted the two of them and hollered, "Come on up here, Margaret. Come on up here, Louise!"

Kennedy shook their hands — and he put the screws to me! I hadn't come out publicly for his presidency yet, and he knew that. So he put me on the spot by draggin' my wife and daughter in front of the cameras. I hadn't said anything to the guys back home up to this point. I felt like he was purposely putting me in a predicament. He had an amazing memory.

Chafin laughed as he remembered the incident, and said, "John Kennedy was a slick and shrewd ol' dawg. Don't let anybody tell you he wasn't."

149

Chapter Twenty-Two

The Strategy Changes

In *The Kennedy Men*, author Laurence Leamer said that with West Virginia's primary looming ahead, the Kennedys were in what they considered the most difficult, most crucial campaign of their lives, and they threw every weapon they had into the fray. Apparently their most effective weapon of choice was capital — cash on the barrelhead. It is still said that the amount of lucre the family spread across the Mountain State in the days prior to the election was simply staggering.

It was the day before the primary — May 9, 1960 — and it was time for the Chafin faction — Perry, Harkins, Curry, and the others — to get together and start reworking their plan at the hotel. Curry ran out and picked up the moneybags at his mother's house and met the rest at the Aracoma. Stacks of off-white envelopes lay on the floor, waiting to be filled with cash.

Campaign couriers had already delivered the political slates, which were professionally printed by the Kennedy campaign.

Chafin recalled:

> Kennedy's people made absolutely sure that their man, JFK, was goin' to be on our slate — 'cause they printed them in New York, and there was Judge C.C. Chambers, Oval Damron, and Okey Justice, too. The slates were there in plenty of time, ready to go, and the print job was flawless.
>
> We then started going over the precinct list and our totals. Where we originally had two hundred dollars designated for a precinct, we might put four hundred or even five hundred, maybe a thousand. Where we had five hundred dollars planned, we switched it to eight hundred, a thousand, maybe two thousand dollars. We eventually got everything ready for the election.
>
> At that time I had a solid organization, which also consisted of loyal voting clerks and "lever-brothers" who were ready do what was necessary once I got the envelopes to them.

He also had a particular woman who helped them in the headquarters. Chafin said that she was the best he'd ever seen when it came to preparing for an election. He stated:

> She was close-mouthed, and she wouldn't lie, either. She'd just say, "They ain't here," or, "I'm sorry. I can't answer that question." When she first saw the money, she asked, "Ah, boys, did y'all rob a bank?"

All of the men in the room laughed uncontrollably at her astonishment. Then Curry told her the story about how it had come to them, about McCahey, the Kennedy people, and the mystery plane with the two bags of currency.

> She helped separate the money into stacks according to their denominations. We had fifty-five or fifty-six precincts, and we boosted money totals in every one of them. Then, using the list of precincts and the money allotted to each

150

location, she delicately put the cash into marked packages, inside manila envelopes and shopping bags. These were to be eventually delivered to precinct captains who were waiting for the drop.

As they got near the finish of their prep work at the Aracoma Hotel room, Chafin called the county sheriff — "Uncle Ed" — and asked him for four stout deputies to guard his headquarters. He told Sheriff McDonald that he didn't want a bit of information to leave the room until the right time.

"We want four of the best men you got. We've got some literature in here, and we don't want anybody to see this information until Election Day," he said, "... because there's some changes being made, Ed."

"That's the way it will be," the sheriff said and nodded. He sent two deputies who were stationed at the doorway to the room during the day and a couple who took their place at night.

"Boys, stay around here close," Chafin told the deputies when they arrived, "and guard our hotel room door, 'cause somebody's liable to try to kill me before this election is over."

Perry said, "Chafe, we're with ya in this! This is going to work out."

The Appalachian boss then reemphasized to the deputies that everything inside the locked room had to be guarded from other factions and local citizens — "Trust no one!"

It was early in the afternoon, and Chafin knew that he had no more time to stall concerning the presidential race. Besides, the slate cards and the notorious envelopes would be delivered by early morning. So he hosted a crucial, last minute get-together at his campaign room so that he could inform his faction who their presidential choice would be.

Chafin's headquarters, Room 220 at the Aracoma Hotel, was full of faction workers and politicians. The room was overflowing with swollen envelopes of cash, slate cards, campaign posters, and literature. Everyone who was working for the faction knew something big was about to take place in a few hours; but nobody knew exactly what.

Chafin retold the story during an interview in 2002, and remembered that once everyone who was important was in the hotel room. Chafin layed back on the bed, put his arms behind his neck, and said, "Gentlemen, I gots somethin' important to tell y'all. By golly, it's gotta be this way: Kennedy's got to COME — or I gots to go!"

"WHAT?" Judge Chambers hollered from among the group of folks. "I ain't goin' to be for *no* Kennedy!"

Chafin jumped out of the bed and shouted, "Shut up, dang you! I got the money ready and everything else is set to go.

"Here, judge, here's one of the slates," Chafin continued, as he threw a card at him. "Read it. Look at the list of names on it."

Judge Chambers, turning brilliant red with anger, pivoted and was about to storm out of the room when Chafin yelled, "Catch him there, boys!"

Perry and Curry moved to block the exit, and physically turned the circuit judge around by grabbing his spindly arms and giving him a quick whirl. He stood there and seethed, as others in the room watched his tantrum.

"Now, judge, you gots to go along with this or your opponent, the current prosecuting attorney, will be wearing your robes. It's Kennedy — Senator John Kennedy. That's the way it will be! Got that, judge? Or do we start scratchin' YOUR name off the slates?"

Chambers shoulders went limp and he sighed. Even though he was vehemently against Kennedy, he knew when he had been whipped. He nodded and slumped down on the edge of the bed, as a man with no vigor, and listened to Chafin's Election Day plans. He placed his head in his cupped hands, as if he were in misery.

After the Democratic Committee chairman told the schedule of events, he asked those in the room for their support. Everyone eventually clapped, except for Judge Chambers and Okey Hager. Neither one could ever truly accept the notion of a Roman Catholic candidate on their slate. However, both knew that what was done was done.

That night Chafin and others hurriedly tore down Humphrey posters and put up Kennedy signs around the courthouse, in town, and throughout the county.

Chafin recalled:

> When Election Day morning came, we started getting everything in place. Workers at the precincts were already on duty. They were fired up and ready for the day. Envelopes and bags were distributed to precinct captains. The half-pints were taken care of, too.
>
> The precincts were well organized. We had precinct captains who would oversee the operation. We had qualified men on the outside and on the inside at the voting polls. It was slick. Some votes cost a dollar or two; some votes ended up costing considerably more.
>
> During the day, several fistfights were reported at various precincts. I would suspect that this was the normal factional fighting we always had, with passionate Democrats fightin' against their own kind.
>
> We spent the evening at the courthouse, waiting for precinct totals to come in. Finally, by the next morning, every one of our men had won — I mean every one. We carried nearly every precinct in the county. Even Okey Justice, a diehard Humphrey supporter to the bitter end, prevailed over Ray Watts.
>
> However the judge, C.C. Chambers, only won by a few votes. We spent about a hundred thousand dollars total, and it all worked out. Besides the Chambers' win, Kennedy took the county, too.
>
> Watts and ol' Claude spent a great deal of money during the campaign, too. They had a little bit of Kennedy's money to spread 'round, too, you know. They didn't do too well, though. Many folks thought they were the most powerful of the factions. Not so. Ray Watts wasn't happy with me — no, not at all on May 11th.
>
> John F. Kennedy took the state of West Virginia by storm. It's now history. However, what people should remember is that it was a presidential race that was bought and paid for — cold cash for nearly every voter. The Kennedys were well aware of our brand of politics. I guess it was their brand, too.
>
> Hubert Humphrey called me at home several days after his defeat. He asked, "Raymond, tell me, what went wrong?"
>
> "Well, I guess you just weren't for the coal operators enough," I told him. "They thought maybe Kennedy was the best candidate."

"Maybe he is!" Humphrey remarked, in a very sarcastic tone of voice. "Who caused the big switch down there?"

"Well, I can't tell ya," I said — "but Jim McCahey had come in here and talked to me."

"Hmm, I believe I see," he mumbled. Then he just said, "Well, I'll be going, Mr. Chafin. Thank you for your time."

When Chafin hung up the receiver, he sat in his recliner and thought about Humphrey. In a way he felt bad for a very capable Democrat. However, he was pleased with the way West Virginia rallied and made an amazing national showing for Kennedy, nearly securing his possible win as the Democratic candidate for president.

Chafin said, with regards to Humphrey:

> Seriously, twenty-five hundred dollars ain't nothin'! Jeez, what could we have really done with that? Humphrey knew he lost his position because he didn't have the kind of finances to pull things off. He gave me a measly $2,500; you can barely buy a used car for that kind of money nowadays.

Humphrey's resources were definitely limited. It was later published that Humphrey spent $25,000 on his entire West Virginia campaign, obviously a skimpy investment in comparison with his opponent's liberal spending. Reportedly the Kennedys spent far more than that on Logan County alone. Chafin said that afterwards he didn't feel too bad about the Humphrey loss, for he "knew deep down inside that Humphrey's political career wasn't finished" and that he would have future victories. Chafin continued:

> He was a very smart man and extremely sly as a politician. A smart cookie is what he was — poor but smart. In spite of the switch, I considered him a friend — and I got my chance to support him again a few years later.

Claude Ellis commented about his faction in comparison with Chafin's:

> I still say we had the stronger of the two factions, especially since we were the first to be promoting John F. Kennedy in this county. We also had the greater resources to work with, thanks to the Kennedys. We had community people like Alex DeFobio, Dan Dahill, and Tom Godby, who were all powerful influences at the time with us. We had the world watching us, and we brought John F. Kennedy to victory.

However, regardless of Ellis' assertion, questions are always answered at the election. The primary was where the real results happened and where the real power was demonstrated in West Virginia.

Through excessive forcefulness, which many of his cronies of the time period called "Chafin's Way or No Way," Chafin was able to manipulate and influence the course of power in the county. However, it was Claude Ellis who made significant strides in the way the county perceived the Catholic presidential candidate.

In a real sense, it was a political standoff. Both political bosses won in 1960. Chafin took the local vote; Ellis changed the minds of the people when it came to the presidential campaign.

Chafin quipped:

> I don't like to lose. It's not in my nature. That's the way it was in 1960. That's the way it is now, too. I was willing to pull the county apart if need be to bring my candidates to victory. Most of my guys won.

Somewhere along the way — possibly through his experience with harsh poverty as a child, or by being the solitary breadwinner for his ailing father and mother — Chafin acquired a great deal of gutsy self-confidence that translated itself well when it came to steering the hard-hearted game of politics in southern West Virginia. He was a fierce competitor by anyone's standards.

Those Two Bags of Money

Because it's been more than forty years since the Kennedy campaign — and the statute of limitations has run out — Chafin was willing to talk candidly about the mysterious bags of money that were dropped off at Taplin Airport before the West Virginia primary:

> Nobody will ever know exactly where that money came from. Never!
> But I'll tell you what we did with it. We bought votes with it! Regardless what you want to believe, that's the way *real politics* works. We used up all that money from the bags and won the whole dang election. It takes large amounts of money to sweep an election. We had it, all right!
> I'd say there were about two thousand dollars worth of two-dollar bills, besides the other money. I wish now I would have kept the two-dollar bills. They'd be worth a fortune now.

Chafin said that it might as well be told, after all these years, that his faction exchanged cash for votes, as all party groups did in the southern mountains. Most of the older citizens remember that free-flowing liquor and crisp bills were commonly involved on Election Day. Whiskey and moonshine were secretly shipped into the area in bread trucks or private pickups and dropped off at specified locations.

"I remember seeing box after box of liquor being unloaded into Chafin's home during the 1960 campaign," an elderly Cow Creek citizen recalled recently. "An old bread truck backed up to Chafin's side door. Several boys unloaded the truck lickety-split."

Chafin reflected about the 1960 campaign:

> There were folks around Logan who would be nearly offended if you didn't offer them at least something for their vote. Something was expected. They were used to being paid. It's the way it was done. I didn't plan to disappoint them.

Tough Boys

Never let your right hand know what your left hand is doing. That's what George Steele told me when I first started in politics. I would have been better off if I had taken that saying a little bit more to heart. But everything eventually worked out.

That Kennedy campaign was a tough one — and a dangerous one, at that. When you go to foolin' around with the kind of folk who were in that campaign, it gets mighty risky. Both sides, Humphrey and Kennedy campaigners, had people involved who would tear you up in a heartbeat if need be. I'm talkin' both local and national politicians, now. Plus, when youse got big money — cash — 'round ya, you get mighty squirrelly.

When you get into a governor's election or a presidential campaign, you have all kinds of groups that want that governor or president elected — church folk, outlaws, gamblers, mobsters, and every imaginable kind of people. Some of them will do anything to get their candidate ahead. Anything!

Chafin said that he believes that historians don't want to record that such vote-buying antics were a normal part of Election Day happenings of the past. However, it was commonplace — in local, state, and national campaigns — at least throughout West Virginia and most of Appalachia.

Chafin added:

All the older politicians know it, too — even those in Washington, D.C. It's an inside secret, of sorts. When you're up in the big leagues, you're dealing with everybody. You don't just go out and get anyone to work an election. You have to be awfully careful whom you pick. You have to be especially cautious of everything you say or do, 'cause people are watching you all the time.

In the ol' days, I guess I can only think of a few fellers who abstained from that sort of thing — one was Bob Byrd. Another was Uncle Ed McDonald. I know they gave money to factions to help in their campaigns, but I doubt that either one ever knew fully how the capital was used. I'll put it this way: I'd be surprised if Byrd or McDonald knew.

The best I can remember, every one of my candidates won in 1960, and won big. The difference in that election wasn't me; it was our team of four. It was because of Bus Perry, one of the most unique politicians I've ever known. He knew where every dollar came from and where every dollar went. Arnold Harkins was a precinct man who had worked for sheriffs in the past as a deputy. He was the best precinct operator I've ever known. Elvie Curry could slip around and find out more inside information than any other three men combined 'cause he wasn't owned by anyone. He could go into any meeting he wanted to. He'd just slip in, and later slip on out.

It was because of Bus, Arnold, Elvie, and me that we won. We made a good team.

There's one thing I learned long ago: If you get too big of an organization, you get into trouble — a heap of trouble. I kept the size down so I could control the circumstances. Sometimes the four of us would nearly get into a boxing match over circumstances in the campaign. We'd get mad. We'd have to recess.

155

We would meet again in the morning. But we kept our disagreements among ourselves — we never spoke about it on the streets.

These boys — who were like brothers to me — are the only ones who really knew about the particulars of the Kennedy switch up until the night before the election. Even then, a lot of the details were withheld from the other candidates.

Chapter Twenty-Three

Claude Ellis: Big Daddy Speaks

Hands down, Chafin's toughest political opponent in the county during the late 1950s and 1960s was Claude "Big Daddy" Ellis — a tall, robust businessman who had proven to be an aggressive and ruthless antagonist in his own right. Born on the thirteenth day of November in 1926, he was named Arthur Claude Ellis. Ironically, his home was not far from Chafin's.

Ellis had always had an interest in the political process, even at an early age, as he told here:

> I was born and raised in a tiny coal-camp house in the Omar area at Chauncey. My dad, Bruce Ellis, worked for West Virginia Coal and Coke. My mother was Violet Ellis, a housewife. I guess I was like any other kid in the camp. We all played along the train tracks, or in the hills along the creek bed, and around the coal tipple. At the mouth of Pine Creek they had a lumber company back then, and we had many days of fun around that lumberyard, too.

> My family lived down at Chauncey for a while, and then moved to Maysburg, where we owned a small house. Maysburg is in the middle, between Chauncey and Omar. I went to Omar Grade School.

> I walked to school in the mornings and I walked home for lunch. Then I moseyed back for the afternoon classes. It was a good experience. I went to school there until the ninth grade. That year my brother had been drafted into the Navy. After my ninth grade year, I talked Dad into signing the papers, and I volunteered for the Navy. World War II had started, and everyone wanted to join up at that time. I was no different.

> After boot camp at Great Lakes, I was stationed at Norfolk, Virginia, at Little Creeks. I stayed there a while and then I was shipped out. I was in the Pacific when the war ended. We were headed to the action when the war ended.

> I guess I first entered politics when I got out of the United States Navy in 1946. I was a deputy sheriff under Frank White.

By the mid-1940s, Sheriff White was a well-established politician in Logan who had formerly been a member of the Logan County Board of Education and served as county clerk. He was also a member of one of the oldest established families in the county. Allegedly, when White served as sheriff from 1945-1949, he was known to demand contributions or "protection payoffs" from merchants and businessmen throughout the county, as many other law enforcement officers had done before him.

Ellis said that after his time as a deputy, he went to the liquor store as a store manager. He made many contacts there, and he has "been in politics in a big way ever since." He also started to understand how tough politics could be and how you have to be able to maneuver and think on your feet.

It was about this time that politician Eddie Baldwin had asked Ellis to come to the local Young Democrats meeting at the county courthouse. Baldwin talked endlessly about how the organization had already picked its man for president of the county group.

"You mean it's already cut and dried?" Ellis asked.

"Yes. Done. We already have our president picked, and he's going to be elected tonight," Baldwin bragged. He then continued to boast about his influence in the party and the strength of his own faction.

Baldwin's braggadocio comments and his pompous behavior angered Ellis. He remembered the incident:

> I got a little p.o.'d at him, so I went to Bill Abraham's place, the Thunderbolt Tavern, at Omar to see Bill. Neither of us had been out of the service very long, and I went there to convince Bill to run for president of the Young Democrats. Bill was well liked in Island Creek, and he was a smart, capable man. However, Bill had no experience in politics at that time. I had to explain to him in detail what the position would mean for him. I also had to describe everything about the organization and what would be expected of him.
>
> Finally, I talked him into running. To strengthen our position, we asked a bunch of fellows to go with us that night. I guess by the time we left the Thunderbolt for the courthouse, we had several truckloads of young men from the Omar area tagging along with us.
>
> When we arrived at the courthouse, Bus Perry was in charge of the meeting. He already had his man picked and was preparing to go through the formality of a vote. He and others who were present thought the victor was assured. But now I had Bill Abraham running, too. Seeing the new challenge before him, Bus called Bill and me off to a side room and suggested that we work together.

"Fellows, I didn't plan on this situation, but we can work this out," Perry said. "Bill Abraham can be named vice president. All right? I guess you agree?"

"Bus, you haven't looked at that crowd in there, have you?" Ellis said sternly, without flinching. "If you haven't, you should take a good, hard look. They are all our people from Island Creek District. Maybe Bill can make YOUR man vice president."

Perry stepped laterally and peeked around the corner of the room at the crowd waiting to vote. He then slowly looked back at Ellis, his shoulders slumped, and said, "Well, Claude, I know what you mean. I guess you got me this time."

Bill Abraham entered politics for the first time when he was voted president of the Young Democrats that night. Claude Ellis was recognized from that day forward as a man to reckoned with. He was able to spar with a seasoned political champ, Bus Perry, and come out of the exchange a winner.

Many residents already knew Ellis as a precinct man and political fighter in several past elections. Now, news spread around political circles concerning Ellis' newfound leadership capabilities. Ellis continued:

I did quite a number on Bus that day. I later did a number on quite a few other people whom I didn't care too much about. I've been in so many battles through the years — some successful and some not.

But when I hooked up with Bill Abraham, I was in Raymond Chafin's stronghold — his territory of influence. We had now moved in, and we were ready to take over his region.

Ellis said he also met a gentleman named Tom Godby shortly after he returned from overseas. At 20, Ellis had been hired as the youngest deputy sheriff in the county at that time — not even old enough to vote. It was during that time that he hooked up with Godby, he recalled:

Tom Godby worked as a salesman for the Windsor Suit Company, out of Cincinnati. We became friends — best buddies — and we were together a lot when he wasn't peddlin' suits to the coal company stores.

I'll tell you one thing: he sold a lot of suits during those days. He was also involved in the *Aracoma Story*, (an outdoor drama in Logan County) playing the character Boling Baker, the lead role in the play. When he and his wife, Mary Lee, got married, they lived in town. We all ran around together.

Tom was a good boy and he was well liked in the county. He turned into a good county assessor, too.

His wife has told me many times that she'd send him out to pay bills, and along the way, he'd run into these bums along the street. He'd hear their hard-luck story and they'd wind up with what money he had on him. He had a big heart for people.

Ellis had been previously married to a woman who had been a nurse, and they had twin daughters. They were later divorced, and she then remarried. A little while afterwards, Ellis met Rosemary Blair. He recalled:

Rosemary, who had always lived in Logan County, was back from Huntington, where she had attended nursing school, and she was working at St. Mary's Hospital. One July, a friend, Isabelle Ollie, who was working at the phone company, fixed me up with a date with Rosemary.

Rosemary and Claude went on a July Fourth picnic to Gilbert, which turned out to be a significant day in both of their lives. They enjoyed that first date. They continued seeing each other, and their relationship flourished. In time, the two young lovers married and set up housekeeping in Logan. By 1959, Claude and Rosemary were living in a small apartment building called the Max Apartments. The apartment complex was located near the Capitol Theatre on Stratton Street.

Claude Ellis was an influential member of the state committee of Young Democrats of America by the late 1950s. It was in 1959 that he reluctantly accepted the lead role in the John F. Kennedy for President drive, as the campaign manager in Logan County. He was also the manager of the Ray Watts faction during this time. He commented:

Watts was our candidate for Logan County sheriff at the time. We thought quite alike, politically, and I thought he would be a strong candidate.

Watts had served as sheriff once before, from 1953-1957, and had held several other major public offices over the years, so he seemed like the most feasible choice for Ellis' faction. Obviously, Watts had already proven on several occasions that he was someone who could muster mass support.

Ellis remembers clearly that no local officeholder at the time was willing to risk being too closely associated with John F. Kennedy because he was Catholic. The individuals on Chafin's slate in particular — mostly incumbents — were extremely cautious about being affiliated with the young presidential hopeful, knowing it could mean political suicide in this area of the Bible Belt known to be largely Protestant.

Ellis had explained the early happenings in a 1964 oral interview for the Kennedy Library, saying:

> I was a national committeeman of the Young Democrats of West Virginia and received a letter to meet with some Hubert Humphrey forces in Fairmont, West Virginia. I went on to the convention and met with some of these people, and, of course, they talked with me about Senator Humphrey at that time. After coming back to Logan County, a good friend of mine who was the executive secretary of the Young Democrats, Matthew "Matt" Reese, out of Huntington, came to Logan on Mr. Kennedy's behalf and wanted to get the ball rolling as far as the Kennedy campaign. Later, I met with Robert "Bob" McDonough at the courthouse.
>
> From there on we met with Bobby Kennedy first, then later, his brother Teddy. They came into Logan. And after that we got the ball rolling.
>
> That year Bob McDonough, JFK's Mountain State coordinator from Parkersburg, joined up with the Young Democrats Clubs of West Virginia, and we all became Kennedy people, so to speak.
>
> Being a national committeeman at the time, after McDonough and I met, we joined up to organize. We got in touch with Ray Watts, who was running for Logan County sheriff. After the meeting, several of us went to the courthouse and formed the Committee To Elect John F. Kennedy.
>
> On the way up the sidewalk to the Smokehouse Restaurant that evening, Ray Watts and I were talking about the campaign, wondering whom we could make the chairman of the Kennedy campaign. Nobody seemed interested. The elected officials wouldn't fool with it 'cause they were afraid of it. We only had one elected official as a candidate, Bill Lockhart, running for prosecuting attorney, who probably would have taken the position if we asked him to — but we didn't insist.

Ellis said that after a lengthy meeting with the faction, realizing that nobody was willing to take on the task, he hesitantly agreed to take on the responsibility.

Yes, I agreed to head the campaign myself. That's how I became the chairman in Logan County, and I soon became active in the whole state of West Virginia. Members in the original Kennedy group included Tom Godby, Dan Dahill, Bill Abraham, and Alex DeFobio, the local theater operator.

Interestingly, Tom Godby, who was our candidate for assessor at the time, was one of the only candidates in this area to put Kennedy literature on his automobile, even though he realized at the time that the situation was risky.

After the election, *The Logan Banner*, the county's newspaper, validated the notion that Catholicism was a minority religion in this area at the time, and that in the early months of JFK's campaign the general public seemed worried about the ramifications of having a Roman Catholic as president. Ellis laughed as he remembered how the county originally perceived a Catholic running for office, when the campaign first began:

One fellow from Rum Creek [near Logan] told me that if Kennedy were elected president, we'd wind up with the Italian pope on the one-dollar bill! Alex DeFobio, who ran the theater on Stratton Street at the time, had his entire marquee lit up with "Kennedy for President" when the family came into Logan. That was the first time I ever saw Alex get involved in politics — probably because Alex was Catholic.

Lots of folks were leery of JFK in the early stages of his run for election. We definitely had problems with the religious issue. John Kennedy eventually came here himself in order to whip that issue down.

First, he sent Edward and other people in here to try to help with that. I can remember when I introduced Edward "Teddy" Kennedy at Midelburg Island at a political rally when he first came to Logan County. I stood up in front of the crowd and told the people a story about two nuns watching a basketball game at a Catholic school. Two sloppy drunks were sittin' behind 'em. Whenever there was a lot of commotion happening on the basketball floor, one or the other of the drunks would say every so often, "We ought to leave this state and go to another state, where there is only two percent Catholics!"

Finally, after hearing the drunks complain and whine more than halfway through the game, one of the nuns had had enough of their comments. She turned and said, "Why don't you both go to H—ll? There's NO Catholics at ALL down there!"

The Logan County crowd laughed and cheered as "Big Daddy" raised his voice and bellowed, "Now, I'd like to introduce to you the brother of the next president of the United States, John F. Kennedy. So everyone, please make EDWARD KENNEDY feel welcome in Logan County! Teddy, come on up here!"

A young Ted Kennedy, handsome and lean with a head full of dark brown hair, took the podium and began to talk to the spectators about Logan County and the many things that could be accomplished under his brother's administration in behalf of the region and its people.

Teddy stayed with us the biggest part of the time. Logan people liked Teddy, and we wanted to keep him here as long as he could stay 'cause he knew how to support his brother. He sold himself good — real good. He spent several months — traveling between Wisconsin and West Virginia — campaigning. When in Logan, he spent most of that time at the Aracoma Hotel.

In those days he became just a common man, and he mixed well with us. I guess he was just like all of us.

Right after one of Teddy's speeches, I remember one fellow from Stollings coming up to me and telling me that if John Kennedy were president, we would all have to start eating fish on Fridays. I told him that it would be a whole lot better to eat fish than to eat no meat at all! West Virginia was having awfully hard times in 1960. As far as I was concerned, there was no other candidate who could turn things around for West Virginia — no one else.

During that time, we formed a Ladies Club for President Kennedy. Roberta Kendall, a schoolteacher who now lives at Midelburg, was chairman of the committee. Rosemary Ellis, my wife, was also a member of the club. Martha Williams and several other women formed a circle for Kennedy, too.

Rose Kennedy and several of John's young sisters came in here and joined up with our ladies club. They had coffee socials and other activities. They all stayed at the Aracoma Hotel. It seemed like every one of the Kennedy people had that magic touch. They could take a situation and run with it at any time. They knew how to sell themselves!

Rosemary Ellis Remembers

There was one incident that stood out in the minds of both Claude Ellis and his wife. Rosemary remembered a certain incident:

I was working in the operating room at the Mercy Hospital at the time, and I was on call — 24-hour call. Because of being on call, I had let the laundry pile up in the apartment. The way the apartment was laid out, all my laundry was piled in the hallway by the door and you had to step over it to come in. So in walked — unannounced — Claude, with Eunice, Ethel Kennedy, and Roberta Kendall! I was terribly embarrassed. However, they stepped over the laundry as if they did that sort of thing every day. I could have killed Claude. They didn't seem to care. It didn't matter if the Kennedy women were carrying a teacup or a Coke bottle — they carried it so well. They were down to earth.

Claude smiled and explained simply, "After they had their coffee at the Smokehouse, they wanted to meet my wife, so we walked up the street and I took them to the apartment."

Memory: JFK Comes to Logan County

Ellis reminisced about meeting John "Jack" Kennedy the first time:

162

I remember meeting with John Kennedy on April 25, 1960, when we brought him into the county. He came in by Williamson, West Virginia, and then came down through Omar. His first stop was at Bill Abraham's Shaheens Shopping Center, where he held his first political assembly in the county.

At that time, Omar was a large community, and it seemed that nearly every citizen in Omar and the surrounding area showed up for the history-making visit. Island Creek men, women, and children jam-packed the store's parking lot. All walks of life were represented: coalminers, lumberjacks, working women, housewives, coalmine officials and superintendents, road workers, truck drivers, and children.

"Kennedy is coming to Shaheen's!" residents hollered, waving their hands at passing motorists while they walked from the coal-camp houses to the grocery store in central Omar. "Don't miss it! John Kennedy's going to be here any minute — here in OMAR!"

Ellis recalled the event vividly:

On this occasion Jack Kennedy came in without his brothers. Bill Abraham, Tom Godby, Dan Dahill, Alex DeFobio, and I were there. We were already completely committed to JFK's campaign. But this was the first time I actually met him — at Shaheen's Shopping Center.

Once the motorcade had arrived at the small grocery parking lot, the crowd cheered as the car door opened and Jack Kennedy stood, grinned, and waved at the people.

After he finished speaking to the crowd, we formed a string of vehicles and traveled down the creek toward the city of Logan. Since I had the privilege of sitting next to him, I asked Mr. Kennedy if he wanted me to introduce him to people along the way.

The compelling young candidate smiled, straightened his tie, and replied, "No, just hold 'em back. I'll take care of myself."

And he did that tremendously! I remember that he got out of the car and went up to people on their front porches in Switzer. He was sharply dressed, looked like a movie star, and created a sensation in these coal camps. He nearly went door-to-door. He would smile and reach out and shake hands with folks along the way. He mixed well with them and did a great job of selling himself.

In an article by Topper Sherwood, in the Summer 2000 edition of *Goldenseal Magazine*, he may have said it best when he wrote, "This is a world that John Kennedy understood very well. His grandfather, John F. 'Honey Fitz' Fitzgerald, had been a bare-knuckles contender in the rough-and-tumble world of Boston politics. And his father, Joe Kennedy, was legendary for his political maneuvering during and after the Franklin D. Roosevelt administration. Wood County industrialist Robert McDonough, who coordinated the Kennedy campaign in West Virginia, called JFK 'the smartest politician in the crew.'"

Kennedy intuitively knew how to campaign in the Mountain State. It was in his makeup and lifelong instruction; and when he reached West Virginia soil, the mannerisms and approach came naturally. He and his entourage took southwestern West Virginia by storm.

Meeting the Candidate

Ellis describes his initial impression of JFK:

> When I actually met John Kennedy, I was surprised. Meeting him at Omar and talking with him man to man, I was able to see his actions and how he could maneuver among the people. He was very self-assured. I was extremely impressed when I saw his movements among the common people. I liked his view of politics and how he viewed Logan County and her residents. It was a bad time for the folks of Logan County. We had houses boarded up at Buffalo Creek, and there was plenty of poverty everywhere you turned. I think when he came to the county he was really concerned about what he saw. That's why he was responsible for eventually introducing the food stamp program.
>
> After campaigning along the way from Omar, we ended up in downtown Logan that evening and had a big rally at the courthouse steps. The most people I'd seen in the city of Logan in a long, long time came to the event — maybe more than I'd ever seen. It was really something!

"When Claude and John Kennedy pulled into Logan," Rosemary Ellis reminisced, "you would have thought it was the Second Coming, considering the amount of excitement, but Kennedy was glad-handing everyone and just being himself. He was a very polished politician, and his accent surely helped here."

Claude Ellis added: "You know, I tried to get an escort for Kennedy from Omar, but the deputy sheriffs and state police were tied up and suspiciously too busy with other things that day. So I talked with the City of Logan police chief, who worked for a Republican city administration at the time. The chief said, 'I'll take care of that!' — and he did. We had a police escort all the way from Omar anyway.

"Sometimes it seems like just a shadow when I think back on the experience now. But it happened. I'm afraid so — it really happened."

After being escorted into Logan by city officers with red lights flashing and sirens blaring, a relaxed, suave Jack Kennedy, wearing a tailored gray suit, seemed nearly larger than life as he stepped out of the limousine and addressed the local crowd from the courthouse steps. A horde of staunch supporters and inquisitive onlookers pushed and shoved just to catch a glimpse of the famed national candidate as he spoke of the various problems that affected the people of southern West Virginia. His voice — with the characteristic Massachusetts accent — echoed above the hushed whispers, seeming to mesmerize men, women, and children alike.

The apparent sincerity and warmth of this orator's empathetic delivery immediately won the hearts of his captive audience that evening, as he promised to send immediate assistance to these people of Appalachia who so desperately needed the message of hope and encouragement he delivered.

Each time he would pause in his speech for an expected response, the crowd would approvingly break out in thunderous applause, nearly drowning out his next words. Several times he smiled and gently motioned with his hands for the crowd to cease their clapping so that he could continue with his remarks.

Ellis recalled the day:

> I think we served 3,500 hotdogs and soft drinks in front of the courthouse that day. I remember that at this same time, Senator Robert Byrd was adamantly apposed to Kennedy throughout the primary campaign. He was a firm supporter of Lyndon Johnson for president and he even tried to convert me. He refused to be a part of the Kennedy campaign in the state, and didn't want to even appear on stage with him. Byrd once told me, "I'm not going to be a part of Kennedy's bandstand, regardless of how popular he is."

Attorney Dan Dahill, a powerful politician in Logan County at the time, who still practices law in Logan, explained in a recent interview: "The whole city came together and it was a carnival atmosphere. Everyone came together, except for Chafin's faction, that is. Chafin and his politicians were all brooding up in the Aracoma Hotel headquarters that day."

Claude Ellis spoke about Dan Dahill's involvement in politics:

> Ol' Dan Dahill was a state senator from this district in 1960. He was also Catholic. However, he didn't have the uphill climb Kennedy had 'cause the people of Logan County knew Dan was born and raised right here in the county. I doubt that most people even realized he was Roman Catholic, and there was never an issue made of it.

Ellis continued to describe the night of the big rally:

> The rally went awfully well. We had a private meeting with John Kennedy at the courthouse afterward. He seemed energized from the crowd's acceptance. He smiled a great deal and there was plenty of laughter in the room. Later we all went to the Smokehouse Restaurant for dinner. He made a lot of contacts with common people at the Smokehouse. He even greeted some who had not heard him at the rally.
>
> Then he eventually worked toward leaving the restaurant, and he spoke with folks all along the way back down Stratton Street. We escorted him over to the Aracoma Hotel for the night. Many Logan residents who had originally supported Hubert Humphrey changed their allegiance the day of the rally.
>
> There was magic in the air. He was very dynamic, and Logan County loved him.

By the next morning, JFK's entourage left the landmark hotel. His first scheduled stop was at Amherstdale — still within the county — where the residents again accepted him warmly. Then his campaign moved on up to the Kopperston and the Beckley area. By April 27th, he spoke at Bluefield State College to a packed house.

It was a whirlwind West Virginia campaign where the Democratic candidate was met at every stop along the way with an unusual amount of kindness. Most of the people at that time were especially curious of this "funny-talking" fellow from Massachusetts.

During the time period, Teddy made his rounds by connecting with Charleston television stations — such as WCHS Channel 8 and WSAZ Channel 3 — and many radio stations. He was already on a first-name basis with most West Virginia newspaper publishers, large-business owners, and coal operators.

Ellis elaborated:

> One of John Kennedy's key men was Jim McCahey, who mixed in good with the coal companies. He was a powerful coal buyer, and he was rumored to be one of the big financial backers for Kennedy.
>
> The Kennedy boys personally sent him into southern West Virginia. He was solely for John Kennedy, and he wasn't too interested in the lower races. But he gained immediate coal company support and acceptance.
>
> McCahey had actually come here some time before JFK had ever arrived at Omar. I first met him down at the city courtyard. He was also staying at the Aracoma Hotel. He said he had a dinner meeting at Island Creek Coal Company that night. So I let him go on ahead to the dinner, but I secretly sent a couple or three people that I had on our side, who worked at Island Creek Coal, on to the banquet to watch over things. I wanted to know exactly what kind of reception Mr. McCahey would receive. I wanted to know what Island Creek thought of him.
>
> These fellows later told me that Island Creek officials said, "Throw the doors wide open to the Island Creek Clubhouse, and make Mr. McCahey welcome."
>
> That was good news for us. He was dynamic and a good speaker. McCahey, and other people like him, met privately with leaders at Island Creek Coal in the coming days. He brought them all over to Kennedy's side. We then took it [the local campaign] from there.
>
> You saw a lot of people from Island Creek District supporting Kennedy by that time, but you didn't see Raymond Chafin or any of his faction coming aboard. He and his people were with Humphrey's campaign at the time. Then, when a few things happened to Chafin later on, he finally came over to our side late in the campaign.
>
> Jim McCahey helped us with Massey Coal Company and hooked up with them specifically to help us with Raymond Chafin. Chafin, who was employed by Massey, was superintendent of its Gilbert operation at the time. Around this same time, Chafin claimed to have secretly met with McCahey and discussed money and Kennedy.
>
> McDonough called me and said he was going to meet with Raymond Chafin and Okey Justice, who was then running for sheriff with Chafin's people. He planned to meet them at the airport on this side of Man, called Taplin Airport. McDonough said he wanted to meet with me at Man after he met with Chafe. I believe that the actual turnover of money for Chafin's help was thirty-

five hundred — *period*. Since then, Chafin has sort of blown it out of proportion when he has said it was thirty-five thousand.

Naw, he didn't have thirty-five thousand dollars — no way. McDonough and several others met with me right afterward and told me what they had delivered in cash.

As for the allegedly inflated figure, Ellis laughed and said, "It's hard to believe that Kennedy would spend that kind of money in Logan County, because he really didn't have to!"

Chapter Twenty-Four
Apparent Contradictions?

It might seem contradictory to hear the burly Claude Ellis speak in such an apparent double-minded fashion. On one hand, he talks about Kennedy's effective campaigning style and concern for the people winning their hearts and votes; then, almost in the same breath, he frankly discusses Kennedy faction money flooding into the state and the organized mischief that went on behind the scenes to assure a positive primary outcome.

Actually, there are no contradictions here; not really — when you take into account the state you're talking about. In the mountain hollows and backward communities of Logan County, swapping money for votes in 1960 was as traditional as pinto beans and cornbread. Natives of the area grew up with voting corruption as a part of their mountain culture, and many believed that a campaign, regardless of how organized and professional it may have seemed, wasn't really a campaign at all unless it included cash or liquor at the precincts.

The outpouring of Kennedy family money into the coalfields doesn't necessarily diminish the fact that John Kennedy truly charmed state voters through his energetic, yet intimate, campaign style and well-orchestrated family support system. Did one aspect of the campaign overwhelm the other truths? No. There was plenty of capital being thrown into the various counties by Kennedy people. Meanwhile, the effectiveness of Jack's many speeches and photo opportunities and his ability to connect with common people can't be denied. Many contend that he could have been just as effective statewide without resorting to buying political-boss support. So, as contrary as the recollections may sound when they come from Ellis' lips, both aspects — campaign brilliance and vote-buying settlements — existed. And these two undeniable truths whirled and swirled around the Mountain State during that campaign season in the land along the Guyandotte River.

Claude Ellis smiled as he continued to give his opinion about Raymond Chafin's claims:

> It sort of surprised me that Chafe would switch candidates so abruptly, but, then again, I know that several folks were applying heavy pressure on him through his employer, A.T. Massey Coal Company. Other folks were puttin' a great deal of force on him at the time, too.
>
> When I think about the money he received, I figure that Chafin may have split that drop-off money with Okey Justice or Bus Perry. But to tell you the truth about it, Chafin probably kept the whole thirty-five hundred dollars for himself. The thirty-five thousand that he claimed to have received would have been impossible, in my opinion. But if Chafe did pick up such a figure, I know where it would have gone — in his billfold.

Since Chafin and Ellis were political adversaries in 1960 and are involved in a friendly opposition even unto this day, it's only natural that the two might disagree on the actual amount of money that changed hands that rainy day at Taplin's airfield. However, both quickly agree that a money settlement took place, and that the cash came from the Kennedys through their intricate — although anonymous — political channels.

It's believed that the bulk of the currency came directly from Joe Kennedy, the immensely wealthy patriarch of the Kennedy clan, who had made several bold statements at the time that implied that money was of no consequence as long as it helped his son.

According to one Logan County source, who only spoke under the condition of anonymity, was a newspaper reporter in 1960. He stated that at least 2.5 million dollars in American currency was delivered on one occasion to the State Capitol.

The former reporter said:

> I arrived at a Charleston motel a few minutes after the money had arrived. Several powerful people were there, and they all were talking and laughing about the cash. I was young and bold at the time. I asked if I could lift one of the containers, an aluminum suitcase. After I received a lackluster nod, I grabbed up one of the bags, and I honestly couldn't believe how heavy the suitcase was. Later the cases were opened and my jaw dropped.

According to this account, the bundles of cash, packed in metal suitcases, were later dispersed among political bosses across the state. Exactly how many money shipments like this one arrived at the Kanawha Motel in Charleston during the primary campaign season will never be known. However, the amount of funds circulating in various counties was said to be astonishing.

Ellis reminisced about the happenings of the time:

> When McDonough told me that Chafin had agreed to come over to our side for a donation, I was delighted. Chafin kept his word for it, mainly because we had McCahey and people from Massey in support of Kennedy. So Chafin didn't really have a choice if he wanted to keep his job.
>
> When Chafin came along with us, it made it a lot easier. We didn't have to use the force that we had anticipated. However, Okey Justice didn't come with us. He went against us and never did support Kennedy. He stayed with Humphrey, which turned out to be his mistake.
>
> Besides the Kennedy family and their friend McCahey, others also traveled to Logan and campaigned in their behalf. Toward the end of the primary crusade, Franklin D. Roosevelt, Jr., came to town several times in support of Kennedy. Robert Byrd, who originally supported Johnson, was later helpful, too.
>
> Now, John Kennedy was hooked up directly with Ray Watts and our local slate. Ray and I went to Charleston and met with McCahey, McDonough, O'Donnell, and others from the Kennedy group on several occasions in order to pick up the funds we needed.

It's been said that it was Joe Kennedy who convinced Roosevelt to travel to West Virginia in behalf of JFK.

Author Laurence Leamer said it properly when he said, "Frankin Roosevelt, Jr., bore what in West Virginia was the most glorious of names. He was the son of the man whose New Deal had, as many in the state saw it, given shoes to people who had walked barefoot, electric lights to those those who had sat in darkness, and bread to those who were hungry."

The visibility of Franklin D. Roosevelt's son was an invaluable tool for the campaign.

Roosevelt Jr. spoke on several occasions for Kennedy, but unfortunately was ill advised by Bobby Kennedy to attack one of Humphrey's perceived vulnerabilities — his war record. On April 27th, Roosevelt told a crowd of West Virginians, "There's another candidate in your primary. He's a good Democrat, but I don't know where he was in World War II!"

Due to that comment and others like it, several newspapers, including the Washington Star, characterized his statements as "a new low in dirty politics." The off hand remarks tarnished his image around Washington from that day forward,

Apparently, he made the comments based upon "reliable information" from the Kennedy camp, and from the extreme mental pressure being applied by Bobby Kennedy. JFK's intelligent younger brother, Bobby, had pushed FDR Jr. for several weeks to make ever-tougher and more aggressive statements against Kennedy's opponent.

The public statement turned out to be untrue and unfair about Humphrey. Roosevelt eventually apologized after the general election to Humphrey for the statement, which some believe dismantled his own character and helped destroy Humphrey's bid for West Virginia.

***

As for the use of the Kennedy campaign money, Claude Ellis said it was used for buying state votes — clearly. He said he put a specified amount into each sector of the county, based upon what the precinct captain figured was needed to "do the job right." For example, he said that he might designate fifteen hundred dollars for Omar's polls to buy the residents' favor. Other precincts might demand much less.

> John Kennedy and his people knew what was going on. This was the way things were done at that time. The amount we received was a substantial amount. Kennedy people put much more than thirty-five thousand into our cause. So, from then on, Ray Watts and I were involved in every precinct in Logan County. I think there were sixty precincts in Logan County at the time. We may have averaged spending one thousand to fifteen hundred dollars per precinct — sometimes more, sometimes a bit less.

> Scripps Howard News Service had reporters in here in 1960. I was working up at Stratton Hollow precinct. When it was all over, a news writer said that we went in and out of the polls more times than the election officers did. It was the way it was done then, and the way we handled it was TOUGH! It was all politics, paid in a bundle, and whoever could buy the most votes wound up with the precinct when the polls closed.

Ellis said that a fellow typically called a "spotter" would bring a voter or family of voters to the precinct. Along the way, the "spotter" would explain the Election Day "procedure" for earning pay or liquor. At the precinct the men who were working inside for the faction were called "lever brothers." They were bought and paid for and were to be on hand to supposedly help voters with the voting machines if they needed assistance.

Suspiciously, everyone that the spotters brought to the precinct needed assistance — being that this was all part of the procedure for the day.

As Ellis clarified, once the request for help was made, the lever brothers sprang into action and ran over to the voting machine to lend a hand. But, in reality, their main function was to steal votes and verify that the voter had stayed true to the faction's slate.

The inside man — the lever brother or clerk — was usually an election official or commissioner who helped verify the vote before the elector was compensated. The verification consisted of the precinct captain, or even Ellis himself, receiving a hand signal of some sort — such as an inside man casually combing his hair back with his fingers — meaning that all had been accomplished.

A compliant voter then received a predetermined cash settlement when an outside poll worker or clerk palmed the person a dollar, five-dollar bill, a ten spot, or more. Sometimes a few dollars were neatly folded and put in a matchbook cover; and the matches were passed to the voter. Cleanly and quickly.

A lever brother or clerk was rewarded handsomely for his willingness to help the illegal voting process. In 1971, Bus Perry wrote in his memoirs that *good* election officers usually held the best political jobs and ranked high in party standing.

> After we got the signal, which meant the voter voted the right way, we then paid the voter; and he or she went on about their business.
>
> I figure that even ol' Chafin was giving away at least five cases or more of liquor at his precinct on Election Day, as well as handing out the same general amount of money we were giving out. We knew exactly who would rather have whiskey than money in every precinct, although you had to be especially careful about dispensing liquor 'cause of the feds. Some voters demanded money *and* booze.
>
> In 1960 Humphrey did it this way, too. I know for a fact that there was Humphrey currency being spread all over the place while we were taking care of our voters, and he and his people were doing the same exact thing in this county and elsewhere in the state. Only difference is that Humphrey had more lint in his pocket than cash, that's all.

It was a complicated, chaotic, and corrupt system that apparently worked well for generations in rural Appalachia. "It's all we ever knew," Ellis said.

O'Donnell Drops Off Cash

Ellis said that the biggest part of the money that he got during the Kennedy campaign came from his main contact at the Kanawha Motel at Charleston, who was a man named Kenneth O'Donnell.

> Kenny was hooked up tightly with John Kennedy and was later named to an important post after the election. Some other smaller monies came from Bob McDonough at Parkersburg. However, the bulk always came through O'Donnell, even though McDonough and McCahey were usually present. Kenny was in charge of that.

Kenny O'Donnell, 36 years old in 1960, had been a longtime friend of both John and Bobby Kennedy. He had met Bobby at Harvard College years before and struck up a friendship. He worked with Jack in 1952 in his run for the senate seat in Massachusetts. From 1952 to '57, O'Donnell was involved in public relations work.

He returned to Kennedy's aid and served as director of the campaign organization for Senator Kennedy's re-election campaign in 1958. By the time 1960 rolled around, O'Donnell was the organizer and director of JFK's presidential campaign schedule.

According to Ellis, O'Donnell often maneuvered discreetly behind the scenes during the primary campaign. Some said he was Jack's right arm, who paid off political bosses and precinct commandos several months before the Kennedy campaign convoy traveled through the state. According to Ellis, with an enormous surplus of financial backing, it was O'Donnell who quietly paid Mountain State political bosses handsomely for their cooperation. It is also rumored that O'Donnell may have been the fellow who supplemented Jim McCahey's enormous resources when he journeyed through southern West Virginia and entertained and bartered with powerful coal operators and union officials.

Later, when Kennedy moved into the White House, O'Donnell's title would appear as "special assistant" to President Kennedy, which in this case most likely meant troubleshooter, political right hand, and bargaining contact. According to published records, O'Donnell was considered the chief political broker in the White House. He was also helpful in guarding the president's notoriously promiscuous and provocative personal life from the news media.

By all accounts, he was part of an exclusive inner circle of Kennedy aides who, along with Lawrence F. O'Brien and David Francis Powers, came to be known as the "Irish Mafia" on Capitol Hill. At least in the first months of the new administration, O'Donnell was arguably the closest confidant to the president, second only to John's brother Bobby.

Ellis continued:

> To my knowledge, no other Kennedy money — besides what Ray Watts and I picked up — came into this county, except for that small money drop to Raymond Chafin at Taplin. I know certainly that Democrats in other West Virginia counties received large sums, too. Kenny even stayed at another location — at the Kanawha Motel — when he came into the state, while Jack and Jackie mostly stayed at the Daniel Boone Hotel.
>
> If it was Jack Kennedy's father, Joe, who was funding the bulk of the campaign in West Virginia, he shipped the bundles of currency to Appalachia through Kenny O'Donnell.

It's also been suspected that Raymond Chafin's payoff came from the hands of O'Donnell, being delivered to Bob McDonough days before the transfer date.

Ellis continued:

> There have been a lot of rumors and blown-up stories that started around that time. It was said around the City of Logan that I received a brand new Cadillac from the Kennedy family. People were calling it the Kennedy Cadillac.

Sure enough, around that time period I did buy myself a Cadillac. I got that car at Colonial Motors at Huntington, and I financed it, if I remember right. None of them — John, Bobby, or Teddy Kennedy — ever bought me a car. That's purely ridiculous.

Ellis explained that Watts and he tried their best to hold the Kennedy campaign and their local faction together during the final weeks before the primary. Also, Bill Abraham helped through the organization and support of his boys at Omar. Tank Williams and James Major were extremely helpful, too.

Bill was a good friend of the black community, as I was, too. Bill went on to become Logan County sheriff, and James Major, a respected black leader from Superior Bottom, went on to be the first black deputy sheriff in the county. Bill Abraham put him on the force. Then, after a stint as deputy, Major went on to become a successful coalmine inspector.

The Kennedy involvement helped make Bill Abraham even bigger than he already was. John Kennedy coming to Shaheen's Shopping Center obviously helped Bill, too.

I truly believe ninety to ninety-five percent of the blacks in our county were for Kennedy in 1960. Kennedy promised many good things, including the food stamp and relief program. There is no reason to tell anyone different — the blacks were a great part of JFK's West Virginia triumph.

Eleanor Visits West Virginia

When all was said and done, Kennedy received 60.8 percent of the Mountain State votes — representing 236,510 votes cast in the May 10th West Virginia primary. Humphrey received the remaining 152,187 votes, representing 39.2 percent.

Ellis discussed the primary:

In the 1960 primary, Okey Justice was elected sheriff. However, Kennedy carried the county. The top of Raymond Chafin's ticket prevailed, from the sheriff on down. It was sort of a trade deal at most precincts. Chafin no doubt made a deal of some sort: "I'll give you Kennedy, if you'll give me Okey."

I doubt that Raymond Chafin ever sent that twenty-five hundred dollars back to Humphrey that he had — NEVER! No way. It's not the way he ever did business in those days. He kept everything he ever got!

After the election, Bob McDonough called me one morning from Parkersburg and asked me to meet him. Dan Dahill, Tom Godby, and I drove over to Parkersburg that day. I picked up a one-thousand-dollar bonus from McDonough because Kennedy carried our county. I was delighted. We then traveled on back home after that.

After winning the primary in West Virginia and eventually moving forward and accepting the nomination of his party, Kennedy continued to campaign hard.

173

He held four televised debates with Vice President Richard Nixon, the Republican nominee. The first was held on September 26th at CBS studios and was carried on all three major networks. The second debate originated from NBC in Washington, D.C., on October 7, 1960. The third television program — "Face-to-Face, Nixon and Kennedy" — aired six days later, on October 13th, from ABC; Kennedy was in New York and Nixon was in Hollywood. The final debate was held on the evening of October 21st, originating from ABC studios in New York.

Claude said that nearly every county resident was glued to the television during the debates. He said, "Nixon looked as stiff as wallboard during the debates. Kennedy was calm and self-assured. I was even more convinced then that he would be our next president."

Claude Ellis said that in West Virginia, the Democratic Party continued to be excited about the possibility of a Kennedy White House. During this approximate time period, Eleanor Roosevelt made a rare visit to the state in behalf of the Kennedy campaign. Although she had been a strong supporter of Adlai Stevenson during the primary, she was a John Kennedy believer by the time the Democratic convention was over.

Ellis remembered her visit:

Tom Godby, Joe Barber, several others, and I went over to greet her. I remember that when we met her at Bluefield airport, it was a sunny day. I had my convertible and Tom had a vehicle that we transformed into a sound car. As we picked her up, Mrs. Roosevelt, a charming woman, made eleven campaign stops from Bluefield to Charleston.

Our first stop was Preston, West Virginia, and there was an extremely large crowd of people there to greet her. I remember that this one particular lady in the audience was trying to reach Mrs. Roosevelt, and she inadvertently got one of her fingers caught inside the door of my car, and I accidentally put all my weight against it. When she hollered, I jumped forward and helped her get her fingers out. When I began to talk to her about her red hand and fingers, she shook her head and said, "My fingers will be all right. I just want to touch Mrs. Roosevelt, and then I'll be out of here!"

We then went on — from stop to stop. Eleanor knew exactly what to say. I'm certain that many people became Kennedy supporters that day because of her and her son, Franklin D. Roosevelt, Jr.

Then, with our final stop, Mrs. Roosevelt's people held a big rally, and she gave a lively speech at the civic center that night in Charleston. For being around 75, she did a real good job.

The Election

The general election was held on November 8, 1960. Results were not certain until the next sunup. In one of the closest elections in American history, John Kennedy carried twenty-three states and received 34,221,344 votes (49.72 percent) to Nixon's twenty-six states and 34,106,671 votes (49.55 percent), a difference of 114,673 votes. In the state of Mississippi, unpledged electors cast their votes for Harry F. Byrd, who carried the state.

In the Electoral College, Kennedy received 303 votes to Nixon's 219 and Byrd's 15.

Ellis said the folks in Logan were extremely excited at the outcome! "I guess nearly everyone was smiling for days," Ellis said. "It was a great time for me and everyone."

Bill Abraham, Joe Barber, Tom Godby, Dan Dahill, and Rosemary and Claude Ellis were with Bob McDonough again during the inauguration.

Rosemary Ellis recalled:

> It was so cold when we went to that inauguration that I wondered what this could have been like if it had been held in the summer. My feet were frozen. If I had been in charge, I would have been ready to switch it to a summer inaugural.
>
> We had reserved rooms in McLean, Virginia, outside the city limits. Then we came into the city, and there was such snow on the ground that we decided to stay at the Ambassador. We met up with Bill Abraham and the others, and we all attended the inauguration together when John F. Kennedy was sworn into office on January 20, 1961.
>
> I never saw so much jewelry and many furs in all my life!
>
> I remember way back, when I first met Claude, he said, "Stick with me. I'm going to introduce you to presidents and kings." I'm still waitin' for the kings!
>
> It's been an awful good ride — most of the time.

***

Claude Ellis said at one point that he wanted to dispel certain rumors:

> In answer to the rumors that I'm still living on Kennedy campaign money, I only received that one-time one-thousand-dollar bonus for my campaign work after the primary. We used up all the actual campaign money on precincts and other campaign needs.

Rosemary Ellis commented:

> You know, I never resented the Kennedy money, position, or the prestige that they brought along with them because they did so much for the people — a lot more than the Hearsts or some of the others who have claimed fame. I never resented their riches. They were always just like us when they were with us. They didn't flaunt their position.
>
> I remember once when John Kennedy had to have someone pay for his hotdog at the Smokehouse. He didn't have any money in his pocket at the time.

Claude Ellis continued:

> After Kennedy was elected, I think he showed his appreciation to all of West Virginia. I remember that he was able to implement the food stamp program, which was something he had promised us his administration would accomplish. He started the program right here in our state. He implemented the Peace Corps and so much more. He especially recognized our needs and spoke loud for our state in Washington.

175

Although I attended his inauguration, I never got to personally meet him in Washington. However, I did meet President and Mrs. Kennedy at Charleston once after he was president. I was with him a long while, and finally we all walked out of the civic center together and they got into his black limousine. Before the limo pulled on out that evening, he rolled down his window and motioned with his finger for me to come over to him. As I leaned down at the window, he smiled and said, "Claude, thanks for everything. I'll be in touch."

That was the last time I personally heard him talk.

In my personal dealings with both of them, I saw Jackie as totally supportive of her husband. She had a classy way about her, and they seemed to adore one another when I saw them together.

I especially treasure a personal letter that I received from Jackie some time after her husband was killed. She thanked me for my help and for making an audiotape of my campaign remembrances. That tape recording is still on file in the Kennedy oral interview archives at Boston.

I'm sure Raymond Chafin doesn't have these types of mementos!

While Kennedy was still president, Claude Ellis was asked by an administrative aide to tape an interview of his campaign remembrances for the future presidential library. Ellis said he started the taperecording a while after JFK took office and finished it up after his death.

The finished oral history interview, which was conducted by William Young, was dated September 9, 1964. It was filed among the various audiotaped oral interviews in the John F. Kennedy Library and Museum, at Boston, Massachusetts. Ellis elaborated:

Several of my friends later traveled to the Kennedy Library and heard it. It was placed in the archives alongside other audiotapes, and I'm sure people from all over the world have heard it by now. I know it's there because my friend Tom Godby once got a copy of the tape recording.

Chapter Twenty-Five

Wrap-up of 1960

On December 5th and 6th, 1964, Robert P. McDonough, in charge of the Kennedy For President campaign for West Virginia, granted an interview to William L. Young, for the John F. Kennedy Library and Museum. He stated then that he first got interested in John F. Kennedy at the 1956 Democratic convention at Chicago.
Bob McDonough talked about the first time he noticed Kennedy:

> I was a delegate [in 1956] and, along with a great many people, thought [John F. Kennedy] was an attractive, capable young man. I did some work among our delegation trying to convince people that they should vote for him for vice president, and West Virginia did, as a matter of fact, give him a few votes.

In an excerpt from the oral history interview, McDonough spoke about southwestern West Virginia and the men who supported the Kennedy for President campaign during the 1960 primary:

> The next is Logan County, great Logan County: (Raymond) Ray Chafin, Claude Ellis (Big Claude), and (J. Thomas) Tom Godby.
> Raymond Chafin was the county chairman at the time and originally the leader of Humphrey For President in Logan County. Then, sometime before the primary election, he changed his mind and ended up by not doing anything. The situation in Logan County, as in a great many counties, revolved around the sheriff. There would be two or more candidates for sheriff, but there were usually just two in a really possible position of winning. Raymond Chafin had a candidate for sheriff, and then there was another strong candidate for sheriff, a meat cutter down there — I forget his name.
> But against Raymond's slate was a slate supported by the candidate ... Tom Godby, and a whole other ticket. When we first went into Logan County, Claude Ellis, whom we knew from Young Democrat days, active in the Young Democrats, liked the senator. Claude saw a real, live political possibility with the senator in his aspirations. So Claude, who was sort of a jack-of-all-trades, working at this and that but mostly politics, became the Kennedy leader in Logan County.
> Raymond Chafin and "Big Claude" Ellis and Tom Godby are what you might call typical of the more active political persons in many counties of West Virginia. Well, I don't know whether they're typical, either, but there are a great number of people in West Virginia, and I suppose in other states, who are in the same category as these people. They're persons of limited economic means, they're not of any particular profession, but they live on politics, for politics. They don't go into politics to get the money deal. They go into politics and, having to eat, they manage to get enough money to eat out of politics. But they develop organizations and blocs of votes and put them together and ally them

with two or three or four or five other groups, hoping to form a group big enough to take over the county offices.

McDonough also said that he relied upon Ellis to represent JFK's interests to his group of people, or bloc of voters, where he had been a major influence. He continued:

> Claude Ellis had been the major factor in putting together an organization and getting to take care of the senator's interests and getting him on the slate. Ellis was successful. But I point out that Ellis was, I think, just as much successful because they, in turn, used the senator to get attention to their faction — and the other faction couldn't find anybody that attractive to help them.
>
> I think it's clear now in retrospect that he [Kennedy] was the most attractive imaginable candidate. He just went up every valley in the state, down every road, and over every hill, and he shook hands by the thousands.

In another excerpt, McDonough recollected a chilly Sunday afternoon pig roast for Kennedy in Parkersburg. John Kennedy's voice had given out and his brother, Teddy, spoke on his behalf. Even though the weather was disagreeable and the hour grew late, the crowd of approximately 5,000 stayed on.

> It took ... nearly a couple of hours for him to meet all those people. They just hung there until they got a chance to shake hands with him and say hello to him ...
>
> You knew doggone well that all these people were going to vote for this man.

Chafin Kept His Political Strength

As he pondered all the political dealings he had been a part of throughout his adult life, Claude Ellis paused and took a few minutes to reflect upon the 1960 election and the local outcome:

> I will have to say that one reason Raymond Chafin was so successful politically in 1960 and throughout the '60s is that he remained precinct captain at Barnabus for his own faction — and even for us in '60. He made the difference. He had good control over his precinct. Because of his influence, there were probably three hundred fifty votes that moved on over to Kennedy, with maybe fifty or less for Senator Humphrey. Chafin really remains in control of the precinct up to this day, as well.

Ellis said that after a few months in his new post, Sheriff Okey Justice became ill and later died while in office. He served from 1960 to 1963. The county court, consisting of W.E. Bivens, William "Bill" Dingess, and Okey Hager, met promptly after his death and appointed J.W. "Jack" Ferrell Jr. to fill his unexpired term in 1964.

In his memoirs, Bus Perry stated that Ferrell did not have a great deal of experience as a businessman, nor had he ever been elected to public office. The West Virginia State

Road Commission had engaged Ferrell as its superintendent of bridges. Ferrell had several employees — mostly political appointments — under his supervision, and he was responsible for repairing and constructing small bridges throughout a five-county area that constituted the district. He was then named Logan County sheriff. The Ferrell administration later ended in scandal.

Some say that jealous political opponents railroaded Sheriff Ferrell out of his powerful position because of their own self-centered agendas — in order to diminish the strength of the Democratic executive committee at the time. Others allege that it was misbehavior in the sheriff's department and during his tenure as bridge superintendent for the state road commission that led to his downfall. Regardless of the true circumstances, the court found Ferrell guilty of misconduct in office, and he was impeached in 1966. Bill Abraham was then named sheriff by the county court.

Claude Ellis continued:

> The same kind of politics — with vote-buying, precinct payoffs, moonshine, and slates — went on here for several more years, even through Bobby Kennedy's campaign, Humphrey's next presidential run, and Senator McGovern's time period. We usually paid 'round five to ten dollars a head. Then, we had to go upward to twenty dollars or so to get more of a family vote. This system stopped dead when former West Virginia Secretary of State Ken Hechler messed around with the state election rules. He put a batch of new rules and regulations into the state laws. It was a downhill battle ever since. We still gave out a little money afterward, but it wasn't as obvious as it was back in 1960.
>
> Although Chafin supported Republicans through the years, like Governor Cecil Underwood, I have always stayed true to the Democratic Party. In all my days, I never switched parties, or jumped across the fence, so to speak. I was born and raised a Democrat, and I'll die a Democrat. Recently the local newspaper in Logan showed a picture of Bo Gibbs and me and identified us both as Republicans. Well, that was a good one all right. I'm a Democrat through and through — always have been and always will be.

He remembered trips to Washington:

> I guess that through the years I went to Washington on several occasions, another one being the inauguration of Lyndon B. Johnson. I went down with several fellows and was so unimpressed that I turned around and came back early. Things were altogether different by then, and I wasn't so pleased with LBJ.
>
> The last time I was in Washington, I went to Jimmy Carter's inauguration. Four of us fellows, including Joe Ferrell, went together. We had a good time, but that was the last time I was in the Capitol.

Chapter Twenty-Six
Memorable Brawls and Tussles

"Arguments and tussles weren't uncommon around Logan County," Ellis stated in a 2002 interview. "They happened even when I was a boy, especially on Election Day."

The whole Mountain State political system was extremely competitive and the players were passionate. While one faction of politicians was at work in behalf of its own slate, the opposing bloc was also on duty encouraging people to cast their vote for its list of candidates. Therefore, the payment for votes often escalated throughout the course of an election, as opposing precinct captains conducted a bidding war for their respective list of contenders. The tension around the polls escalated as well.

Ellis recalled one incident:

> I remember once we had another fight going on when Louis Nagy, a precinct helper, was working over in Black Bottom, called lower Mt. Gay. I was in charge of that precinct at the time. The Republican chairman in Logan County kept coming over and picking on people that I had in the house [a mountain term for the election place], and I finally told him, "Don't come back here and start stuff anymore!"
>
> This fellow owned a car dealership at the time, and he lived across the street from where the precinct was. He eventually walked back over and got into another quarrel with Nagy. I guess Louis took all he could take and finally poled him [struck him with some type of crowbar or billy-club in the abdomen], and his hat flew over the fence and he went down. We had no more problems from him after that.

Ellis said there were precincts where he worked in past years where things went on that he didn't particularly like. "Hey, but they happened anyhow, and I dealt with the circumstances," Ellis commented matter-of-factly. He went on to explain:

> I imagine my wife, Rosemary, worried about me a little bit when I was working politics — but not necessarily too much. She was accustomed to the dangers. I was a little rough in those days, mind you. Once there was a fellow, a former deputy sheriff, who caught up with Bill Abraham and me over at Randy's Steakhouse, at Holden. He started a fight with us over his job. He wanted to know why we had him fired. Bill was soon to be sworn in as sheriff, and we explained to him that the reason he was let go was purely political, a normal change that was made 'cause a new administration was coming in. I guess he didn't like our answer.
>
> While he argued, he kept fooling around in his pocket, and I knew he was about to get something out — but what, I didn't know. Finally, I knew. He pulled out a knife and cut a deep gash in my side. I then jumped up and tore the entire place apart — along with him.

Ellis, although bleeding from the wound in the side of his abdomen, immediately tossed the deputy over several tables, causing him to lose his knife in the scuffle. After he picked himself up, he grabbed hold of a wooden chair and broke it over Ellis' back and jumped on him. Meanwhile, Abraham frantically landed punch after punch into the man's jaw and side, as Ellis rose up and brawled with the man once again. The sound of dishes and glasses shattering and the yells and screams of frightened customers racing for the store's front door were nearly deafening as the three men battled, tumbled, and fought around the room.

There was a big gasoline heater that hung on the wall in the establishment. At a certain point, with all the force I could muster, I slammed him so hard against the wall that, when he crashed against the wall, the heater fell off the wall onto the crown of his head. That heater was totally flattened by the time I finished up with the deputy. He ended up at Veterans Hospital at Charleston that night; I went to the emergency room at Logan General Hospital. From there I called my wife and I told her that this former deputy had cut me up and I needed to get sewn up. Rosemary didn't worry too much about it. She didn't even come over to the hospital. I ended up with seven or eight stitches and a few bruises here and there.

I've been in quite a few scuffles. I was over at the Smokehouse Restaurant once. I remember a big fella came to Logan from Wayne County. He was inebriated. He was in the restaurant that night and started mouthing off at me. I tried to walk off and get away from him. By the time I got out on the street, he came outside and hollered, "Come back here, Ellis! I'll be the one to tell you when you can leave and when you can't!"

I turned around, and I said, "That's it!" I ended up tearing him up pretty bad and destroying a parking meter that night. When the deputy sheriff, who was a friend of mine, came by the restaurant, I told him what had happened. He picked the guy up and put him in jail. I later told the deputy to let him sleep things off and let him go home to Wayne County in the morning. That's what he did, too.

***

Another time, when I owned and operated Ellis Union-76 Station, next to the train tracks and the intersection at Logan, I remember that I was just loafing around with Tom Rose Tomblin, a local politician, and several others. We always had some loafing time around there, since the station was open 24 hours a day. That particular night two fellows in a car with Ohio tags drove up and blocked the pumps. I asked one fellow, the passenger, who came inside the station, to move the automobile. He left and a few minutes later the driver, who was pretty drunk, came in the station and said angrily, "Who is it that wants me to move my car?"

"I do," I said.

"Maybe you think you can make me?" the car owner said.

"I suspect I can," I responded.

Within seconds, the Ohio driver pulled back his fist. Ellis instantly grabbed hold of the man, and a tussle ensued. Ellis countered every punch the Buckeye State visitor threw. Big Daddy then finished him off with a powerful uppercut. The force of the final blow hurled the unconscious driver through the plate-glass window in the front of the store. When he landed, he lay helpless in shattered glass. Ellis went out the door, brushed him off, and doused him with a paper cup of cold water.

> Once he regained consciousness, I bent down and talked to him a minute. I finally asked him, "Son, what are you drinkin'?"
> "I … uh … I best not tell ya," the trembling fellow answered, as he attempted to get his footing enough to stand up.
> Well, I was wondering what it was, so I'd know what to give my precinct workers during the next election. Musta been awfully good stuff!
> Never saw the guy from Ohio in the City of Logan again.

Chafin Is Attacked

Ellis remembered another incident in the early 1960s when he was sitting on a wooden slat bench early in the morning with a friend, directly across from the Smokehouse Restaurant, at the entrance to the White and Browning office building.

Raymond Chafin and a few political buddies had been eating breakfast at the Smokehouse, which was a rather routine occurrence. By the time they were preparing to check out and leave the establishment, there was a man, a distant relative to Chafin, lingering outside the restaurant.

Ellis remembered:

> My friend and I watched this fellow. He was acting very peculiar. Several of us knew that this guy had a beef with Chafe — something of a personal nature. Therefore, we sort of kept our eye on him.

Instead of being a political rivalry, Ellis implied that the fellow was incensed over a situation concerning his wife. Tom Godby and a group of fellow politicians walked out of the eatery with Chafin following close behind, grinning and chatting with the others.

When Chafe stepped outside the double-glass doors into the sunlight, the fellow ambushed him, drawing a knife out of his front pants-pocket.

"I'll cut your throat," he snarled at Chafin, as he waved the blade in Chafin's face.

Chafin, terrified by the attacker, nearly fell backward as he tried to move away from the glistening weapon. Once he regained his balance, he swung his fists wildly toward the aggressor. He landed a solid punch and then another. However, the assailant shook off the punches and kept lunging forward with the blade.

Ellis remembered the incident:

> My friend and I immediately jumped up and ran over to the scene. We broke up the fight. Chafin came close to being hurt badly that day.

182

Another time, when Chafin was county clerk, he got into a fight with the same fellow at the bridge down where he lives. I was the justice of the peace by that time. The deputies had the case brought before me, and Chafin was carrying on like he was mean and tough that day — actually like a madman. But truly, Chafin was lucky he didn't get himself purely killed, 'cause the guy was extremely jealous over his wife.

Business Tycoon

Claude Ellis was involved in several flourishing businesses over the years. For a while, he even owned and operated the popular Smokehouse Restaurant.

Through the years, many famous individuals have had dinner or spent significant time in the once-famous diner, including John, Bobby, and Teddy Kennedy, Rose Kennedy and her daughters, Senator Hubert Humphrey, Senator Jennings Randolph, Senator George McGovern, Franklin Delano Roosevelt Jr., Senator Robert C. Byrd, Congressman Ken Hechler, Governor Jay Rockefeller, Senate President Earl Ray Tomblin, Governor Arch Moore, Governor Hulett Smith, Governor Cecil Underwood, and Governor William Barron.

There were occasionally movie stars, as well as nationally known entertainers and country music stars, who stopped by the eatery while traveling through town, including Roy Rogers, Gabby Hayes, Lorne Greene, Stonewall Jackson, Bill Anderson, Ronnie Milsap, and Hank Snow.

The restaurant wasn't particularly fancy. It included a casual breakfast counter located across from stainless steel ovens, deep fryers, warmers, and a cooking area.

The counter space had a row of chrome-legged and bright vinyl-upholstered swivel stools. The main dining area had round wooden tables, chrome and plastic-back chairs, and a heavily waxed black-and-white-checked linoleum floor. The floor was later replaced with gray-colored linoleum. Along one dark-brown paneled wall was a well-stocked newspaper and magazine rack. Along the opposing side from the kitchen was a thirteen or fourteen-foot blue marlin hanging on the wall, which a Logan County resident, Ed Wood, had caught, mounted, and presented to the restaurant as a conversation piece.

There were also framed photos of the Logan High School Wildcat basketball and football teams of yesteryear. Interspersed among the team photos were portraits of famous people and framed newspaper clippings — featuring local and national political leaders who had dined at the restaurant at one time or another.

The diner's menu included Mountain State favorites, such as pinto beans and buttermilk cornbread; chili dogs with slaw; cube steak and gravy; a variety of soups; a sandwich board; eggs; fried potatoes; gravy and biscuits; pancakes; apple fritters; homemade apple, lemon, chocolate, and coconut cream pies; and chocolate cake.

It seemed like everyone who worked in town ran to the Smokehouse at lunchtime, hoping to grab up one of "the good seats." So many tried to squeeze into the restaurant on certain occasions that the place was often standing room only from noon until around two o'clock on weekday afternoons. Then the crowds thinned out for the evening business.

The place also had a supper club and a private meeting room with a Main Street entrance in the back. It was said at the time that anybody who was anybody ate at the

Smokehouse. Unfortunately, due to poor management, the social hub of Logan County closed its doors in the early 1980s, and an era ended.

Ellis reminisced:

> It was an important location in town. It's hard to determine how many political deals and how many dollars have changed hands inside that small restaurant. Now that it's gone, there are still folks who say they miss it. A bit of Logan died when the Smokehouse closed.
>
> I ended up letting Sam Mureddu, a businessman, have the Smokehouse some years ago. At the time, Sam and his friend Phil Glick, who was the owner of Lewis Furniture, had some prime property across the river at Triangle Addition. This property now includes several professional offices and the Peking Chinese Restaurant.

During that time period, in the 1970s, Ellis developed severe diabetes, and he was looking to slow down and get out of the business. He sold the restaurant, settling on a certain amount of money and the property at Triangle Addition.

Besides the Smokehouse Restaurant and his Union-76 filling station, Ellis owned several pieces of real estate and has had partnership dealings with several other flourishing businesses through the years. Even though he is now retired, Ellis still owns the Triangle Addition land and several pieces of rental property.

> I wish someone had the insight and the capabilities to bring the ol' Smokehouse back to Logan, as it once was. I believe the importance of the facility can't be overestimated.

Chapter Twenty-Seven

Dan Dahill Tells It Like It Is

"With five thousand dollars you can elect any man to any office except sheriff in this county — that costs forty thousand dollars. Why, heck, all you need to do is have the right boys pulling the levers and you can't miss," Dan Dahill, an outspoken lawyer and House of Delegates member at the time, stated in a controversial 1960 article in *Life* magazine. At that time, Dahill was working on his own campaign for state senate and enjoyed a huge amount of popularity and power among the voters in Logan County. However, Dahill was never considered a political kingpin, and he never held control of a county faction. In many ways he was considered a loner and mostly concentrated on his own campaigns. Nevertheless, he was quite effective as a politician and an attorney.

By late 1959 and into 1960, Dahill was an advocate of John F. Kennedy and his presidential campaign movement, working in conjunction with Tom Godby, Alex DeFobio, and several others to establish a foothold for the young Massachusetts senator within the county's boundaries.

Dahill, who is now 84 years old, lives with his wife, Jean, at Ethel, West Virginia, in Logan County. With a strong voice, muscular build, and a square jaw, Dahill looks and acts much younger than his years. However, if you trace the deeply sunken lines in Dahill's face, you can almost read the graphic tale of a lifetime dedicated to political and legal confrontation.

As he spoke about his years in Logan County, he boasted that he is working on his fifty-fourth year as an attorney and still handles a few cases here and there.

Dahill spoke about his life:

> I'm working on a couple of cases against the state right now — one personal injury in Charleston, a child molestation case, and a few others. I try to do just enough, 'cause I figure that once you quit, your mind — poof — there it goes.
>
> I came to Logan when I was three years old from Huntington. Dad — Daniel Ryan Dahill — got a job as a bookkeeper with West Virginia Coal and Coke, at Omar. Dad had a sixth-grade education, but he was naturally intelligent and could work out complex algebra problems in his head. We lived at Omar until I was seven.

Dan D. Dahill was born on September 28, 1919. Dahill says that one of his earliest memories of living at Omar was being the five-year-old master of ceremonies for a minstrel show. Traveling minstrels were popular at the time; all the entertainers in the roaming troop wore blackface. Dahill's mother, always ready to encourage him to excel and to step up and be counted, dressed him up in a "Little Lord Fauntleroy outfit" and pushed him onto the stage to announce the various acts.

The crowd of spectators, who were mostly standing in the dark, smoky room, would laugh, hoot, and holler during the loud and raucous vaudevillian-like show; but when little Dahill marched out on the wooden-plank stage between acts to announce the next performer, the audience would instantly smile and hush. Everyone was eager to hear the little boy's words. Even at such a young age, Dahill loved the attention and spoke loudly.

Then we moved to McConnell (near Logan), and that's where I actually grew up. I guess I lived like we were rich when I was growing up. I traveled to Europe once and did many things. We weren't rich, but Dad had had such a hard time growing up that he wanted me to have everything. He sternly told me when I was getting out of high school, "You're either going to be a lawyer, a doctor, or an engineer. I don't really care if you ever practice a day. But during the Great Depression, I never saw a professional man in a bread line."

Mother quickly suggested, "Choose doctor! That's what you should be!"

Well, I couldn't see myself as a doctor, sitting and pushing around all those papers at a big old desk and dealing with all those illnesses. So Mom's idea was out. So, I said, "Mom and Dad, I'll be a lawyer."

As a hardy, overly confident teenager, he entered Notre Dame right after graduating from Logan High School.

I was soon carrying nineteen to twenty-one hours per semester while I was at school. I was diggin' ditches and then washing dishes for two hundred men once a day. For all that, I got one hundred seventy-five dollars for nine months. The money was taken off my college bill, mind you — I never saw cash. I did it to work my way through school.

I was carrying all the hours because I was taking the seven-year law course crammed into six years. In my third year, I started taking a few classes for law school. Under the particular program I was in, you didn't get a bachelor's degree in the fourth year; you got it in the fifth year. From there, I would have to spend a year in law school.

As Dahill neared the end of the semester of his fifth year, he signed up for and eventually spent several years in the U.S. Marine Corps.

I actually signed up on February 3rd, right after Pearl Harbor. I made a deal with my recruiter. I agreed I would go straight to flight school, but it was with the understanding that I wouldn't go until the end of that final semester of my fifth year. I even made him write it clearly in my paperwork. So, after that final semester, I graduated. If it hadn't been for the war, I would have gone on and gotten my law degree the next year.

When the war broke out, we were all eager to enlist and fight. I specifically joined the Marine Corps because they promised to send us overseas.

In those days, they would usually give a person eight hours of flight training, and if you were fairly competent, they would let you solo. I ended up liking it so much that right after I started taking lessons, I was sitting in the cockpit one day and I got into a nasty argument with the flight instructor about how to best fly the plane — and the motor was running at the time. At that point, I only had about five hours of actual training under my belt. He got so mad at

186

me for my mouthy overconfidence that he said, "If you're so dang smart, Dahill, why don't you fly this contraption by *yourself?*"

"Why don't you get your [rear-end] out of the plane and I will!" I retorted.

Sure enough, he got out and I took off, without a hitch! I accellerated down the airstrip and then pulled back on the throttle. I was instantly airborne!

Dahill's first solo flight was perfectly executed. He soared above the airstrip with surprising ability, demonstrating the kind of control one would expect from a seasoned flier. Dahill reflected:

In all my life, the one thing that I really, really loved to do was fly. It came natural to me. I soon became a fighter pilot — flying a bent-wing F4U Corsair.

Hello Mary Lou

I got out of the Marines on June 8, 1946. I was home visiting. My family is Catholic, and [the church] was having a combination meeting of the altar society and the [Catholic] men's club at Mr. Salvatti's home at Holden, West Virginia. Because Dad and I were so close, he asked me to go with him, and I went. That night I met a wonderful girl, Mary Lou Salvatti. I didn't know it at the time, but in her diary that night she wrote, "Tonight I met the man I'm going to marry."

Mary Lou was going to school at West Virginia University. I had already had five years at Notre Dame before the service. After I was released from the Marine Corps, I moved to WVU for my last year of law and we dated.

While at WVU, I didn't go to half the classes. I didn't give my best effort. My honor degree at Notre Dame didn't transfer. All the grades transferred as straight Cs. So I said, "Oh, horsecrap!"

I guess I eventually graduated from WVU with a C-plus. Besides my anger over the transfer of my grades, I didn't like the WVU dean at the time, either.

Mary Lou and I later married. We were married only twenty-eight months and three days, and she died. She passed away on March 3, 1952. We had two lovely girls in that span of time — Susan Gray and Nancy Lou.

By this time, Dahill's two-room law office was on Stratton Street, next door to Lillys' Crown Jewelers, in Logan. As a widower, he raised his two young daughters to the best of his ability. His home — once a county landmark — was situated on a knoll beside the entrance to what is now Chief Logan State Park, in Justice Addition, four miles outside Logan.

As a consequence of what Dad had said about a professional man, I always worked at law to make a living after I graduated. I guess I always wondered why I was put here on Earth, because there was nothing I really ever wanted. I practiced law, but all I really ever enjoyed was trial work. I liked my work at times, but I wasn't exactly crazy about it. I practiced mainly because I wanted to send my daughters to college, and I hoped to send them on a trip to Europe or something like that, and to take care of simple obligations. I worked at making enough income to take care of those things, and then I would take time off when

187

I raised enough money. Then, when funds started running dry, I would get back to work.

I went on from there for about fifteen years and then married a local girl who was as good-lookin' as heck, but she liked to run around. We ended up in a divorce. Then I went another twelve years or so, and I married Norma Jean Moore. Norma Jean and I have been together ever since. I always say I've had two good wives and one bad. Norma Jean is a wonderful woman.

A Vibrant Political Career

Dahill talked about the beginnings of his interest in politics:

I started in politics to give me something to do after my first wife died, I guess. I had been elected to the House of Delegates in 1956. During that time, Paul Winter, the superintendent of schools, gave me a copy of the bill for community colleges that some other states had already adopted. I introduced it to the House and couldn't get it through. I guess the speaker originally thought I was going to be his stooge, but I wasn't. So West Virginia Speaker of the House W.E. "Bill" Flannery told me at the time I would serve two terms in one — my first and last.

Flannery was a brilliant man — but a possibly a bit crooked, in my estimation. Two years later, probably with Flannery's encouragement, Claude Ellis ran against me for House of Delegates. I squeezed in and just barely, and I mean barely, beat Claude by around 166 votes, because the organization was against me. So I was just narrowly elected again. If you read *The Charleston Gazette* during that time, the newspaper reporters portrayed me as a maverick. All I knew at the time was that I wasn't going to be anybody's stooge.

Interestingly, to this day, Claude Ellis disagrees with Dan Dahill on this issue, declaring that it was not Speaker Flannery who was behind his candidacy for House of Delegates at the time. He says that Flannery was already deceased by that time, and that it was a decision made locally by his faction, which placed him on the slate.

Dahill continued:

Right after the election, Claude was walking up the street with Tom Godby and some other people. I was standing in front of the Logan County Courthouse. Claude walked up to me and said, "You only got four votes from my precinct. I know who two of the [sons of guns] were, but I don't know who the other two were. But when I do ..."

"I'll tell ya who they were!" I responded angrily. "They were two more guys just like me who don't give a sh— 'bout YOU!"

Angered by his words, Ellis moved toward the attorney. Dahill gritted his teeth, reared back, and clenched his fist, ready to punch Ellis in the jaw. However, Tom Godby, who was an exceedingly tall and lanky man, immediately jumped between the two politicians to stop the impending scuffle.

188

"Whoa, boys, you don't need to do this!" Godby shouted, as he stretched out his arms, putting one hand on Ellis' massive shoulder and the other on Dahill's chest, pushing the two men apart. "Why don't you two try to simmer down and let this election be over and done with, okay?"

After tempers cooled and fists relaxed, Godby moved away and allowed the two men to break things off and walk away from one another. They both mumbled obscenities as they departed, but at least the disturbance was over.

Dahill continued:

> That was one of the first times I met Tom Godby and got to know him a little. He had also run for the House of Delegates that year. We eventually became close friends.
>
> That year I introduced the community college bill again. This time I got it through the House of Delegates, but Glenn Jackson wouldn't help me in the Senate. I was extremely mad, and I went over to the clerk of the Senate and told him he might as well clear Jackson's desk out and pack up his stuff, because he wouldn't be coming back after the next election. I told the clerk, "I'll bust Jackson's [rump] at the next election."
>
> Meanwhile, Tom and I started discussing the next election, and Tom was considering running for the Senate. I told him, "No, Tom, you have to have income."
>
> "Well, you're right ... maybe I'll run for assessor," Godby responded.
>
> "Yes — then I'll run for Senate!" I proclaimed loudly, determined that I could win the state office and hurt Jackson.

Dahill says that he was completely immersed in the Kennedy For President campaign in Logan County. Claude Ellis once stated that one of the main reasons Dan Dahill became involved with Kennedy was that "he could identify with the uphill fight a Roman Catholic would have in these mountains."

In one 1960 interview, Dahill stated, "... in the presidential primary, folks are saying there's enough Freewill Baptists alone in this county to whip Kennedy."

There were many in southern West Virginia who questioned whether an Irish Catholic could garner enough Mountaineer votes to beat any opponent, besides overcoming someone as politically savvy as Hubert Humphrey.

Dahill expounded:

> It was an amazing time. Tom Godby and I were the only two elected officials in the county who were for John F. Kennedy at the very beginning, in early 1959. Even Claude's hind-end was hanging out at that time. So Tom and I talked about it, and I told Tom, "Go talk to Claude Ellis and bring him in."

After that meeting, Tom Godby met with Ellis quietly at the Smokehouse and talked about the presidential race. After some slick convincing, Ellis was brought into the fold — eventually to take charge of the entire local campaign.

Dahill went on:

That's the way Claude really got connected. I met John Kennedy personally — face-to-face — only once, at the Smokehouse Restaurant. I instantly liked him. As a matter of fact, I always liked John Kennedy. But honestly, I never cared much for Bobby, the hatchet man, or for the other brother, Teddy, especially after that Chappaquiddick incident. While we're on the subject, I knew one of the fellows who attended the party that Ted attended that night. The young woman who eventually drowned was supposed to leave the area and head home the day before. However, she was urged to stay for that party. It was a sad day.

JFK Memories

Dahill recalled certain situations during the 1960 campaign:

When John Kennedy came to the City of Logan, I remember that Judge C.C. Chambers snuck out the back door of the courthouse and hightailed it out of town. He was a strong Humphrey man, and he wanted no part of a Catholic president.

Although the height of the Ku Klux Klan movement had ended many years before, it was rumored that Chambers had once been an organizer for the Klan, when Logan County was an organization stronghold. It's been said that many of the businessmen and merchants in the county were also involved in the KKK in the 1930s and 1940s, and it was alleged that Chambers still held onto many of their core beliefs into the 1960s.

Dahill said in those days that lawyers called Judge Chambers "Alimony Slim" behind his back because of his harsh actions in divorce proceedings. He elaborated:

I once mentioned that to a *Life* magazine reporter who was doing a feature story on the Kennedy campaign when he asked me about the judge. I then suggested that the reporter should go see the judge. After we talked, the reporter went down to talk to Chambers. The judge put on his best robe, and I guess he figured *Life* magazine was going to make him out as a hero. But when the magazine came out on the stands, they ran his black-and-white snapshot. Near his photo was his name — "Alimony Slim."

When the magazines first came into the Smokehouse, the restaurant manager wouldn't put them out on the rack for several days 'cause he was afraid to. Five or six years later, the judge was still saying, "You should have made that right!" He never could forgive me for that. I believe he died hating me.

I also remember when Raymond Chafin came into the Kennedy group. Raymond — "Cathead," as we always called him — originally had Humphrey's money and was a big Hubert Humphrey supporter. Then, I distinctly recall that Jim McCahey came in from Chicago with a suitcase full of money. Next thing you know [the Kennedy people] made "Cathead" give Humphrey's money back — 'cause he must have got some of Kennedy's at the time, I guess. Let me say that Raymond was supposed to have sent the Humphrey campaign money back.

We all have our doubts whether the cash ever left his billfold. Believe me, I know him well.

As I said, Tom Godby was running for assessor for the first time that year. I was running for Senate, to whip ol' Glenn Jackson. Claude Ellis wasn't for me. He and the boys were for Glenn, who was a fiscal agent for the county. He had also been chairman of finance for the Senate for around twenty years.

Big Claude and the boys were all against me and waited up until 3 o'clock the night before the election. Glenn Jackson was supposed to bring money up to Cora, West Virginia, but he never showed up. Glenn thought he had everything sown up, so he conveniently forgot about delivering any money to Cora. So Cora went for ME out of spite!

Tom won big. He was one thousand votes ahead. Yet he was in my office crying a river while final precinct numbers were being tallied. However, I was barely one hundred votes ahead in three counties! In the Senate race I had to worry about all of Lincoln, all of Boone, and all of Logan County. Tom was way up and crying. I was celebrating with my measly hundred votes!

When all was said and done, Tom won the assessor's race by a landslide. Meanwhile, I had one of my men, carrying a .45-caliber pistol, standing at the walk-in safe at Lincoln County Courthouse. I wouldn't let the county court get the ballot boxes out until I showed up to watch. I had two other guys with pistols in Boone County, too, but Tom was watching out for me here in Logan County. When everything was tallied, I won the three counties by … 153 votes.

I barely lost Lincoln County. I barely lost Boone County. I lost Chapmanville District altogether. I won Logan District by 100 votes, and my ol' buddy Joe Manco, of Triadelphia District, brought me in eight hundred votes! With those eight hundred votes, I was victorious.

It was always the same for me: the other candidates had the support and the cash to run on — I only had the B.S.

The B.S. worked for me.

Two Bucks for Your Candy

Kennedy won by a giant margin. Tom and I went with Claude when he went up to get his bonus from Kennedy's main state man — Bob McDonough — because the county went for Kennedy. We went into McDonough's office and sat down.

When Dahill sat down, he curiously looked around the room. At his side was an end table with a wrapped box of candies. While Ellis and Godby talked to McDonough, Dahill casually leaned over and opened the box and helped himself to a piece of caramel, then a second, and a third.

After he paid Claude the one thousand dollar bonus, McDonough looked over at me and asked me, "Now, what do *you* want?"

191

"Not a dang thing from you — but here's two dollars for your box of candy!" I answered sternly, as I reached into my trouser pocket and tossed two worn bills toward McDonough.

McDonough looked at Dahill with a puzzled look, and nervously said, "Uh … okay, thanks."

McDonough hastily turned back to Ellis and continued his conversation about Kennedy and his county-by-county tallies.

All the while, Dahill sat back in the office chair and smiled, as he casually munched on the remaining few pieces of candy and tossed wrapper cups carelessly on the table. Within fifteen minutes or so, they all got up, shook hands, and left the office. They returned to Logan that day.

As far as his recollections of Raymond Chafin's faction, Dahill said he remembered hearing about a big Kennedy payoff. He added:

> If Raymond Chafin did get a wad of cash from the JFK campaign, you can bet he kept most of it for himself. I never saw ol' Cathead, Raymond Chafin, buy anything with his own money. The only time he ever had a brand new car was … suspiciously … AFTER every primary election.

***

> I always liked Cathead; but you could never believe a thing he said. I remember being in his office in the basement of the Sears Building in Logan, while the new courthouse was first being built around 1963. He was an office-holder at the time. A fellow, who was really down on his luck, came in to ask Raymond if he could get him a county job. Raymond immediately responded, "You're a hardworking guy and a good Democrat. Yes, sir, I certainly can. I will make a phone call while you stand here and set it all up. Trust me."

According to Dahill's account, Chafin called a high-ranking politician while the unemployed man listened as he spoke into the phone receiver, "I have a great young fellow in my office and he needs a good paying job on the road department crew. I need you to put him to work! Thanks for the favor. Yes, I will tell him you'll call him next week."

"It's done!" Raymond said as he put the phone earpiece down.

The unemployed man was delighted and thanked Raymond for his kindness. Raymond and the gentleman shook hands; then he left Raymond's office smiling, expecting to receive a phone call in the next week from the road crew supervisor.

> As soon as the fellow left Raymond's office, he looked over at me, smiled, then picked the phone back up and called his political friend back and told him to forget the job request and proceeded to say what a scoundrel the unemployed fellow was.
>
> Now that's how Raymond was as a politician. That fellow never got a phone call or a county job.

Chapter Twenty-Eight

Chafin Visits the White House

In January 1961, after Kennedy had taken office, a secretary at the White House called Raymond Chafin at his home.

"Mr. Chafin? Is this Mr. Raymond Chafin, of Cow Creek?"

"Yes, I'm Raymond. What can I do fer ya?" Chafin answered.

"I'm calling from the White House, sir. President Kennedy would like to see you."

"Huh? Uh … well, the president, you say? Well, can I think on this? Can you call me back in an hour?"

At first Chafin thought the phone call was a practical joke from one of his cronies in Logan. He immediately began to tell his wife, Louise, about the prank call. After discussing it, Chafin decided to phone Bus Perry about the caller.

"Bus, I'm not sure, but I may be going to Kennedy's house," Chafin said animatedly. "It might have really been the White House that called me a few minutes ago. This woman on the line sounded awfully professional to be someone local. But what would Kennedy want me up there for — what did I do?"

Perry hurried and ended the call so that he could run over to Chafin's house to await the callback.

"This is something, if it's true!" Perry reminded Chafin. "Do you realize how many people get to visit the president of the United States at the White House? Not many, Chafe! Not many!"

Sure enough, about an hour and a half later, the same woman called back and asked, "Mr. Chafin, when could you come to Washington? President Kennedy would be honored to see you."

"Shoot, you … you name the time," Chafin said, stammering. "I can make it."

She set a day and time and explained that a motel room would be taken care of for him. As the day approached, Chafin went out and bought a brand-new suit, brown wingtip shoes, and a new red bow tie for the occasion.

He then spent a great deal of time worrying about his appointment.

"What will I say? What if I stutter? What if I clam up altogether?" Chafin thought. "What if I trip walking into the Oval Office and make a fool of myself?"

It seemed like every conceivable scenario and bumbling possibility ran through Chafin's head as he nervously thought about what it would be like to walk through the corridors of the White House — the former home of such great men as Abraham Lincoln, Teddy Roosevelt, Franklin D. Roosevelt, and Harry S. Truman. It was impossible for him to imagine what it would be like sitting across from the leader of the free world.

"If Dad could see me now," Chafin mumbled audibly as he stared in the mirror and practiced saying, "Good morning, Mr. President … uh, Good morning, Jack …uh … Mr. President, your gracious honor, how's you doin'? …"

Chafin knew that this upcoming moment would be much more intimidating than his earlier meetings with Mr. Kennedy. He hadn't been so nervous or panicky when he first met Senator Kennedy in Charleston, right after he announced his candidacy, or when, a few months later, he met with him at the Aracoma Hotel. When Chafin and JFK stared out his hotel window at the street below, he was calm as could be.

Now Chafin was going to meet President Kennedy on his turf, not in little Logan, West Virginia. The White House. Things seemed altogether different this time around. Chafin was petrified. To him, Washington, D.C., seemed like a large city that could swallow up fellows like him for breakfast.

Louise tried her best to encourage and support her husband through the tense days and restless nights before the meeting. Slowly, Chafin worked up his nerve and readied himself for the trip to the nation's capital.

When it was time to leave Cow Creek for Washington, Bus Perry drove Chafin to Charleston for the night. After a fidgety night in a motel, they left Charleston the next morning in Perry's Cadillac, arriving at the capital by evening. They checked into the Mayflower Hotel, where reservations had been made in their names by the White House staff.

> The next morning, we both took a taxicab over to the White House. Unfortunately, Bus was unable to see the president. The president's calendar only showed my name. So I was the only one able to see President Kennedy in the Oval Office.

When Chafin first entered the White House, he was ushered into the reception room, an elegant space with exquisite wood flooring, luxurious rugs, priceless ornaments in every corner, paintings hanging on the wall, and a sparkling chandelier in the center of the span.

He was overwhelmed with the splendor of the president's home and the number of well-dressed people moving about like restless worker ants. He was so nervous that he could barely hold his two hands still or keep his right eye from twitching. Chafin wondered if he'd be able to say a word when he finally did get to walk into the president's office. His mouth was dry, and it was hard for him to swallow.

Eventually, the moment came. Chafin took slow, deep breaths as he was escorted up to the Oval Office. There, President Kennedy was sitting behind his desk — the famous Resolute Desk that was originally given to President Hayes by Queen Victoria. Kennedy seemed totally at ease on the far side of the room. He was nearly in silhouette as the morning sun peeked through the window from the world behind him. Once Chafin started to move toward his desk, visual details began to come into clarity. Chafin could see that he was well groomed and slightly tan, and grinning. The president was dressed in an expensive, fastidiously tailored black suit, a heavily starched white shirt, and dark print tie.

Kennedy stood up and walked around the desk toward Chafin, and said, "Raymond, I'm so pleased you could come to Washington to talk with me."

Leaning forward, he firmly gripped Chafin's hand and shook it unhurriedly. After greeting him warmly, he showed Chafin a chair in front of his desk. The president then pulled around his own rocking chair, setting it across from Chafin's seat.

"Again, it's so good to see you again, Raymond — and I trust your trip was a pleasant one?"

"Well, yeah … it was a heck of a long drive, ya know, from Cow Creek," Chafin mumbled as he nervously searched for words.

Within seconds, an attractive woman wearing a navy-blue business suit and holding an office clipboard entered the room and told the president that he had approximately ten minutes to spend with the Logan County native.

"No. This man is Mr. Raymond Chafin from Logan County, West Virginia. I asked him to come here to talk with me," Kennedy said, as he smiled at Chafin and winked. "He has all the time he needs. Reschedule or reshuffle my appointments if necessary."

Kennedy turned his focus back toward Chafin and started the conversation by saying that he remembered their discussions in Charleston and Logan, and that he still wanted to find a way to help the people of southern West Virginia.

From the moment the secretary left the room, Chafin felt somewhat at ease with the president. His hands eventually stopped shaking, and the muscles in his neck and shoulders relaxed a bit. For the next hour or so, the two of them discussed mountain politics, West Virginia people, and their immediate needs.

As Chafin discussed the sluggish coal industry, coal-related businesses, and the serious hardships of West Virginia coalminers, JFK sat and rocked in his chair and seemed to be listening intently to every word. Chafin mentioned how so many miners were out of work at the time and families were all truly suffering — men, women, and children. He also spoke about how it had affected the entire state's economy and morale.

Chafin painted a rather gloomy picture of the state, as he said, "These people want to work, but most can't even find a job. Many of the people have run out of unemployment compensation. They have no food pantry or medical care for their families. Miners are literally dying from black lung disease, and people are in desperate need.

"... We want your help, Mr. President. We need help back home," Chafin pleaded.

Kennedy then talked about the various relief programs that he was commencing, including the immediate increase in the commodity levels for people in need as one of his first initiatives.

"Mr. President, I've been on welfare before," Chafin interrupted. "Let me tell ya. People don't like that commodity flour, butter, cornmeal, or thick-tastin' cheese. I mentioned that to ya when we talked in Logan. They might take it, but they wind up givin' it away or feedin' it to their hogs."

Kennedy frowned and seemed astonished at his words. He hesitated for a split second and then vowed that the quality of food would improve so that people would have nourishment and good flavor, too.

"What I'm tryin' to say is that people don't want that ol' commodity stuff, sir," Chafin respectfully disagreed. "In the ol' days — under President Roosevelt's administration — my mama got a grocery order that she could take to the store and buy real food right off the store shelf."

Chafin went on to explain the procedure behind the program that his mother utilized.

"I know how relief folk think," Chafin added. "I've been there, sir. They want dignity most of all. Let them shop at a normal grocery and choose their own food, like the more fortunate folks do."

At that point, Kennedy grinned and motioned with his hand for Chafin to pause for a moment.

"Whoa, Raymond. I want some others to hear this," he leaned forward and whispered.

He then stood up and pressed the transmit button on the intercom at his desk. He called his secretary into the room and told her he needed to see several officials from his

195

administration right away, and named each of them. Within five minutes, several men walked into the room. One woman, who is thought to have been Assistant Secretary of Labor Esther Peterson, also walked into the room within minutes. All stood around the president as he sat back down in his rocker.

President Kennedy then asked Chafin to retell his story about his mother and her assistance program.

He began to tell the account again. At one point, Chafin even advised the listeners to "get rid of the stinkin' commodities program. It's not a good thing."

"You have to consider the farmers in the country," one of the gentlemen interrupted, speaking directly to the president. "That would hurt them a great deal if the commodity program were discontinued."

"No, I disagree with you," the woman from his staff protested. "If you give people money or some type of grocery order list, you are essentially helping the farmer — through legitimate grocery sales."

Then Chafin motioned for their attention and mentioned the importance for dignity in the coalfields. "This type of plan, like ol' Roosevelt had fer us, offers self-respect to mountain people, who are mostly down-and-out."

Several of the people in the room looked toward the president and nodded. Kennedy smiled and said, "Raymond, you have been most helpful today — to all of us. I assure you that this is not the end of this issue. I like what you've said here today. Would you consider visiting me again?"

Chafin stood up and shook the president's hand and said, "I would be honored, Mr. President. By the way, you are equally welcome to come to Barnabus anytime, too."

"I may do that someday. I may do just that," Kennedy smiled and said.

Chafin was escorted from the room by White House aides. He walked back down the hallway of the White House with a childlike smirk on his face, realizing that he had just managed to talk coherently with the head of the United States of America. More importantly, he was able to share what he believed to be the pressing issues that affected his people in Logan County.

Perry and Chafin drove back to West Virginia that day. All along the way Chafin told about his meeting and the president's interest in the grocery-list welfare that his mother had known.

According to Chafin, it was only a few weeks later that the West Virginia Department of Welfare started coordinating the first food stamp program — a trial project created and encouraged by the Kennedy administration.

The plan began on April 26, 1961, in Welch, West Virginia, in McDowell County. Edward Levy, a 48-year-old unemployed coalminer, was the first person to sign up for President Kennedy's food stamp initiative.

Regardless of whether it was simply coincidental or specifically because of his chat with the president, Chafin feels confident that he was instrumental in enacting the food stamp program for West Virginia.

"After the food program had been started in McDowell County, Kennedy invited me back to the White House sometime later."

Again, Chafin said President Kennedy was a perfect gentleman and even more gracious than during his first visit.

"He gave me the feeling that my ideas were important to him. He also said that the people of West Virginia were especially dear to his heart. I want to believe that this was true and that he wasn't just shootin' the bull," Chafin reminisced.

In that meeting the president asked Chafin if it would be possible for him to personally travel through McDowell County to give his assessment of the new program, by talking to residents, merchants, and businessmen. Chafin could tell that JFK was excited about what had been developed through his administration and that he wanted an evaluation from "someone who understood the importance of the program."

"What can I do to help you as you evaluate the county? What will it cost, roughly?" Kennedy asked.

"No help needed," Chafin said. "I would be honored and pleased to drive over to McDowell County and look over the program. It won't cost y'all a dime."

After returning to West Virginia, Chafin took a friend, Orin Beaufort, with him because Beaufort was a truck driver who delivered soda pop to nearly all the merchants in that area of the state.

"He knew McDowell County and the business owners like the back of his scrawny hand," Chafin said jokingly.

Several weeks later, Chafin returned to Washington a third time to tell about his program findings. With only a few exceptions, merchants were thrilled about the program. He gave the stamp plan the "thumbs-up" to Kennedy administration officials.

Then in 1962, at John F. Kennedy's insistence, Congress raised welfare expenditure, renaming the aggressive program Aid to Families with Dependent Children. Under the new law, states were allowed to necessitate recipients to do community work and be present at government-approved training programs.

Kennedy uttered what has since been a central objective of government welfare policy: to end poverty, not just alleviate it. Welfare should be "a hand up, not a handout," in Kennedy's own words.

"In a funny way, he took many of the things we talked about and made it public policy," Chafin added. "Pretty amazing, huh?"

Chafin Works Toward Retirement

After the 1960 general election was over, Kennedy was in the White House, and the Chafin faction candidates took their respective political positions, life returned somewhat to normal in Logan County. Chafin returned to his full-time commitment for Massey's Gilbert, West Virginia, operation. Business was flourishing, and Chafin's position was secure.

Chafin stated:

> We were producing an incredible amount of coal for Massey, and I was able to make some good changes — building roads, organizing the men at the site, and turning the "cancer of the company" into a profitable business.
>
> One day while I was sitting in my office, John Asbury came to see me. It was good to see him. Years before, I had been his assistant superintendent; we took state road exams together.

197

Asbury had once left the state road, in the early 1940s, to work for Black Rock Asphalt, at West Logan. Through a series of circumstances, he returned to the Department of Highways some years later. At this time, in early 1961, he was repairing a wooden bridge that crossed the river near the mine entrance and Bailey Lumber Company.

While Asbury visited Chafin, he said, "Raymond, do you realize that you've accumulated fourteen years with the highway department? They've started a new policy with their retirement plan that would give you fourteen years in the plan. Here you are the Democratic county chairman, and you could have just about any job you wanted with the state, and you're here at Massey. You're going to lose fourteen years! Can you make any kind of arrangements with Massey so that you can go back to the state road and take advantage of the retirement you've already earned?"

"Well, I'll have to check on that," Chafin answered, as he pondered the situation. Now that he was getting older, he knew that retirement was an important factor to consider.

Asbury and Chafin spent the rest of the afternoon discussing old times and reminiscing about what they had accomplished together in the late 1930s and early 40s while working for the West Virginia Department of Highways.

> Later, after I thought it over for several weeks, I called Morgan Massey and asked if I could talk to him privately. He flew in and I met with him at the cottage. The cottage, located at Chauncey Hollow, was Massey's private hideaway where many of Massey Coal's largest decisions had been made. By this time period, E. Morgan Massey was nearly running the entire operation. His father was phasing out of the day-to-day operation of the corporation.

> When we met, there was no one there but Morgan and me. We discussed the situation, and Morgan said, "Now Raymond, I don't really want you to quit. But if you want to go back to the state and work your retirement out, we would also like to keep you under our employment."

> I went back to the state, working part time for the West Virginia Alcohol and Beverage Commission. I was a beer inspector. I also worked for a while with the Labor Department.

> I was still Logan County Democratic chairman. I continued to work for Massey, as well. I never did go back to the state road.

Chapter Twenty-Nine

It Was November 22, 1963

It was a brisk, overcast morning when Bill Abraham, dressed in a dark charcoal suit, picked Chafin up at his home. When Abraham blew the car horn, Chafin, who was just finishing his breakfast, wiped his mouth and rolled down his shirtsleeves. He jumped up from the dinette, and Louise helped him put on his tattered overcoat. He pecked her on the cheek, dashed out the front door, and hopped inside Abraham's automobile.

"Ready?" Abraham asked.

"Go ahead. Hit it. We're already running' behind, and we haven't even started."

As the two left the Omar area, they discussed the schedule for the day and the list of issues they planned to discuss with Governor Wally Barron that afternoon. Abraham and Chafin took their time as they navigated along the sixty-eight miles of zigzag roadway leading to Marmet, West Virginia, and onward toward Charleston.

Chafin recalled the day and certain events:

> Bill was never one to worry about such things as schedules and such. He was almost always fashionably late for any appointment he ever had. As for me, I was an early riser and had a tendency to be early for meetings or duties. This particular day Bill was the driver, so I knew we wouldn't be too concerned with the time it took to get to Charleston.
>
> Bill and I headed to the State Capitol. Thinkin' back, I don't even remember what we were specifically going to see Governor Barron about, now. However, we used to spend a dime or fifteen cents at the tollbooths if we were in a hurry — we could save time by heading across the West Virginia Turnpike, near Marmet, and going on up to Charleston, but you have to pay to drive on it. Although we weren't particularly in a hurry, for some reason we drove the turnpike anyway.
>
> As we drove onto the highway, we stopped to pay our toll. The young fellow at the toll window said, "Did you hear President Kennedy was shot in Dallas? But they think he is still alive."
>
> I answered by saying, "Oh, no! What?"
>
> I glanced over at Bill. He was pale, and I thought he was goin' to die. We were both stunned by the news.

After the toll was paid, Abraham drove up a way and then pulled his car over to the highway shoulder.

"Oh, this is awful," he said, as he looked over at Raymond. "... Oh, my Lord!" Abraham said.

Chafin continued:

> We had never heard of anything like that before — at least not in our lifetimes. Both of us being politicians, we couldn't help but wonder what in the world would happen now. We sat there for three or four minutes and talked

about what we had just heard. Bill turned the car radio on and tried to pick up the latest news.

A newscaster on a Charleston radio station, who was barely able to keep his composure, said that President John F. Kennedy had been shot at Dealey Plaza, in downtown Dallas. The approximate time of the shooting was 12:30 p.m. Central Standard Time.

On the radio, we heard about a Dallas parade, something about a man named Lee Harvey Oswald, a motorcade, a grassy knoll, and that President Kennedy was shot in the back of the head with a high-powered rifle. We then learned he passed away. I immediately got physically ill over the news.

We weren't the only ones pulled off along the turnpike that day — there were cars, trucks, and semi-tractor trailers pulled off the highway as far as we could see in either direction.

When we got to the Statehouse, everything was closed and locked, including the governor's office. The parking lot 'round the Capitol complex was empty. An extremely unusual and creepy feeling came over me. That was a sad, sad day for America.

Louise and Margaret were both weeping uncontrollably when Bill dropped me off at my home that evening. I know that they felt like they knew him so well. We were all distraught. Since I met with him in person on several occasions, looked him directly in the eyes, and talked to him many times on the phone, I felt that I was close to him, too.

In later news reports, the country found out that it was Kenny O'Donnell who had the grim task of reporting to Vice President Lyndon B. Johnson that the president had passed away. O'Donnell went into the waiting room of the hospital where Johnson was waiting. As he entered the room, the vice president looked up at Kenny and asked how President Kennedy was doing. O'Donnell muttered, "He's gone."

Reflections On JFK

Chafin recalled:

Let me tell you this — whenever I called the White House, I got through to President Kennedy within five to ten minutes, unless he was out of town. If he were out, I would get a personal call at least by the next day. I talked directly to him. I felt honored to have had that kind of relationship with him.

On that November 22nd, I believed things would never be the same for West Virginia. In a way, they never were, either. By November 25th, he was buried at Arlington cemetery. I remember staying home to watch the blurry picture of the funeral procession on our black-and-white television; our reception wasn't very good. I think we walked around for weeks in a daze over what had happened.

We were just getting' the things done that we needed — including county roads, highways, and the food program. President Kennedy was a friend to West Virginia. He reminded me more of a governor than a president of these United

States in the way that he cared about us locally. We talked about him like he was family.

I guess I can only thank Senator Robert C. Byrd through that period of time. Senator Byrd courageously stepped up and took over after John Kennedy was gone. He fulfilled many of the same things that Kennedy had planned to do for us. Senator Byrd even went way beyond what anyone else would have done in the same situation.

After the assassination, Chafin was asked to give a recorded oral history interview, just as Claude Ellis had given for the Kennedy library archives. According to the John F. Kennedy Library and Museum, repeated attempts were made to secure an agreement with Chafin governing the use of the project once they had the finished interview. Nevertheless, they were never able to secure a full legal agreement with him. The library director eventually made the decision that the transcript files remain open for research purposes.

Chafin explained:

Well, I was extremely cautious of what I said at that time. There were still open wounds in this county over what I'd done in 1960. Some of the complete facts were too sensitive to include in that interview. I said as little as I could get by with.

Ellis Remembers the Assassination

Claude Ellis remembered exactly where he was when he learned about the assassination:

I was park supervisor for Chief Logan State Park at the time; the fellows I was managing, along with myself, were putting the public swimming pool in. I was on the side of the hill, building a water tank to catch enough water and then hook it up with the pool. I lived at the park at the time. My wife, Rosemary, came up to where we were at and told me what had happened. It was a terrible experience — terrible.

I immediately left the other workers and went home to watch what was happening on the television set. I didn't go back to work that day. I couldn't.

Looking back now, I think about what he could have accomplished had he lived. It was a terrible loss to the country, and to West Virginia.

Chapter Thirty

Abraham Runs on Republican Ticket

Recently Raymond Chafin sat back and reminisced about his lifetime political career from his dark maroon, well-broken-in sofa in the living room of his modest Cow Creek home:

In my political days, I've had some hard, hard decisions to make. Long ago, beginning even before I was county clerk, Bill Abraham was one of my best friends. He had a gift for smooth-talking people on a one-on-one basis. He was an outstandin' politician, and he had a big heart.

Bill helped me get organized at Omar. He was well liked when he ran for the Logan County Board of Education on the nonpartisan ticket. However, first time he ran, he was defeated. The second time he ran, I was in a little better position to help him. That time he won.

In my opinion, he was probably one of the best politicians we ever had in this county. He was on the school board and did a good job. He also helped me a lot personally, like when I was first elected as county clerk in 1963, since Bill was also a Democrat.

In 1964, there was a big political upheaval in the county. During this time, I was still county chairman as well as the new county clerk. The struggle escalated, developing into a partisan battle and a nightmare for my faction.

It ended up with the impeachment of the sheriff, Jack Ferrell. Ol' Jack had gotten into the bridge construction business while he was serving as sheriff of Logan County. Running a business of this type while maintaining this position of authority was considered to be a conflict of interest, so it was illegal. The Logan County Commission voted to impeach him.

I had to preside over the commission's county court: Red Bivens, Okey Hager, and William "Bill" Dingess. We met at my house. In order to get the Democratic organization unified, they first offered the position of sheriff to me.

I was already the Logan County clerk. I never yearned to be sheriff because at that time, after being elected and serving your four years in, you were out! You couldn't run for re-election.

Here we all were, in my living room, when I turned it down. Bill Dingess jumped up and said, "Well, if you're turning it down, I wanna be sheriff!"

What else could we do? I had other ideas, like nominating Bill Abraham, but Bill Dingess was on the court with us. So I remained quiet about Abraham and said, "Well, as far as I'm concerned, it's up to you two other members here. If they want to be fer ya, then I'll be fer ya, Bill."

"OK, we'll vote for Dingess," I remember Bivens and Hager stating.

I guess old Bill served as sheriff for the shortest term we ever had — maybe one, or no more than two days.

Bill Dingess had been in business putting in new power lines for the mining operations.

He did a lot of work for them. As you know from before, at that time you couldn't be a construction worker like that and be sheriff, too. After all, I guess that's what happened to the former sheriff — that's how it ended for him — although personally I don't think he [Jack Ferrell] had really done anything wrong.

Bus Perry once wrote concerning the issue: "In all fairness, I believe the impeachment of Jack Ferrell was strictly a political maneuver to break the power of the Logan County Democratic Executive Committee and let the anti-state group gain control of the organization."

Chafin stated:

Bill Dingess wanted Jack Ferrell's position. But once he was sheriff, he was left with the decision of whether to give up his construction business and stay with the position of county sheriff, or to give up the political power and prestige and go back to work for his construction operation.

His lawyers told him he'd be crazy to sell all of his holdings to be county sheriff.

When Dingess "slept on it" and thought about the difference in the pay and what he was going to lose, he decided he didn't want to be the sheriff after all. So we had to have another meeting at my house. We came up here so nobody would bother us.

The men, including Bill Dingess, Red Bivens, Okey Hager, and Bill Abraham, got together at Chafin's, out back of his home on his wooden deck, "under the rock cliff."

According to published accounts, the only thing that was different this time was that before the meeting, Chafin had already started lining up support for Bill Abraham.

Chafin remembered:

I asked ol' Bill Abraham, "Bill, I turned it down and Bill Dingess had to give it up. You're young in politics — how 'bout us supportin' you?"

"I kind of hate to give up the Board of Education position," Abraham answered. "But if they [the Democrats] are for me, I'll accept it."

Chafin said that they put Bill Abraham in as sheriff. It made some of the Democratic Executive Committee members upset. Chafin said that, "it also made a certain state senator mad. I won't mention his name because he's now dead and gone, God rest his soul."

Abraham went on to finish out Sheriff Ferrell's unexpired term. When the next election came near, it looked like another political storm was brewing.

When it was time to put Bill Abraham on the ballot for sheriff, the committee wouldn't put him on. They voted me plumb out as chairman for what I had done — placing Abraham in the sheriff position in the first place — and they named Dr. J.W. Ferrell, Sr., Jack Ferrell's dad, to the ticket.

Most of the people of the Democratic Party wanted Bill Abraham instead of Dr. Ferrell. I did, too, obviously. So when we couldn't get Bill on, Lloyd Brumfield, a leading Republican who had always been my friend in politics — except in the general election — came to see me.

"Raymond, if I can get the Republican Committee to put Bill Abraham on their ticket and persuade the majority of the Republicans to back him, what would you say?" Brumfield asked, as the two men stood in Chafin's front yard.

"Hey, you're puttin' me on the spot! The best friend I've got is Bill Abraham, and we're even neighbors! It will probably end my political career, but I could not be against Bill Abraham. If you put him on your ticket, I will support him," Chafin said, swallowing hard, barely able to believe the sound of the words coming out of his own mouth.

"Give me a little bit of time," Lloyd Brumfield requested of Chafin.

Immediately Brumfield went to work, hunting down prominent local Republicans, including Bob Samson, Neil McCloud, T.K. Killen, and Dallas Morrison, and explaining the situation in precise detail to each man. After discussing the pros and cons and then formulating a proposed political agenda, the group decided to meet later at Chafin's home to talk over the possibility of backing the Omar resident.

It didn't take long for the group to decide what their best option was — they would place former Democrat Abraham on the Republican ticket, to run in direct opposition to the Democratic Executive Committee's candidate for sheriff, Dr. J.W. Ferrell, Sr.

Chafin Supports Bill Abraham's Sheriff Bid

During that time, many of the Democratic leadership laughed at the thoughts of Bill Abraham flip-flopping and running as a Republican. They also chuckled at Chafin's awkward political position. However, they had underestimated the extensive cooperation that Abraham and Chafin were able to coordinate with the Republican Party.

Numerous rallies and town meetings were planned, while a massive door-to-door campaign was undertaken. Posters and brightly colored campaign signs were erected throughout the county. Literature was distributed. Faithful Republicans, including some of the most influential residents and businessmen, began making sequential list phone calls, until virtually every household was eventually contacted.

"We talked to people and gathered up money to fight with!" Chafin said. "Big money."

Loyal precinct captains were chosen carefully. Word of mouth was especially effective as Chafin and his cronies traveled from town to town, up and down hollow after hollow, spreading their party's platform. "Vote Abraham" was the war cry for the election season. Thousands listened, liked the message, and voiced their support.

Chafin recalled Bill Abraham being on the ticket:

We had the election, and Bill Abraham clearly won — by more than 1,000 votes. That made that whole bunch of Democrats sore at me, 'cause I supported the Republican cause. But, hey, he was a Democrat — he wasn't a Republican! He was masquerading in a Republican suit, for a very special reason: to win the election. Still, they [the controlling faction] got sore at me.

Chapter Thirty-One

Chafin Stops His Campaign

After Abraham won his bid for the sheriff's race in 1966, many of the local Democrats were mighty steamed at Chafin, who was county clerk at the time, for abandoning their candidate, J.W. Ferrell, Sr., and successfully campaigning for the GOP pick.

Chafin remembered:

> The next time I ran, in the 1968 primary, two years after this episode, I could sense the problems I had with the local Democrats. First, this one was against me, and then that one was hostile to me. They finally came out and decided to back Bill Anderson, a Logan County politician and businessman, to run against me! Now, he and I had always been the best of friends. I had supported him twice for the House of Delegates. I would have called myself fair with him.

Bill Anderson walked up to Chafin and said, "Now, Raymond, what are we going to do? The faction wants me to run against you! We got to make some kind of deal here."

"You go ahead and file," Chafin told him. "Then, Bill, we'll decide later on what we're going to do about this situation."

Chafin recollected:

> So Bill filed agin me for county clerk. At that time it only paid around $600 a month. I had to do other things to make it [during the previous term when I was county clerk]. If it hadn't been for my wife, Louise, teaching school, I could never have survived on that salary anyway.
> As a matter of fact, Bernard Smith and Red Hager came over, and we all went over to Charleston to talk to Governor Hulett C. Smith about this matter.

Hulett Smith moved into the governor's mansion in 1965, serving only one term. Chafin had supported and campaigned locally for Smith. Since Smith won the governor's race and because he was thankful for Chafin's assistance during his run for election, he had taken a liking to Chafin and kept close tabs on the state of politics in the county.

Smith, Hager, and Chafin jumped in Chafin's white Chrysler and drove over to the Capitol on a sunny Monday morning. When they arrived at the governor's doorstep, he was waiting for them and invited them into his office.

The men began to explain the situation in the county, and they asked Governor Smith for advice in the matter.

"Whatever you want to do, we're with you," Governor Smith said, as he made eye contact with Chafin. "But Chafe, if you want to go with the West Virginia Road Commission, we have a big position for you. We need you. We'll give you a job."

Chafin continued the story:

I agreed, and they set my salary at more than twice what I had been getting! I came back and told Bill Anderson, "I am quitting campaigning. You win! When this primary's over, I'll resign, and you can take the county clerk's office."

So we made a quiet deal — hush, hush. All I asked of Bill was, "Please don't change anybody in my office. These people were loyal to me, and they each did a good job. Keep them on."

We shook hands, and Bill agreed to honor my request. He said, "You're welcome in my office whenever you take a notion. My girls will be happy to help you."

I quit campaigning, and Bill won by 800 or 900 votes. That didn't embarrass me too much because, being a practical politician, I had learned that you don't storm off and cuss when you lose. Instead, you just wait for the next one and cut him back.

I went to Charleston to go to work as the new highway construction supervisor for the West Virginia Interstate System. I was satisfied.

Senator Jennings Randolph and Chafin

"He's dead now, but we need to remember ol' Senator Jennings Randolph," Raymond Chafin reflected, as he recalled spending personal time with the portly political leader.

One time I was in my office at the Logan County Courthouse, serving as county clerk, in the later 1960s, when the phone rang. I answered it, and it was United States Senator Jennings Randolph. It was two, maybe three weeks before the primary election.

"Raymond, I'm going to speak in the morning at 11 o'clock in Bluefield. Then I'm coming to Welch," Randolph said. "I need someone to meet up with me in Welch and bring me up there, to Logan, after I speak."

"Senator Randolph, it would be an honor to come and get you," I answered him. We continued to talk for a few minutes to make plans for the upcoming meeting, and then hung up.

Arnold Harkins was sitting in the office at the time I took that call. He had just recently bought himself a new car. After hearing me talk to Randolph, he said, "Why don't ya let me go with ya? You and the senator can ride in the backseat, and I'll be your chauffeur. Then you can talk to him on the way back here."

I agreed.

The idea of a private audience with the important senator thrilled Chafin. His political gears began to turn as he considered all he could talk about. In addition, his own jalopy was a little run-down at the time, and he knew he would have to get a tune-up if it was to make it to Welch and back.

Even though arrangements had already been taken care of, an exhilarated Chafin, almost giddy from the thought of being alone with Randolph, decided to call the senator back to reconfirm that he would indeed be in Welch the next day, "chauffeured in a brand-spankin'-new car," at whatever time he was needed.

I remember that Arnold and I went on over to Welch the next day. That car drove like a dream. Senator Randolph was already standing up and speaking when we went inside the Welch auditorium. When he saw us, he introduced Arnold and me to the crowd, telling them that we were eventually taking him to Logan.

After he finished his speech and greeted and shook hands with the people, we all left Welch and headed for Logan.

Arnold purposely drove a bit slow so that his friend Chafin could enjoy more time with the United States senator.

After an enjoyable trip, during which Chafin was able to casually talk about local politics and his concerns for the area, they finally arrived within Logan's city limits.

"R.W. Raike, the president of the First National Bank, met us," Chafin said. "I remember it as if it were yesterday."

Raike pulled Chafin off to the side when he got out of the car and whispered, "Hey, Chafe, why don't you bring Senator Randolph over to the Mezzanine for dinner, at Aracoma Drug Store? He can talk to all the guys there."

"Well, R.W., I can get him to come, but I don't want all you daggone Republicans jumpin' on him at one time!" Chafin retorted — half joking, half seriously — as he brushed Raike's hand off his arm. "If y'all start anything while we're there, I swear to goodness I'll grab up the senator and we'll go! I'll then deal with you later, Raike."

"Ah, we won't do that!" Raike promised, as he laughed. "I guarantee that none of us will say anything out of the way."

After they unloaded the senator's luggage, Chafin and Harkins took Senator Randolph over to the Mezzanine. Sure enough, Joe Fish, a powerful and vocal businessman and Republican at the time, was there with many of his colleagues. Fish was extremely well read on all the latest issues. Most of the others sitting around were diehard Republicans, too. Chafin, Harkins, and their guest, Senator Randolph, must have felt like field mice that had just walked into an angry lion's den, being that they were the only Democrats in the place.

As they walked across the threshold, the diner suddenly became silent. Everyone stopped whatever he was doing, and every eye in the restaurant became fixed on Randolph, Harkins, and Chafin. With each step, the wooden floor creaked and cracked as they made their way across the room. Attempting to greet people along the way, their voices seemed to sound abnormally loud — booming, echoing, and bouncing around, in stark contrast to the utter stillness from the other patrons. By the time they reached an open table, Chafin's cheeks were bright red from embarrassment. Chafin said that the room was just a little too quiet for his liking.

Arnold Harkins, Bill Abraham, and I were the only Democrats in the whole place, besides the senator himself. Bill Abraham then introduced Randolph to the crowd, adding that the senator was the chairman of the Senatorial Roads Commission.

"... and so, let us all give a round of applause to the good senator," Abraham announced. At that point, all the men in the room began to clap out of respect for Senator Randolph.

After Randolph greeted everyone and said a few carefully chosen words, R.W. Raike and others started to ask questions and discuss roads and highways with him. Joe Fish knew more than anyone else in the room about the inner-workings of the federal roads commission. Joe and the other Republicans in the room suggested a variety of ideas — surprisingly good suggestions — for creating a road program that would specifically affect southern West Virginia.

"They were well-behaved, as promised," Chafin said. "I was pretty dang surprised!"

Chafin, Hawkins, and Abraham were delighted that the local Republicans, who were well-known for heckling other Democrats in days gone by, were respectful and had used the time wisely to come up with several worthwhile proposals.

The rest of the night went well for Chafin. Visiting with this political idol, he was able to help persuade Senator Randolph to spend several days in Logan. He continued to discuss the possibilities of a workable highway plan with both Republicans and Democrats. It seemed that Randolph had stumbled into a nonpartisan situation where all concerned were willing to work together — maybe for the first time — in order to help West Virginia move forward.

Chafin smiled as he recalled:

> When Senator Randolph returned to Washington, D.C., a few days later, he introduced a bill for the Appalachian Road System. The aggressive bill consisted of many of the specific ideas that had been presented at the Mezzanine in Logan. Working together, Senators Randolph and Byrd got it approved! That's when the corridor system really started. It's kinda funny, and I hate to admit it, but it all started at a Republican meeting in Logan.

Since President Lyndon B. Johnson did not seek another term in office, Chafin figured he would probably support Robert F. Kennedy in his run for the White House in 1968.

Chafin was especially excited about the idea of campaigning for another Kennedy. He felt certain that he could connect with Kennedy, just as he did with his brother eight years previously. Although he didn't know Bobby well, he felt that surely he would have the inside track. He even wondered if maybe there might even be political cash — big money — coming his way again.

In the spring of 1968, Bobby Kennedy, who sharply disagreed with the course of action of President Johnson and Vice President Humphrey, campaigned for the Democratic Party nomination. By June, he had won major primaries in Indiana, Nebraska, and California. Upon departing a political celebration in Los Angeles, after the victory in the California primary was certain, the now infamous Jordanian Sirhan Sirhan shot the young presidential hopeful. He died the following day, on June 6, 1968.

Chafin was distraught by the news of another Kennedy's death. He wondered, along with many other Americans, what was happening in the United States of America — a nation in turmoil.

It was a stressful and discontented time in our nation's history. Only a couple of months before, on April 4, 1968, a sniper had assassinated black civil rights leader Dr. Martin Luther King, Jr.

Now both Kennedy men had been shot and killed. The world seemed as if it were churning out of control. Students were demonstrating at campuses across the nation, displaying peace signs and chanting slogans of "Make Love, Not War." The militant Black Panther Party was growing in significant numbers. Some African-American groups around the nation — intending to protest inequality — participated in marches that often turned into violent rioting. Bizarre cults and sects were springing up across the country. As far as Chafin was concerned, the hippie culture, flower children, and the rock-and-roll lifestyle were changing the face of a nation he loved. In his eyes, society seemed to be crumbling.

Besides the country's internal unrest, Walter Cronkite described the atrocities and carnage of war nightly on the 6 o'clock news on CBS. Over 36,000 young men and women from West Virginia were serving their country on unfamiliar soil, in a strange tropical place called Vietnam. Many of these Mountaineers never returned home to Appalachia.

As Bob Dylan's lyrics during that era appropriately said, "The times, they are a-changin'."

Claude Ellis & Raamie Barker Remember Bobby

Claude Ellis still has vivid memories of Robert Kennedy:

I remember that I was with Bobby Kennedy one week before he was killed. I doubt he had the contacts that Jack Kennedy had during his campaign. I also don't think Bobby was quite as personable as his brother — although he did have a dry sense of humor. You know, I doubt that anyone could have beat JFK when it came to his ability to be likable and charming. I have never seen anyone put himself across to the people any better than John Kennedy. But even though they were very different people, Bobby still did a good job in his own right. Bobby was campaigning in the state, and he made a short stop here in Logan.

It was a sharp young dark-haired local politician, Raamie Barker, the son of influential Chapmanville educator Shag Barker, who handled the Robert Kennedy For President campaign in Logan County.

Raamie Barker, who is now the administrative assistant for Senate President-Leiutenant Governor Earl Ray Tomblin, spoke about the time period:

It was a very bright and sunny day in downtown Logan on the day before Easter 1968 when I met Bobby Kennedy on Stratton Street in front of the Logan County Courthouse.
He was sitting on the top of the back seat of a mid-size convertible. It was at the end of a short entrance-into-Logan parade when we were introduced briefly. One of my assignments that day was to escort him to the platform, a flatbed truck, parked just around the corner where about 7,000 Logan Countians and

West Virginians were waiting to greet him. It was an electric moment. People were packed in around us 10-15 deep. It was one of those events you never forget and can relive many times over just as vividly as if it just happened.

It had been about a week before I was informed by a Logan Democratic faction led by Tom Godby, Bill Abraham and Claude Ellis, that Kennedy was coming to Logan and that by virtue of Claude Ellis' longstanding relationship with the Kennedys, this faction of Democrats would host the event. They considered it a big political coup in the primary election because of the status of the Democratic presidential candidate coming to Logan, and the county's history and involvement with Kennedy's slain brother, John F. Kennedy, and his successful run for the presidency in 1960. Kennedy's chances looked good for a repeat of his brother's success because it had only been a few days since Lyndon Johnson announced he would not seek re-election in order to focus on a peace initiative to end the war in Vietnam.

The visit provided a great deal of free publicity in the media, associated the candidates being backed by that faction with an almost god-like figure, politically speaking, and how else could you assemble a crowd that large for a partisan gathering?!

I was informed of the visit and my role in it by Godby, Abraham and Ellis at a meeting with Kennedy's advance team, which included a world ranked amateur tennis champion, Donald Dell, among others. They told me they wanted me to serve as co-chairman of the New York Senator's Logan campaign along with Man resident Roberta Kendall. Of course, I was elated—I was a dyed-in-the-wool Kennedy man, and about to vote in my first presidential primary, just a shade under 21 years of age.

During the meeting they explained I had been picked to introduce Senator Kennedy — a complete, but very well received, surprise. I was selected because of my draft age status and because of the facts that I was a college student, ready to graduate, someone with young Democrat status, active in politics, and that I was a non-Catholic — more specifically, a Baptist. The opportunity was something I literally dreamed about, but was absolutely certain would never happen. They just didn't let a kid like me do those things — they are usually reserved for the "big boys" in politics, and heck, I was so wet behind the ears they couldn't keep enough towels around to dry me off.

I was told Senator Kennedy wanted to be identified with those particular demographics in politics because of the nature of the times and because a great many new voters were entering the body politic with the same demographic description I possessed. It made no difference to me — I was getting the chance to meet and to introduce the man whom I felt would be the next President of the United States of America—Robert Francis Kennedy.

Told to keep the introduction short, I knew I had to tie him to the effort JFK brought to us in 1960, even though I was then only in the ninth grade at Chapmanville High School. I had also been told to meet him at the convertible and personally escort him to the stage. He didn't like police escorts and wanted an average person to accompany him. They also told me that because people want to touch and shake hands with him, that they sometimes would literally grab at him, and that he had actually even fallen to the ground on occasion. They told me that if that happened to grab him around the waist (they even showed me how to do it) and just plow through the crowd.

As he disembarked the vehicle, he stuck out his hand and said "How are you doin', Raamie? Glad to have you on board with us. Which way do we go?" I said something stupid, I am certain, but pointed the way and we began to move. The Logan police chief and a county constable came up to the car and took him by the elbow to move him through the crowd, but he pulled away, saying, "Raamie will get me to where we are going." I moved in and we moved on slowly through the crowd, which performed as expected. I did have to help keep him on his feet. At six-foot-two inches tall and a good 40 pounds heavier than he was, I had no trouble keeping him going. One of the things which amazed me most was how much smaller he was than I.

When we topped the stairs to the flat bed truck, a roar went up from the crowd that was deafening. I was struck by how many young people had camped in closely to the flatbed to get a chance to shake his hand. He would reach down and 20 arms would come to meet him. I scanned across the crowd and it was a mass of human beings as far as the eye could see down each street, even into the side streets—no way for automobile traffic to move in or out.

On the rooftops of a couple of buildings you could see some police with rifles or shotguns. There had been a few threats phoned in, but no one really took them seriously. I could just imagine in my mind what would happen if someone set off a firecracker and some dummy with an itchy trigger finger would begin firing at the platform, killing us all. How little did I realize then that my fears would become reality in the kitchen of a Los Angeles hotel about six weeks later.

There were a few formalities in the program that had to be taken care of and it was, as a matter of fact, a pretty heady experience to that point. I was rehearsing what I would say when it came time to introduce Senator Kennedy, but in order for some of the politicians to get their chance to be recognized, one introduced another, who introduced me, and then, shaking in my shoes, I managed to speak into the microphone: "My fellow Logan Countians, eight years ago today a young man from Boston came to Logan County with a dream — a dream for you and I. Today his brother comes to fulfill that dream. Ladies and gentlemen, the next President of the United States of America — Robert F. Kennedy…" The crowd cheered and Kennedy took the rostrum.

I really don't know how it could have been shorter or sweeter — the Kennedy legacy, picking up the torch for the next generation of Americans; the ideals and icons of the succession of brother to brother was interwoven in those words, which, after all the brooding I did about it, were just spontaneous remarks. I was glad to be past that part and to just get to hear the great man speak.

As he prepared to wind his way to his stump speech, a collection of statements about the issues he wanted to focus upon, Senator Kennedy took the time to thank Claude Ellis for his help that day, as well as for his help in getting President Kennedy elected. He noted in his remarks that West Virginia made the

211

difference in the election because it shot down the walls of religious prejudice — a 97 percent non-Catholic population supporting a Roman Catholic — not by a mere margin, but by a landslide. He referred to being in Logan and in West Virginia as "it's good to be here, back home in West Virginia."

He also took time to mention several on the platform including Tony Hylton, son of Logan Banner Managing Editor Charlie Hylton, who was on his way to Vietnam. It provided an excellent backdrop for Senator Kennedy's views on ending the war.

And, in a surprise to me, thanked Roberta Kendall and me for the work that we were doing — and would be doing — for him in the weeks to come. He even asked the crowd to give me some applause, and it did. My head was inflating by the seconds.

As he talked about housing, the war, the need to improve the quality of life for all Americans and what we should be doing in the struggle for Civil Rights, Senator Kennedy peeled on and on, intermingling the popular quotations he often used in speeches of great philosophers and poets of times past. I was listening, but I was also observing — the crowd and the stark devoted attention they were giving to his every word and to him as he spoke.

I was seated immediately to his left and could see the crowd and see what he saw. I noticed the little shake in his hands as he spoke — I think the man actually was experiencing a little stage fright. Then, I also noticed, scratches on the back of his hands and some small scars and bruises in the same location — the toll of shaking hands with folks in a large crowd, which put things in perspective that this is a human being and not some sort of infallible and indefatigable figure. There is a price to pay for fame and for public service.

In about 15 minutes it was all over and Senator Kennedy began the handshakes and moved toward the end of the platform. My job was over and so was my special place in the history of Logan County. It took him longer to get off the platform and to his vehicle than it took him to speak, but just as he began to step down, he turned around and caught my eye, waved and said, with thumbs up, "thanks for your help."

I saw him later in Charleston, at the Municipal Auditorium, where I was invited to sit on the stage with him where he would make a major address on foreign policy. I had the choicest seat, just to the left of the podium, looking out on a packed house of some of the best known names of Democratic circles, including a young member of the West Virginia House of Delegates at that time, by the name of Jay Rockefeller.

As an aside to the story of the events that day, I was enabled to go to Charleston with the help of Assessor Tom Godby. The old heap of a car that I owned was broken down and I was, in the popular vernacular, "without wheels." Tom asked me after the rally in Logan if I was planning to go to Charleston, to sit on the stage while Kennedy spoke, and I told him I couldn't because of car problems; he pointed to his car and said "hop in, we're going." And, we did. I had a lot of fun with "Big Foot" that night and learned a lot about politics, and some of the old war stories he shared with me would make another book. But, it was the end of a long and memorable day I shall never forget.

***

Kenny O'Donnell was handling Bobby's national campaign, as he had organized and scheduled Jack's run for the presidency. After JFK's death, O'Donnell was named chairman of the National Democratic Executive Committee in 1964. But at first word that Bobby was ready to throw his hat in the ring, O'Donnell became involved and committed to the cause.

Claude Ellis recalled Bobby Kennedy's arrival in Logan:

> By this time Bill Abraham was the county sheriff. Sheriff Abraham sent Deputy Sheriff James Major and another deputy to pick up Robert Kennedy at Taplin Airport. They brought him into Logan.

Much like a replay of the 1960 campaign, nearly all of Logan County came to see another Kennedy up close. This time it was Bobby, the former attorney general, who was ready to speak to the people of Logan about a need for change within the Democratic Party.

Ellis remembered the event:

> Bus Perry, a very young Raamie Barker, and I were on stage with Bobby at the courthouse, near McCormick's department store, and the people of the city were extremely excited to catch a glimpse of a Kennedy at the rally.

In his speech, Kennedy clearly outlined his own ideas for a better America before the crowd of onlookers. Logan County heard, applauded, and approved.

Ellis continued:

> I met with him that day and introduced him around. Several of us took him down to the courthouse, and he met with people along the sidewalk. He had a captivating smile.

After his visit in Logan County, Kennedy left and worked his way up the curvy road to the State Capitol. Ellis went on:

> A bit over a month or so later I was at the Daniel Boone Hotel in Charleston with other politicians when we got the word that he was killed in California. I was completely devastated. I knew all of them — John, Bobby, Teddy, Sargent Shriver, and even the Kennedy sisters — and it was like losing a close family member. I had been in touch with all of them and had worked with each of them in one way or another.
>
> In that period of time I was still working with the same basic faction I had been with in 1960. Earlier, it hadn't been too long after John Kennedy's death that Robert started out on the campaign trail, and he ended up here in Logan. To me, that's how his campaign really started out. Like his brother, he placed an emphasis on West Virginia.

Raamie Barker also remembered Bobby's untimely death, and added:

> Of course the news of Robert Kennedy's death came as a shock, but really not a surprise, even though it is as tragic as news can get. Nothing really surprises me these days, but many things are shocking. We lost the hope and promise of two great, but yet, unfulfilled lives. It is tragic in and of itself, to lose leadership in a time of great national chaos and danger, even more tragic because the action of individuals or an individual denied us the choices we should be allowed to make in a democracy.
>
> Lost as well were Robert Kennedy's chances of fulfilling his late brother's dream. It is ironic that he entered the race too late in West Virginia to be involved in the Presidential Preference Primary and was stumping for delegate votes. It proved to be difficult to gain a majority of those votes with delegates who were directly elected, because they were not identified on the ballot as to which candidate they supported, a requirement now made effective in current law.
>
> And, with Lyndon Johnson's dislike for Robert Kennedy and the organization which stayed with the Senator, the White House and that faction of national Democrats were supporting Vice President Hubert Humphrey's bid, and they were delivering delegations enmass to Humphrey's side. It would have been a long and hard uphill battle for Kennedy to win the nomination in Chicago. But, those questions were answered with the sounds of bullets and gunfire and the sudden and unexpected silence accompanying an end to a hopeful campaign. Of course the rest is history: Hubert Humphrey was nominated and lost in a very close election; Vietnam continued another four years; Watergate ended in Nixon's resignation; and the country stagnated economically until the 80s, when conservatism took control of the ballot box and the Reagan "revolution" began.
>
> Personally, though, it was like a part of my own life had died, leaving memories, the dreams of what might have been, and the challenge to try to always do the right thing by the people who share the same hope, as well as to guarantee collectively the great blessings of living in the United States of America — many who believed that RFK held the answers to the national pain we were enduring.

Chafin Chooses Humphrey, Again

After Robert Kennedy's murder, Raymond Chafin wasted little time. His faction had not yet officially endorsed anyone for president. Therefore, he quickly moved all political support toward Vice President Hubert Humphrey. Even though things hadn't worked out in the 1960 campaign between Humphrey and Chafin, Chafin actively pushed to see Humphrey in the White House this time. The majority of Logan County's registered voters also supported Vice President Humphrey now that Robert was gone.

Chafin said:

> I liked ol' Humphrey. He was a slick ol' politician and a fine Vice President during the LBJ administration. Sometimes I think he had more political savvy than John Kennedy. I believed with everything in me that he would take the presidency in 1968. I wanted to accept as truth that he trusted me this time 'round, too. I know he had the support of Logan County. I didn't make the famous switcharoo this time, either.

Humphrey eventually became the Democratic Party's nominee, but Richard M. Nixon narrowly defeated him in the general election.

Chafin recalled the election:

> The Nixon and Humphrey race was pretty darn close, but our man lost in the end. Then we had Richard Nixon in power again — and everybody knows what happened there: Watergate. What a fiasco.

After the defeat, Humphrey returned to Minnesota to teach at the University of Minnesota and Macalester College. He returned to the U.S. Senate in 1971, and he won re-election in 1976. He died January 13, 1978 of cancer. After Humphrey's demise, the governor of Minnesota appointed Humphrey's wife, Muriel Buck Humphrey, to fill the vacant Senate seat. She served until November 7, 1978, and was not a candidate for the unexpired term.

Chafin continued:

> Once Humphrey lost his presidential bid to Nixon, I knew his chances for the White House were over. I think at first he was a flogged pup; however, he soon pulled himself back together. I hate that he never had the opportunity to serve in the Oval Office. I believe he would have been a great president. I'm certain that things like that Watergate debacle would have never occurred. Humphrey was too slick for that. It was hurtful for Louise and me on the day he died.

Chapter Thirty-Two
Headed for Florida

Chafin said that by the late 1960s, when he reached his midlife years, he started thinking about retirement. Around that time, he and his wife Louise started talking more and more about slowing down — especially after each summer vacation. After a lot of consideration, they decided that he would retire first because of his pension and investments. Besides, he hadn't been feeling well for a while.

They knew that they would travel as long as their good health held out. They reached a decision that Chafin could head down to Florida alone in November, after his retirement, and return when the weather warmed up, and that this would probably be an annual event up until Louise was ready to retire, too.

Chafin described his retirement:

> I retired in the early 1970s, and we bought the motor home we always dreamed of. Actually, I bought the "Cadillac" of all motor homes. Ah, it was a nice 'un, too.
>
> By the time I retired I had been working for Seth Phillips at Belva Coal Company. I was feeling mighty sick all the time. I had a bit of black lung, and it was workin' on me — bad. The doctor had refused me when I tested for the mines, but 'cause Seth needed me in the worst way for his strip job, I was able to work there for about two years anyway. When I started there, Belva was running fifteen railroad cars of coal a shift or less. When I left, we were running fifty-five cars on the second shift, with a total of approximately eighty cars of coal a day. Now, you didn't have the one-hundred-ton cars like they have nowadays. We only had fifty-, sixty-, and seventy-ton cars at the time. They may have just come out with the eighty-ton cars around the time I ended my career.
>
> I think retiring to Florida really helped me. Up until that time, I don't believe I ever took a vacation — well, not a relaxing vacation. When I took vacations I always had so much on my mind, usually politics, that I found it hard to rest and relax.
>
> I think a lot of men can't take a real vacation because they worry too much about what's happening at the job. However, when one really retires, you can finally, finally, finally let go.
>
> First thing after I retired, I went on down to Florida and stayed for two or three months. But without Louise, I decided this wasn't the life for me. Louise was still teachin' at the time. So I came back — cuttin' my whole trip a little short — and I told Louise, "Hey, you gots to quit and go with me."
>
> "Well, the teachers just got a raise. I'd like to teach another year or two and build up my pension," Louise answered.
>
> "Forget about that ol' pension. You are going south with me! I don't like goin' down thar all alone. I want you to go down with me and enjoy it!" I told her. I continued to "bellyache" and aggravate that poor woman for several weeks until I finally persuaded her to retire, too.

Louise worked one complete school year after Chafin retired. Then, according to Chafin, they had a great time:

> Finally, when Louise retired, too, we toured all through Florida. We had a Chrysler Simca that we towed behind the home on wheels. We had a hook on the back so that we could hook up the car in a minute and take her loose in a half-minute. We just went anywhere we wanted to go in the state. Mom was still living at that time, and she was still in pretty good shape. She sort of watched out for everything in Barnabus while we were gone.
>
> When we got to Florida, we'd often pull into these supermarket parking lots and spend the night there. If it weren't too hot, we wouldn't worry about cooling the home down. We had air conditioning, but we didn't want to sit there with the motor running all the time in order to get it. So we did without when we were on a parking lot. We might stay at a store's parking lot for a night or two, then we'd go find ourselves a campground. We'd drain the sewage tank, fill up with water, and get our bottled gas. After a night or so, we'd search for another parking lot, maybe at Kmart, A&P, or Krogers.
>
> This motor home was all self-contained, using bottled gas or electric for cooking and refrigeration. It also had an electric grill. We even had a deep freeze, maybe two foot by three foot. We could freeze that contraption up when we stayed at the campgrounds, and it would keep all our meats and other things good for several days, before we hooked 'er up again.
>
> We made our headquarters in Fort Meyers. That's where we actually got our mail. But we traveled a whole lot. We went to Fort Meyers every November, and we returned to Cow Creek in April. Of course, I was involved in politics year 'round. But in the winter months, I did all my work by telephone.
>
> Louise would often cook while we were goin' down the road. She'd throw a big ol' towel on the kitchen table so nothing would vibrate or scoot off the table while I drove along. If we had another couple with us, one might drive while the others ate, and then we'd switched places.
>
> We went to a lot of big shows while we were down there. We got to see a lot of big-name movie stars during that time. We'd watch the newspapers. When we read that a movie actor was going to be somewhere close that night, or maybe the next week, we'd call ahead and get ourselves tickets.
>
> My cousin Henry Justice and his wife, Pearl, did most of the traveling with us in the early days. Henry was the retired principal from Chapmanville High School. We all got along real well, and we had a heck of a time on our trips.
>
> When we went, we split the expenses. Anything that we spent on the motor home — gasoline, oil, or food for the deep freeze — we'd split fifty-fifty. When we wanted to stop off and get us a meal at a restaurant, we made us an agreement: everybody pays fer their own. If I wan' a steak, I wan' a steak! If somebody else wants a little hamburger, let him or her have that ol' hamburger — as long as I'm eating my T-bone. That's the way we operated.
>
> My brother Elbert, Jr. lived up in Indiana. In the early summer when we would get bored around here, Louise and I might head for Indiana to visit him

for a week or so. Henry and Pearl would follow us, too. When we'd get there, we'd pull into his yard and hook up the motor home to Junior's trailer, and we'd sleep out in the home on wheels.

Chafin said that whenever he would travel to Elbert's, he'd visit the Amish villages in the area.

Henry, Pearl, Louise, and I all loved to go out to the Amish region. I always loved farms, and Louise did, too.

We went out there one time, and one of the families asked us in to eat with them since they had seen us around there so many times in the past. We went into their dining room and sat down. They didn't have electricity, but they used oil lamps. It was like ol' times when I was a young'un.

When Chafin, Henry, and their wives walked inside the screen door, they couldn't believe the dinner table. It was chock-full of wonderful-looking meats, gravies, cooked vegetables, casseroles, assorted desserts, and homemade breads. The various smells were equally delightful. They all hurried to take their seat, and the head of the home said the blessing, "Heavenly Father, thank you for this wondrous bounty and for these special friends who have come to fellowship with us today. Amen."

Chafin reminisced:

They had smoked ham — oh, ol' fashioned smoked hams like my g'ma and grandpa used to smoke. My dad and mother smoked 'em, too, right here on Cow Creek.

They made us fried potatoes, as brown and crisp as you ever ate! They had black-eyed peas, cornbread, and rolls – 'bout any kind of bread you could ask for. They had a big, long dinner table. When Louise, Pearl, Henry, or I wanted something, one of the farmer's daughters would wait on us. She'd pick up a giant platter and bring it around. She'd get the meat or vegetables off for us, or we could rake it off onto our plate. Everything was heaved high on platters — including pork chops.

Chafin said they were a large Amish family — with a bunch of children "stair-stepping" in height and age — ranging from approximately five years old to twenty.

He said that, in his opinion, dinner would have to have been the best meal he'd ever had. When they were nearly finished with supper, Chafin told the head of the home that he would like to purchase one of those smoked hams.

We got up and he took me outside and showed me his hams and bacon, with maybe eight or ten hams hanging in his smokehouse. The hams were tied up tight in burlap sacks, and I asked him, "What's this burlap for? Why do you do that?"

"Well, that's to keep flies and insects off the meat," he answered.

I told him again that I'd seriously like for him to sell me a couple of the hams and a side of bacon, but the ol' farmer said, "No, sir, I'm not interested — those are fer my family."

"I'll pay you a good price for 'em," I said.

"Don't try to bribe me," the farmer responded, almost angrily.

"Sorry, I wasn't tryin' to entice ya. I just thought it would be nice to have a real Amish ham or two. That was so good."

"Tell you what I'll do," he purposed, "... later in the year, when I kill my hogs and everything is smoked, cured, and I got 'em ready, I'll send you a couple hams and a couple sides of my bacon. I'll send you the meat and a bill, and you send me a certified check for all of that."

Then he called his oldest daughter into the smokehouse to get our West Virginia address. He promised he would try to get the hams to us before November 15th, when we usually left for Florida for the winter, then we shook on the deal.

After we visited for a while longer, we thanked the family for their hospitality and left the farm.

Several months later, I had nearly forgot about ordering the Amish hams. One day UPS pulled in here when we were packing up and getting ready to travel south.

When I opened up this big, heavy box, I was never so surprised in my life — beautiful smoked hams and sides of bacon, just like I'd asked for. The bill was inside, all right, but the price was really low — nearly nothing per pound. Henry and Pearl came up, and we went fifty-fifty on the meat.

I asked Henry what he thought we should do with all this meat because we were getting ready to go. We finally decided what to do.

Ol' Kirk Halstead lived across from me in a trailer that he rented from me. I called him over, and when he got to the house, I asked him if he wanted one of the hams and some of the bacon.

Kirk said, "Lord, have mercy. Yessiree-bob, if I can afford it. How much you want fer it?"

When I told him the price, he laughed out loud and yelled, "Yessir! Yessir! You better believe I'll buy it!"

We put the rest of the Amish bacon and ham in the back of Henry's car and took off for Florida for the winter.

I believe that was the first time I took Interstate 75. We definitely had plenty of wonderful food for the trip, thanks to that kind ol' Amish family.

Vegetable Stands and Bartering With Tomatoes

Raymond, Henry, Louise, and Pearl were amazed at the number of produce stands and fields with "Pick Your Own..." signs along the road to Florida.

You could just drive along the road anywhere and buy yourself some fresh vegetables — beans, tomatoes, strawberries, peaches, anything! I guess they outlawed that now — no peddlin' on the roads. But it was much different back then.

I told the rest of them that I was going to drive on out to see those Everglades. Along the way we saw a tomato patch about a mile long and a mile wide. There was a sign in the field that said, "ALL YOU CAN PICK: 10¢ A POUND."

Shoot, tomatoes were forty, fifty, even sixty cents a pound back home. We were pretty excited!

He pulled beside the road, and the older fellow who owned the field walked over and motioned with his arms to the left, and said, "Hi, folks. Over here is one kind of 'mater," and then he motioned to the right and said, "Way over yonder 'tis another. Y'all get them with your hands, or we have baskets you can borrow. Get all you want."

Chafin said he jumped out of the motor home and went out and picked four or five good ones and came back to the owner to have the tomatoes weighed.

Chafin said, grinning as he told the tale:

Henry, Pearl, and Louise got carried away. They came back packing all that they could possibly carry in their arms and sweaters — maybe five, six, or seven pounds apiece. By the time they finally got to the checkout, we had forty or fifty pounds worth of 'maters!

Chafin laughingly asked them what they were going to do with that many tomatoes. They all shrugged. However, they all seemed pleased and especially content that they had gotten such a good price.

We went on down the road a little further, and there was a field of sweet corn. Henry turned over toward all of us and said, "Now y'all listen here. Let's just pick us a few ears of corn here — not another fifty pounds worth. We're not loadin' down this time."

We all laughed, but Henry especially tickled me. He was a trader from way back. He was raised over at Delbarton, West Virginia, up the head of a long holler, and he was used to barterin' when need be. When we stopped, Henry asked the young caretaker of the field, "How much is it an ear?"

"Five cents an ear," the teenager said. "That's if you pick 'em yourself."

"Hey, you wouldn't consider swappin' some of that corn for some of our tomatoes, would you?"

At that point, every one of us inside the motor home snickered at Henry, and his wife, Pearl, blushed.

"Yeah, you got tomatoes?" the boy said. "I'll trade with ya!"

So Henry traded eight or so tomatoes for some of the fellow's sweet corn, while we all watched in amazement. Eventually we pulled that twenty-eight-foot rig back out onto the highway and drove a little farther down the road. After about five or six miles, we came up along an enormous field of pole beans — with straight rows of beans as far the eye could see. Henry nudged me and whispered, "Pull on over, Chafe. Let's get us some pole beans, too."

Tough Boys

There was a little Mexican man out by a roadside stand by himself at this one. Henry yelled out the passenger's side window, "Sir, we ain't got a lot of money. Could we trade you a few 'maters for some of your beans?"

Henry held up some of the nice tomatoes. "Si! I take tomatoes! Gracias. Take beans you want! Si! Come!" the farmer answered with a heavy accent.

Over the course of a few hours, we were able to get rid of at least thirty pounds of ripe tomatoes, keeping only what we felt we could use. Ol' Henry, the hillbilly horse trader of the group, was able to trade for plenty of corn and beans. We had enough fresh produce to last for the next week or so!

We always had the best time with Henry and Pearl. We were almost like kids again.

Chafin recalled other memories about his travels:

A haircut was seventy-five cents down in Florida back then. Henry was the first one to find the bargain. The fellow he found was a barber and a watermelon farmer. But he was good. We paid as much as eighty-five cents to a buck and a quarter back home, so that was a deal.

We saved money by going down South. You won't believe this, but Louise and I went to Florida and lived the life of Riley in the 1970s for a lot less. One could go out there and get nearly anything that you wanted to eat, right along the road. We could also stop along the road and fish in the canals. We liked to catch these certain fish that Louise called jailhouse fish 'cause they were striped all the way around.

We would catch a mess of fish, and Henry and I would filet 'em and fry 'em, and by dark, we'd have somethin' good to eat. They were the best eatin' fish that you ever had. We also learned all about oysters, found in big clusters in the canal. They looked like "red dog" [a form of coal] to me when they were all joined together. They were good when you rolled 'em in flour and fried 'em up, too.

The motor home had everything you could ask for. Later, I sold it and bought a big thirty-foot camper. It was nice, too. So, through the years, we've had it all.

According to Chafin, the best thing to have when you're traveling is a good CB radio. As he explained, you can get "three or four miles away from one another and still not get yourself lost."

We kept a CB on all the time. So did Henry and Pearl when they followed us down. My handle on the radio was "Shovel-Runner," and Henry's was "Mr. J" 'cause that's what the kids used to call him at school.

We were once traveling through Florida. The motor home had a sign on the front that said "Raymond and Louise Chafin."

All of a sudden I heard somebody say on the radio, "Breaker, breaker, break…."

221

I looked over at Henry and laughed. I recognized the voice coming through the CB speaker. It was one of the radio personalities — a disc jockey from WVOW radio in Logan. We talked a lot on the CB when we were in Logan County. He must have been vacationing, too. So I got on the CB and responded back to him, "10-4, good buddy, come on — who we got here?"

"This is the Radioman! So whom do we have here? 10-4."

"You gots the Shovel-Runner!"

"Boy, looky at this signal! I am really gettin' out!" Radioman answered. He was wonderin' how he could be in Florida talking to Shovel-Runner all the way back in Logan County.

"Yessir, you sure are, good buddy!" I answered him.

Then he asked, "Where you at?"

"Up on Cow Creek at my base station, where else?" I told him, as I tried to keep from crackin' up. Within a few minutes, only a few miles ahead, the Radioman was sitting alongside the road as we whizzed by in that big ol' motor home with our names on the front! I laid on the horn for several seconds and waved.

"Hey! Wait a minute here, you ol' coot!" Radioman hollered on the CB microphone.

We all busted out laughing as we headed on down I-75.

"So long, good buddy, the Shovel-Runner's gotta go!" I called back, as I let out a big chuckle. "Over and out!"

Chapter Thirty-Three
Where's Hoss?

The year was 1972, and South Dakota Senator George McGovern had not yet won the Democratic presidential nomination. Raymond Chafin was back in Logan County showing his support, campaigning locally, for McGovern — all the way through the primary and into the general election. Chafin and Hubert Humphrey had long patched up their differences from the 1960 campaign. However, even though Humphrey again ran for his party's nomination, Chafin didn't think he could win, so he chose to support McGovern for president.

Chafin said that one time, maybe a month before the general election, he got a call from campaign headquarters to meet McGovern at the top of the hill, at a strip mine operation at Rum Creek, near Kelly Mountain. Everything had already been organized for McGovern, and everyone in Logan expected him to speak on the courthouse steps that afternoon.

Then a while later, Raymond got a second call from the same campaign worker, saying that McGovern unfortunately couldn't make it. However, Lorne Greene, the handsome, white-haired actor who played Ben Cartwright on the television show "Bonanza," was going to come to Logan County to speak in McGovern's behalf.

As soon as Chafin's daughter, Margaret heard the news, she said, "Oh, Daddy, I wanna see Lorne Greene!" Chafin remembered the occasion:

> My daughter, Margaret, and her son, Joshua — my little grandson — went with me to meet Lorne and his wife. Joshua was still in diapers then. I also took Bus Perry with me, 'cause Bus was smart and educated. He had a degree in every kind of political science.
>
> It was a cold, windy day, but the sun was shinin'. We went up there to wait on them. For the occasion, we got us one of those big cars to chauffeur him back to Logan with. Lorne liked those big limousines, ya know.

When the small aircraft topped the mountain, Margaret was extremely excited. Chafin straightened his tie, took a deep breath, and rushed toward the plane as it prepared to land on the mountaintop in order to welcome the famous visitor to West Virginia.

Because news had traveled fast, there were several dozen cars and pickups full of people waiting at the same spot. All were hoping to catch a glimpse of the patriarch of the Cartwright family when he arrived on West Virginia soil.

Chafin continued:

> Lorne knew all about me even though he had never met me before! The McGovern campaign people must have pointed me out to him, on the inside of that plane, 'cause Lorne came walking directly to me. He took Joshua up in his arms and he greeted us all. His wife was a full-stock American Indian and a very nice person, too. We stood around and talked for about five minutes, up on that hill that overlooks the valley below. Then I escorted him to my car so that I

could take him down to the county courthouse. We were already late, so I hurried.

Chafin pulled out and all the other cars on the mountain followed. Within seconds, there was a large, unplanned caravan of vehicles driving through Rum Creek, with Chafin leading the pack in a shiny white Oldsmobile that he described as "the biggest they made." He continued:

> Mr. Greene was a real gentleman, but you could tell he liked that limelight. On our way to Logan, I suggested that his wife speak to the crowd, too. He smiled and said sternly, "Nope, she doesn't get out front. I'm the star."
>
> When we got into town, I introduced him at the courthouse, and the crowds went wild. There were guards stationed up on top of the courthouse with guns. When you get to be in a presidential campaign, you have to be guarded all the time.
>
> In a way, Lorne Greene was a lot more popular to our people than ol' McGovern was. Everybody was tickled to see Ben Cartwright. I couldn't wipe the grin off my face when I saw the crowd reaction.
>
> Everyone wanted to know where Hoss was. When someone would ask how Little Joe was doing, Lorne would look over at me and wink, and then smile and say, "He's doing just fine, thank you!"
>
> After his speech, Lorne and his wife joined Louise, Margaret, Joshua, and me at the Smokehouse to eat. We laughed and laughed about people asking him about the Ponderosa and his "sons."
>
> I enjoyed talking to Mrs. Greene. She asked me, "Do men really go back in these mines in the mountains? Do women go back in the mines, too?"

The Greenes were amazed by the area's picturesque beauty, but they were also concerned about the disproportionate poverty they witnessed as they traveled through the countryside. As they slowly ate their simple meal, they chatted about how they thought Senator McGovern could make positive change happen for all of Appalachia.

The other customers in the restaurant gawked at the Hollywood television star and his wife — watching their every movement — as they sat near the front of the restaurant. According to Chafin, Lorne Greene was exceptionally friendly and gracious to all who spoke to him.

Chafin went on to discuss the rigors of campaigning:

> There were times during that campaign that I had to put on two suits within the course of the same day — and several different bow ties — because I would be politickin' from morning till night. It was a real job to keep on top of the faction and to keep the candidates in front of the people. It was also hard to keep the candidates from squabbling among themselves sometimes.
>
> I got a real education out of politics. With the people that I've met and the politicians I knew and watched through the years, I've had a real learning opportunity.

Even though McGovern coordinated a grassroots campaign that appealed to the country's most liberal politicians, he lost the election to Richard M. Nixon by a landslide.

Chapter Thirty-Four
Camping, Truman, and a Bumper Sticker

Chafin is convinced that there is a special, uncanny magic that West Virginia residents create when traveling out of state. Circumstances in his own past, and the friendly nature of others, have convinced him that the charm emitted from a Logan County native is especially detectable outside the state's border.

> During my traveling, I never found a person anywhere who didn't want to sit down and talk to a West Virginian or hear about our state. Regardless of whether I was in New York, New Hampshire, Arizona — or anywhere I ever ended up — people seemed to love mountain folk.
>
> This is hard for a lot of people to believe, but you'd be awfully surprised how many different places where I was asked to speak publicly along the way. Many times if somebody was going to have a big party, maybe somebody I'd just run into — like a big movie actor or businessman with a big, fancy home — I'd end up gettin' myself invited. Henry and I would both go!
>
> We'd go just to get that stuff that costs so much money ... let me think for a minute ... oh, yeah, caviar. That's it! We'd go for that caviar! I really didn't care much fer black fish eggs, but we'd go get it anyway, just 'cause we knew it cost so much. During the party, I would usually end up with a group around me just wantin' to hear me talk, I guess. People in other places enjoyed hearing 'bout Cow Creek and West Virginia. I think sometimes they just liked our accent.

Go West, Young Man!

Chafin continued to talk about his travels:

> I guess we all traveled to Florida for thirteen or fourteen consecutive winters — with such wonderful memories. We even traveled out West with Margaret and her husband at that time, James "Mick" Robinson. It was a good time in life for us.
>
> Florida was especially an educational thing for me. Louise kept records of where we went, where we got gas, and how much we paid for gas. She kept perfect records – or journals — of all the trips we made through the years.
>
> Louise and especially ol' Pearl worried about getting lost when we first started going down. But as long as I followed the power lines, I knew that they would take me somewhere — to a town, a housing development, a business, or somewhere. I never felt lost as long as I followed the electric poles. Plus, I always kept our tank full of gas. I never worried.

One August, after Chafin had traded in his RV for a pop-up camper, Louise and he talked and decided to travel in a different direction entirely. They agreed that they had seen the South many times. This time they wanted to see the American West — as far as they could go.

As part of my planning for the trip, I asked my son-in-law, Mick, who was a certified welder at the time, to come up one weekend and put a hitch on my car. I wanted that hitch so solid that I wouldn't have to worry, regardless of wherever I traveled with my camper.

Mick came over on a Saturday and welded that hitch to the car at the service station across the road from my house. After he finished, he said, "This thing is solid enough that it will take you anywhere. You can even take the camper to Wyoming and back if you want to go."

I came back to the house and told Louise that Mick had welded the hitch on the car and he said it would take us all the way to Wyoming if we wanted to.

"Wyoming? Hmm. Maybe we can do just that," Louise answered, and kinda took me by surprise.

Not long after that, we started to actually make plans to take off for Wyoming. I marked out a plan on a road map.

I asked my brother Cliff and his wife, Vergie, if they wanted to go with us. They said they couldn't go at the time because they had two kids. So Louise and I decided to travel alone. After I thought it over, I decided it would be great for us. As the days went by, I started to look forward more and more to the chance of being alone with Louise and making traveling memories by ourselves.

However, not everyone was thinking the same way he was. Chafin continued:

When I think back on this trip, I can't help but think that I got double-crossed by Louise. The evening before we were supposed to go, here came my daughter, Margaret, her husband, Mick, and my baby grandson, Josh.

"Where are you going, Daddy?" Margaret asked as they walked in the front door. "Why are you packing up? You going on another trip?"

"Your Mommy and I are taking a little vacation — alone," I answered firmly.

"Daddy, where are you going?" she asked again.

"Well, we might go out West," I mumbled.

"Take us with you," Mick joined in. "We've always dreamed of going out West."

"Josh is just eight months old. We can't take him that far. That would be too hard on him … and me," I tried to explain. "How would we do that?"

"OH, DADDY! We can work that out. Daddy, he's a g-o-o-d baby!" Margaret pleaded. "You know he is!"

Next thing ya know, here came Louise, slowly scootin' across the room, and she went over and stood with Margaret and Mick. They all began to beg me to please let them all go.

I knew what was happening. I was being pressured… but it wasn't too hard to persuade me. I sort of liked the idea myself after I thought about it, even though I had originally wanted to be alone with Louise. So I agreed, and said, "Okay, okay. Let's all go. Just quit the bellyaching!"

Margaret threw her arms around Chafin's neck and said, "Thank you, Daddy! We'll have a great time."

"Now we can sleep every night in the camper," Mick said excitedly. "We don't even need to eat in a restaurant. We can cook at the campsite."

Chafin told the story about the trip out West:

We checked our supplies. We loaded up and took off the next morning — Louise, Margaret, Mick, and little Josh. We first drove to my brother's house in Indiana for the first night.

The next day we actually started driving westward. It made me think of the ol' wagon days. Here we were with only a few bags of belongings, and we would all be camping under the stars, so to speak. We stopped at campgrounds every night of our trip. We bought a clothesline rope for Josh 'cause he didn't want to stay still at the camp.

He had a little plastic ducky riding toy that he liked to sit on and play with. So when we pulled in for the night, he would want to get on his duck, and he was tied to the camper so that he didn't accidentally stray too far.

Louise was always a strong Democrat, probably most of all 'cause her daddy was killed by fellows that headed the Republican Party in Logan County when she was young. When we got into Missouri, Louise especially wanted to see Harry Truman's house at Independence. So we stayed at a campsite near President Truman's hometown. They had a lake, plenty of firewood, and everything you could ask for. Margaret and Mick even did a little bit of fishin' while we were there.

We built a big campfire and roasted hotdogs and marshmallows and imagined what it must have been like for the early settlers in the Missouri frontier.

The next day we finally found it. Harry Truman's home was located in downtown Independence. We parked near the house, and a guard came out to see what we were up to. I explained who I was, that I was the Logan County Democratic Executive Chairman, and how I had supported President Truman in Logan when he was in office. I also told him how much Louise and I thought of the President and that we had hoped to at least meet him while we were in the city.

The guard said, "He can't come out. I'll tell him who you are, Mr. Chafin. Then he might wave through the front window if he's up to it. OK?"

We all stood on the sidewalk and watched the guard walk back up to the house, looking up at the front window and hoping to see just a faint shadow of a hand on the window glass.

After a few minutes, much to our surprise, President Harry Truman actually walked out onto the front porch. He waved at us all from the first step of the porch. We all waved back excitedly. Margaret was absolutely thrilled as she grabbed hold of my arm. Louise's eyes filled with tears as we gazed at Truman, now a frail ol' gentleman who had once meant so much to all of us as our Commander in Chief.

Mick seemed speechless. As for me, I couldn't do anything but chuckle nervously. Within a minute or two, he turned 'round and went back inside. However, I will never forget that important moment in all of our lives. President Truman waved at little us.

After we calmed down, we left Independence, Missouri, and resumed our trip to the land of cowboys and Indians — Wyoming.

We went on and came to a place miles and miles up the road. We were all tired, so I decided we better just pull off the road for the night. We came into an Indian village, and there was a young-looking Indian sittin' in front of this building in a police uniform. He was apparently the head of the police department on the Indian reservation. Next to him was an ol' Indian who looked like he was at least 250 years old. We later found out he was the chief of the tribe.

I says to the chief, "Me no have place to stay."

The police officer turned toward the chief and snickered, then told him what I had just said. The chief slowly stood up and looked over our car and trailer. On the back bumper I had a "McGovern for President" bumper sticker.

As soon as the Indian chief saw the sticker, he looked at me and said in broken English, "You gots McGovern — he friend?"

I smiled and pointed toward my heart, and said, "McGovern is *my* man."

The police officer smiled and patted the elderly chief on the back, then said several words to him in his own tongue. The chief smiled and made some sort of hand gesture toward the sticker on my car.

The officer then looked at me and said, "Mister, I will get in my cruiser. You and your family can follow me. We'll find you a place for the night. Our entire village is for Senator McGovern. Our chief says that if you are for McGovern, you are welcome."

I bowed and leaned over and shook the chief's hand, and said, "Many thanks — I mean, heap big thanks, chief!"

As Chafin and his family followed the police car, they drove four or five miles outside the village until they came to a remote area where there was a small adobe and wood house, a large yard, and a solitary light pole. The cruiser coasted to a stop.

The officer got out of his car, walked up to Chafin's car window, and said, "You and your family can stay right here where the Chief lives. This should be considered an honorable thing. The Chief likes you. You may stay all night."

We set up camp under that light. In the distance we could hear the Indians playing eerie music all night long, until at least 4 o'clock in the morning. Margaret and Louise were scared to death. Mick and I laughed, and I finally told them, "The Indians aren't going to scalp you'ins! Calm down. They invited us here. Remember, me heap big McGovern man."

They all laughed at me and then tried their best to sleep. We stayed there that night. Before long there was a cloudburst. It must have rained all night long. It rained so hard that we all started to get shook up. Between the Indian music and the rain, none of us got much sleep at the reservation.

By morning we pulled out and drove that entire day. We finally reached Wyoming by sunset. It was a beautiful place. Mick was driving by this time. He drove us by several cattle ranches and then drove us up a mountainside to a campsite. The temperature must have dropped a good twenty-five degrees as we headed up the hill.

Luckily, Chafin had packed plenty of blankets, enough for little Josh and the rest of the weary travelers. They had a wonderful evening. Chafin and Mick built a giant fire, and they all sat near the flames and listened to the dry firewood snap and crackle as the intense heat consumed it. Surrounding the site it seemed as if thousands of grasshoppers were kept busy chirping at the sight of the bonfire. In the far distance they could hear a lonely coyote crying at the full moon.

We loved the Wild West. It was a trip that none of us ever forgot. When we finally headed back home, we traveled slowly and again enjoyed the experience of camping every night. It was also great to spend time with little Josh. My, how he grew during our travels!

We had so many good times over the years. After that trip, we traveled to Florida several more times and did all the things that we wanted to do. Every trip seemed to be an adventure. Sometimes we went with Henry and Pearl. Margaret and her family met us in Florida several times, too. However, in the early '80s, we had to give it all up due to Louise's fadin' health.

Chapter Thirty-Five

The Saddest Day of My Life

"During our retirement, we were havin' the best times that we ever had in our lives," Raymond Chafin said. "However, in 1983 we were spending the winter in Florida, at what we called our headquarters at Fort Meyers. Our son-in-law's mother and dad had just come down to spend a couple of weeks with us.

"That was the beginning of an unlucky time. Micky's dad got sick when he came down, and he had to have surgery on his kidneys. After the operation, he was taken back to West Virginia.

"It wasn't very long after he and his wife went back home to recover that Louise got sick, too. Her stomach was killing her. I remember that it all started on a Saturday. By Sunday, I took her to a clinic. The head doctor told me that if she wasn't better by morning, I should take her to a hospital.

"By the next day she was still hurting a lot, so I took her to the hospital, and the doctors who examined her said she needed an operation. They said she had a stone in her kidney.

"They went ahead and admitted her, and when they operated on her the next morning they had to remove one of her kidneys."

Louise's primary surgeon, Dr. Goldman, who was an older gentleman, asked an attendant at the nurse's station to call Chafin into his small office after the surgery was over so that he could give a full report of the operation. When Chafin heard his name called on the intercom, he nervously stood upright and headed for the nurses' desk.

He felt as if his heart were hammering through his chest as he prepared to hear about the surgical procedure on his mate. Chafin had many concerns that day. For one, he was troubled that Louise might be slow to recover, considering it was such a serious kidney operation. He also wondered if she would be the same physically. Would she always have a kidney problem? Were there any complications?

Henry jumped up and followed his best friend. They were escorted through a maze of cubicles and hospital rooms. They soon arrived at the doctor's meeting room. There, a grim-faced gentleman stood by his cluttered desk. He removed his dark-rimmed glasses and stethoscope as he glanced toward the doorway. When Chafin and his friend entered, he removed and folded his blue surgical robe and laid it on the back of his chair as he greeted them warmly and motioned for them to take a seat.

Seconds seemed like hours as the surgeon wrung his skilled hands, looked solemnly to the floor and slowly shook his head. Searching for the right words to say, Dr. Goldman finally broke the silence: "Mr. Chafin, when we went in, we had to remove your wife's troublesome kidney. There was no other alternative. She survived the operation and she's resting right now. But I'm sorry to tell you this: your wife also has cancer, and it's bad."

"How bad?" Chafin whispered, as his face turned pale.

"The way I see it right now, she has maybe six months to a year. I am so sorry, Mr. Chafin."

After a few more questions, Henry and Chafin left the office. They walked down the long hall to the waiting area outside the recovery room in total silence. The waiting room was empty, and the lights seemed to be unusually dim.

As they sank into their seats, still numb from the shock of the news, they began to quietly chat about the many memorable events they had experienced in Florida over the last twelve or thirteen years. They talked about Louise and her sickness and what it might mean for the future. Chafin finally broke down and sobbed as Henry wrapped his arm around his friend and comforted him.

"It was probably the saddest day of my adult life," Chafin remembered, as he wiped his eyes. "I knew there was nothing I could do to change things. My contacts or influence couldn't really change things."

During that time, Chafin's daughter Margaret was teaching in Logan County, at Whitman Creek. Chafin called his daughter at the school from a hospital pay phone. The school secretary pulled Margaret out of class, and she walked down to the office to accept the long-distance phone call. When she lifted the receiver, Chafin said, "Margaret, sweetheart, this is your dad. Your mother's surgery is over. They had to remove one of her kidneys. Also, when they were inside, they found cancer. Honey, it doesn't look good for your mother. Your mother and I have always said that if anything like this ever happened to either one of us, we would tell the other. I'm obligated to do that. So I'm going to tell her about what the doctor found."

"Daddy, let me fly down, and I'll go in with you," she said, as she began to whimper.

So that evening she boarded a 32-seat turbo-prop from Yeager Airport, in Charleston, on a scheduled flight to Fort Meyer. When she arrived in Florida and walked into the terminal, she dropped her luggage and ran over and hugged her father. They embraced for several minutes, and then they left for the hospital to see Margaret's mother.

Chafin and his daughter had decided to wait until morning to break the news to Louise. Neither one of them were able to rest through the night. Nevertheless, the next morning they both went into her room.

Louise was awake and alert by the time they walked in. As he held her hand, Chafin explained what the doctor told him the day before. Margaret stood behind her father, with her right hand on his shoulder. While her husband talked, Louise sniveled quietly. When he finished, he took a deep breath and squeezed her hand lovingly.

"Why, Raymond Chafin, do you think you're going to get rid of me that easily?" Louise snarled, after she heard the news. "I'm not going anywhere — I'm going to stay with you, boy!"

Then she leaned up from her bed and said, "I'm going to whip this, ain't I, Margaret?"

"Yup, Momma. You've always done anything you've ever set out to do. I suspect you will beat this, too," Margaret said softly, as she peeked around from behind her father.

The next day Chafin and Margaret went back to the doctor's office to discuss what Louise had said when she heard the news.

"Well, with proper care," the doctor said, as he smiled, "and with good doctors, she might live a year or two. It sounds like she's a fighter. She'll need to be a scrapper to overcome this."

"Yes, she's a fighter, all right! She's a Chambers. I'd like to take her back to West Virginia, doc," Chafin said.

"Sure, that might be a good idea, Mr. Chafin. Once we release her, get her to a specialist immediately. I've heard a lot about West Virginia University. If you can get her there, they might be able to see things that I don't see," he responded as he reached out for Chafin's right hand. "Good luck to you, sir, and to your family. Please call me if there is anything more we can do in the future."

Going Back Home

Chafin immediately went back to his camper and called Senator Robert C. Byrd. He was a special friend of the family – both politically and personally.

Byrd said, "Let me see what I can do."

Chafin said that it was around three or four days later when Robert Byrd called him back and said that he was sending a specialist — a cancer doctor — over to Charleston, West Virginia.

"We'll make a way for him to treat your wife," Senator Byrd said compassionately.

Margaret flew back to West Virginia and went back to work at the school. Louise eventually got out of the hospital and was taken to their camper at Fort Meyers, where she rested for about a week.

Chafin recalled:

> After the week, she got herself ready and we drove the long drive back to Cow Creek. Henry and Pearl followed behind us. She did as well as she ever did on our trips. Then I took her over to Charleston to see the cancer specialist that Senator Byrd had arranged for us at Charleston Area Medical Center.
>
> She started getting chemotherapy and a few other treatments. I stayed with her at CAMC for ten days and ten nights. They fixed me up a private room over there, next to her room. I brought my clothes and stayed right beside her, 'cause when they started treating her, the nurses wanted someone with her all the time.

Chafin said that occasionally he would go downstairs and walk outside the large CAMC building to "get a little mountain air" while she slept, but then he would "shortly race back to her side so that he was always there" when she woke up.

> Some of my people — my relatives — would come to see her, and they'd relieve me for an hour or so at a time. They visited with Louise and kept her spirits high. They were all helpful and so good to do that. Margaret would come on over on the weekends and help me.
>
> Louise was a real trooper. She was tough, I'll tell you!
>
> After the ten days, her doctor said, "She's stayed here long enough. She needs to get out of here and go on home."
>
> "What? What do you mean, go home?" I asked.
>
> "Yep, we'll move her into a wheelchair, and we'll bring her to the front door of the hospital this afternoon. You take your time and drive her on home. That'll do her the most good right now, because she told me she really wants to go home," the doctor added. "If you have any problems, call me or bring her right back in."

I had Louise home for a few days, and she was lying on our living room couch when she started to raise up and fell out on the floor. I thought that was it — it's all over. I called the ambulance to pick her up. It was a rule at the time that the ambulance would first take a patient to Logan General Hospital for treatment.

I was a little upset and I didn't want her to go to Logan's hospital first. I wanted her taken right back to CAMC. So I called Roger Bryant, the director of the Logan County Ambulance Authority.

He was a kind friend to Margaret, Louise, and me. I told him the situation, and he said that under the circumstances, he would take Louise straight to the State Capital, bypassing the ambulance authority's normal procedure.

When she got to the hospital, the doctor started treating her again. I had a chance to talk to the doctor the next day, and he said, "Mr. Chafin, don't let things like that scare you. That sort of thing goes with this sickness she has. It's actually pretty normal, considering."

Tragedy Strikes the Chafin Home

I know it's hard to believe, but she beat it. Louise was eventually cured of the cancer. But we were afraid to go back to Florida anymore. So we spent all of our time at Barnabus, at Cow Creek. It wasn't too bad. At least we were home and Louise was here to share life with.

Apparently, being a feisty and determined fighter helped Louise to overcome terminal cancer. Doctor reports indicated that the cancer had vanished because of the aggressive treatment. However, Chafin always believed that she overcame the cancer because of Senator Byrd and because she was "too bullheaded and headstrong to be defeated."

Several years later, she started having more kidney problems, with ever-increasing pain. Though the cancer was gone, she got steadily worse until she had to have regular dialysis treatments. She became bedridden.

By this time, Margaret had quit teaching school and studied to be an engineer. She liked construction work like I did. She was working for the West Virginia Department of Transportation as an area maintenance manager at the same time they were building and finishing Corridor G in Logan County. She lived up the creek, at a little farm that we owned. Louise and I bought that farm sometime before, and we had always planned to give it to her.

Chafin explained that by 1997, Louise had to have around-the-clock custodial care, since she was totally confined to bed. Margaret stopped by frequently to spend the night so that her father could get sufficient rest. There were two beds in the master bedroom. Louise had a hospital bed in the room, and Chafin slept in a full-size bed next to her. There was a third bed on the other side of the hall in a small room usually reserved for Margaret when she stayed the night.

One night while Margaret was staying up to care for her mother, she went into the bedroom — the room across the hall from where Louise and Chafin were lying — in the early morning hours and apparently decided to smoke a cigarette before she fell asleep.

Chafin recalled the horrible events:

> I heard a terrible noise that woke me up. When I looked toward the hallway, I saw a flickering glow. There was a fire in the house! When I looked across the room, Margaret was trying to put out the flames on her mattress. When she turned sideways, I saw that the back of her flannel gown was on fire.
>
> I yelled frantically, "Margaret, you're on fire!"
>
> She looked down at her side and saw the flames and screamed as she ran past our room and into the living room, where she stood in the center of the room, engulfed in flames.
>
> Everything happened so fast! I remember that I immediately ran after her. I shoved her down on the floor, and I ran back to the bedroom to get something to smother out the flames with. I wrapped her up in a sheet to put out the flames. By the time I got the fire out, it was really bad.
>
> The house was so full of smoke and ash by that time. It was so bad that I could hardly get back into the bedroom area. Louise was still in there and she couldn't get up!
>
> My neighbor and his daughter, who were members of the Barnabus Volunteer Fire Department, got my back door open and rushed in. They saved Louise and what was left of Margaret. They may have even saved my life 'cause I was trying to get Louise out when they burst in.
>
> Margaret was taken to Logan General Hospital first. She was burned so bad that they sent her on to Huntington, a much larger facility. Then, from Huntington, they sent her to the Cincinnati Burn Trauma Center, at Cincinnati, Ohio, where she passed away.

Chafin's only beloved daughter died on her 48th birthday, in the early morning hours of Thursday, October 30, 1997. According to official reports, Margaret (Chafin) Williams suffered third-degree burns over sixty percent of her body during the fire which broke out in her parent's single-story, masonry home on Cow Creek. Chafin and Louise were treated for minor burns at Logan General and released.

Fire officials at the time said they believed either a cigarette or a burning candle started the fire.

According to the obituary in *The Logan Banner*, West Virginia Senate President Earl Ray Tomblin and West Virginia Senator Lloyd Jackson served as honorary pallbearers, along with Department of Highways officials Sam Beverage, Wilson Braley, Tim Pullen, and Curley Belcher. The honorary pallbearers also included Art Kirkendoll, Alvis Porter, Rick Abraham, Paul Hardesty, Truman Chafin, J.B. Phillips, Hobert Day, Bob Wolfe, Andre Nick Shaer, Rick Grimmett, and Charlie Grayley.

Pallbearers were her sons, Joshua Robinson and Jesse Williams. Additional pallbearers were Michael Pennington, Gene Curry, George Curry, Todd Chafin,

Raymond William Chafin, Kemper Chafin, Minnis Chafin, Charlie Chafin, and Mark Thern.

Chafin spoke candidly about that time in his life:

> When the fire happened, a big part of me died in those flames. Besides that, all my records, including the journals and notes that Louise wrote over the years, were all destroyed. All of our history was in the two bedrooms in this house — our years in Florida, the places we'd traveled, gasoline price documentation, and most of my political records and pictures. The blaze destroyed things that I wouldn't have taken thousands and thousands of dollars for. But I would have gladly given everything I owned to be with Margaret one more time.
>
> After Margaret died, we had to leave the house and stay with my brother down the hill, here at Cow Creek.
>
> Fire is a terrible thing. Days later, when I went to tell poor Louise that Margaret died at Cincinnati burn unit, she never did shed a tear. She quietly said, "Raymond, if she was as bad as you all say she was, she's better off."
>
> That's all she ever said about the entire fire incident — period. She just couldn't speak of it. However, she asked me if there was any way that she could go to the funeral home for the visitation when the funeral arrangements had been made. She was completely bedfast by this time, but I made a call to Roger Bryant at Logan Ambulance. I believe he liked Louise better than anybody.
>
> Bryant said, "Yes, Mr. Chafin, I'll send an ambulance there, and we'll take Louise to the funeral home chapel and she can stay there through the visitation hours."

That evening an ambulance arrived at Chafin's brother's house. The men in the ambulance put Louise on a cot and took her down to Collins Funeral Home. They wheeled her up to the foot of Margaret's casket.

Chafin recalled:

> She lay right there, on a gurney, and she greeted everybody who came in. She shook hands and hugged every person who came up to the closed coffin. No tears.
>
> That was the biggest crowd I ever saw at that funeral home. There were cars parked all the way down to Donny Steele's Market, and all along the other way up to the bridge. Every place you could get a car parked along the road was filled. People came from Charleston, Huntington, and everywhere. I saw people there that I hadn't seen in over twenty years.
>
> The next day, Louise decided to stay home for the actual funeral. She said, "I did what I wanted to do. You go, Raymond. You go."

Services were held at Switzer, West Virginia, on Sunday, November 2, 1997, at Collins-Slater Funeral Home Chapel. The Rev. Robert Pritchard and the Rev. Charles Blankenship officiated. Burial followed at Highland Memory Gardens at Godby, West Virginia.

Chapter Thirty-Six
Louise Is Called Home

Raymond Chafin discussed his wife's declining health:

> Louise lived a year or so after Margaret died. I never heard her say as much as "ouch" in all my life with her. She never did complain. She was jolly regardless of how hard things got for her. She would be talkative to visitors and friendly to all who came over.
>
> She had some of her treatments at Man, West Virginia. The nurses and the mayor's wife, Mrs. Perry, were so good to her up there. She even felt bad going up there so much, making them work so hard. She had to go quite often — sometimes twice a week — to have her artery opened up for the dialysis treatments. Then at other times she'd go over to Charleston by ambulance to have her dialysis.
>
> In all those years, she never complained. I went to the bedroom every night, and she and I would watch television together. I'd go in and lie down next to her and say, "OK, hon, what are we's going to watch tonight?"
>
> We'd laugh and talk about all kinds of things. We always remained best friends, as well as husband and wife. I never went off and left her other than to run necessary errands at Logan every once in a while. But I had someone here all the time if I ran to town. Unfortunately, she continued to get worse, but she never gave up. Finally, on one of her treatments at Charleston, she didn't return.

Louise (Chambers) Chafin died Wednesday, April 7, 1999, at CAMC General Division at Charleston, West Virginia. She was 81 years of age.

The obituary said that Louise was born January 5, 1918, at Dehue, West Virginia, the daughter of Art and Cynthia Raines Chambers. Funeral services were held at 2 o'clock in the afternoon on Saturday, April 10th, at Collins-Slater Funeral Home at Switzer, West Virginia. The Rev. Charles Blankenship and the Rev. Robert Pritchard officiated.

Her nephews were her pallbearers. Burial followed at Highland Memory Gardens at Godby, West Virginia.

As he recalled the experience, Chafin leaned forward and whispered:

> Son, death is a funny thing. It can change anything and everything in a split second. I have had partners, good people I worked with, and even acquaintances taken unexpectedly. One day they're okay and planning the future — next minute they're gone. *Poof.*
>
> I've seen it happen in politics, too. I've seen candidates spend big, big money to plan this and that for a campaign. Then when they win an election, they never get to serve any of their time — 'cause they're gone ... in a flash, in an instant.
>
> Death is that way, sneaky and sly; there's no guarantee of any tomorrows. It's as painful to lose a six-month-old child as it is to lose one who's 55 years

old. If there's love there, there's nothin' that you can do 'bout it. It will be painful.

Mom Still Lives In My Memories

Chafin also shared recollections about his mother:

> My mom, Lucinda Curry Chafin, was the luckiest woman in this whole world. She had eight of us. Her sons-in-law were as good to her as her boys were. They all did things for her all the time. None of her sons-in-law or daughters-in-law ever said a harsh word about her, not that we ever knew of. Every holiday — Christmas, Thanksgiving, Easter — or her birthday, my mother thought she should get a present. Not from one family member — from ALL.
>
> However, if she got a new dress as a gift from one, she might even give that dress away to another daughter-in-law before the night was over. But she expected a present anyway, from every last one of us. We had great family moments and memories. Our family was close. We were raised that way.
>
> When she departed this life, a part of me was never the same. Now that Margaret and Louise are gone, and Mom and Dad, I spend a lot of time just thinkin' about the good times that we all had, everyday. The ones that have passed on to the other side are still with me. I guess I have them right here — through my memories.

Airplanes, Washboards, Outer Space, and Politicians

When one is young, his or her dreams, thoughts, and goals are usually found in the future. However, the aging process can eventually change the focus. As the Scripture says, life is like a vapor, which appears for a few seconds and then vanishes away. The years can steal away the dreams of the future. There are some aged who have nothing left but the past to reflect on. The future may seem limited, unsure, and gloomy. However, the accomplishments, successes, and goals of the past remain the highlights of a life.

One afternoon as Chafin spoke about the many developments that have happened in Logan County and in the world since his youth, he was obviously down in the dumps. Not typically an emotional man, he was nevertheless moved when he considered the many things he has seen and experienced during his lifetime and how he has lost so many loved ones, friends, and colleagues along the way. He also realized that the interview process was nearing an end.

Chafin has experienced great heartache and pain in the last few years — pain that no political victory or personal accomplishment can erase.

Nearly all of his immediate family have "gone to the other side." Most of his friends and political cronies from the old days — people such as George Steele, R.W. Raike, Bill Abraham, Arnold Harkins, Bus Perry, Ott Holliday, T.R. Workman, and Jack Ferrell — are all gone now, too. Most of the men he worked with on the state road have passed on, as well as former business partners and associates.

Even the deaths of President John F. Kennedy and his brother Robert seemed to weigh heavily upon Raymond's mind — as did that of the President's wife Jackie O.'s years later from cancer, and more recently, their son, John Kennedy, Jr., and his bride in a tragic fatal plane crash. In ways Raymond felt that the Kennedys had become a part of his extended family. Now his dealings with John F. Kennedy in the Oval Office at the White House are but a hazy memory. The remaining glory of the Kennedy years — what was once called "Camelot" — has been tarnished through unpleasant findings of moral infidelities among family members and the untimely deaths of others.

When Chafin takes the time to sit and think about the past, he, like everyone else, tends to get a little depressed. Though his phone rings constantly, there are moments when he can't help but feel isolated and alone. Perhaps he sometimes feels as if he alone is left to continue the family and political legacy.

Chafin reflected upon his life:

Every Memorial Day, and on other occasions, I plant flowers at the graves of Louise and Margaret. Growing older isn't all it's cracked up to be, especially if you live to be my age. It's tough to watch your loved ones and friends pass on. Life goes by much too quickly.

I still find pleasure in my grandsons, Josh and Jesse. I enjoy spending time with my nephews, cousins, and friends. My brother still lives next door to me. Cow Creek neighbors come and visit all the time. Gorgeous spring days and warm sunshine still feel wonderful on this ol' tired body. I especially enjoy dabblin' in my politickin'. But still, it's never easy to lose your immediate family. I guess a lot has changed over these 86 years.

My grandson Josh is now grown. It seems like only yesterday that we all laughed as he played on his little ducky ridin' toy. He has now graduated from Marshall University, and then after that, he went to law school at West Virginia University. He recently passed his bar exam. He is now a flourishing attorney in Ashland, Kentucky. He followed his father's footsteps, for Mick continued in school through the years and became a successful attorney. It broke my heart, and Louise's, when Mick and Margaret divorced years ago, though they remained on good terms afterward.

My grandson Jesse, from Margaret's second marriage, is now 22 years old and totally different from Josh — as much as day is from night. However, he likes construction work and working with his hands. I don't know if that's what he will always do, but that seems to be what he wants to do right now.

All is different now. When I was a small boy, we didn't even have paved roads 'round these parts. No water or electricity. Regardless of what was happenin' elsewhere in the county, very few folks had cars or trucks around Main Island Creek. I 'spect there were more buckboard wagons, spring wagons, and horses than cars in Omar, Pine Creek, and Cow Creek when I was a small kid.

I remember that liquor was supposed to have been illegal, but moonshine stills were plentiful in the hills, and gambling dens were 'bout everywhere.

It was a slew of years before I would even see an inside toilet. We used privies or outhouses, along with newspaper or the pages from a Sears catalog for bathroom tissue. I had never even dreamed of such things as electric refrigerators, freezers, air conditioners, plastic-wrapped meats, or big supermarkets when I was a young'n. We didn't have electric washers or dryers. We had washboards and creek water, clotheslines, and ol'-fashioned elbow grease.

I can't even imagine what my grandsons will see and experience in their old age.

Chafin also explained that things such as televisions, tape recorders, stereos, and personal computers were beyond anyone's imagination. The thoughts of traveling in space would have been something set aside for silver screen matinee serials or comic books — not intended for real life. That would have been considered ludicrous.

Most people around us had it hard, and we wasn't no [sic] different. We learned how to make do with what we had. Daddy did the best that he could, and that was surely fine with all of us.

We never really knew that we were poor, because we had a roof over our heads, always ate well, and us kids always found plenty of things to do for enjoyment. Everybody 'round us lived pretty much the same darn way.

Chafin remembered that when he was young, if an airplane happened to fly over Cow Creek, all the kids in the hollow would stop whatever they were doing, look up, and point at the biplane — usually a single-prop crop duster hired to spray some large farm in a neighboring county, a politician flying into the region, or maybe a pilot just out on a joyride, playing daredevil.

We were kind of awestruck, you might say. It was such an unusual thing that we couldn't wait to see the next one come 'round. We tried to imagine what it must have been like for that fearless pilot zooming around the blue sky, with the wind beating him in the face — being able to look down on the tiny world from way up yonder. We figured that people and animals must have looked like fleas and potato bugs to him as he soared among the clouds.

Biplanes were one thing. Space travel was something entirely different. Never in my wildest dreams did I ever think I'd live to see someone actually step on the moon, but I saw Neil Armstrong make a believer out of me. I wonder what the next eighty-five years will hold.

Chafin pointed out that besides the inventions and technology he'd seen come to pass, he had also been a witness to many miraculous changes for the good in the Mountain State that had been accomplished by certain political figures — referring to people like Franklin D. Roosevelt, Harry S. Truman, John Kennedy, Lyndon B. Johnson, and Jimmy Carter.

Chafin reflected on his long career in politics:

I have been fortunate to hobnob with people like Governor Wally Barron, Governor Hulett Smith, Governor Arch Moore, Governor Jay Rockefeller, Governor Gaston Caperton, Governor Cecil Underwood, Senator Jennings Randolph, and others.

240

Through the years, there's been a lot of things that Senator Robert Byrd, in particular, has done for us right here on this creek. But not only here — go look at Harts Creek, for example. Take a look at the new bridge at Chapmanville. Take a look at the things that have been accomplished in southern West Virginia. Look at the different things that we have gotten from our United States senators over the last fifty years. Some people have made a great difference for us all. I will also say there have been a few politicians — scoundrels — who haven't given us diddly squat.

It's because of outstanding people like Senator Bob Byrd and local boy, Senate President-Lieutenant Governor Earl Ray Tomblin that we now have what we have. And I 'spect more is on the way. I remember noticing Senator Tomblin when he was just a boy. I guess I always figured he'd do somethin' important.

Incidentally, the nice thing about Senate President Tomblin is that when we have a need — a real necessity — Earl Ray is always here for us. He's a good man and a good politician. He's just like us; he's country.

Earl Ray Tomblin is a resident of Chapmanville, in the 7th District. He was elected to the West Virginia House of Delegates in 1974, 1976, and 1978. Then he was elected to the West Virginia Senate in 1980, 1984, 1988, 1992, 1996, and 2000. He was elected January 11, 1995, as the 48th president of the West Virginia Senate. He was then re-elected in 1997, 1999, and 2001.

Born in 1952, he is the son of Earl and Freda (Jarrell) Tomblin. His father, Earl, was once a justice of the peace, Democrat Executive Committee member, and sheriff in Logan County

In 1979, Earl Ray married Joanne Jaeger, who is currently president of Southern West Virginia Community and Technical College and also an influential leader in the Logan County Chamber of Commerce.

Earl Ray has been helpful in putting Logan on the map, as far as I'm concerned. I know fer a fact that he has spearheaded program after program, bringing diversification and jobs into this area of the coalfields. Plus, there is one important thing about Earl Ray: he is pro-West Virginia ... all the way. He is a shining example of what one person with determination can do for our region.

Regardless of one's view of Chafin, it's hard to deny that in spite of his lack of a formal education or a large vocabulary, he has been acquainted with the elite of our generation and counseled many local and national political giants of the 20th century.

In the past, dignitaries such as Senator Robert C. Byrd have spent many nights at Chafin's home beside the trickling creek at Barnabus.

Chafin remembered Byrd's visits:

He's a very religious man, ya probably know. Years ago, during one of his first visits, Louise and I had to rush to the neighbors in order to find a Holy Bible for him. He reads his Bible every night. He's a good, good fella.

241

Whenever folks knew he'd be stayin' with us, there would be a constant line of citizens coming in and going out our screen door. It seemed like everyone wanted a chance to make his or her request of Bob Byrd. Some just wanted to shake his hand and wish him well and such. He was always gracious and accommodating to the people of Cow Creek, Barnabus, Omar, Chauncey, Switzer, Monitor, and Logan. He played his fiddle right here at the house on several occasions for the public.

Then, on other times, Senator Byrd came in secretly, and no one even knew he was staying here. That's the times I personally enjoyed the most. He's just a nice man to be 'round. He's also a good thinker.

He doesn't have time to come here anymore and seldom calls personally, but I still call him a friend. He's like me — old age is setting in.

Through the years, quite a number of the Mountain State's governors and other governmental leaders have sat around Chafin's dining room table, enjoying Louise's country breakfast. There, while filling their bellies with home cooking, unlimited cups of hot coffee, and lots of Southern hospitality, these political leaders were also served a heaping helping of Chafin's ideas.

"There's nothing better than a captive audience," Chafin said.

Chafin has always been vocal about his desire to see Omar and Cow Creek people treated fairly. Other visionaries, such as United States Senator Jennings Randolph, knew Chafin well, feeling comfortable enough to stop by his house unannounced on many occasions. They also went to several political engagements together over the years.

I still have barbecues every so often with county fellows like Rick Abraham, Art Kirkendoll, Paul Hardesty, Rick Grimmett, Alvis Porter, and the like. I still fool around with the political big boys. Buck Harless, [West Virginia timber tycoon, businessman, and multimillionaire philanthropist] from Gilbert, still drops by every so often, and we talk up ol' times. He's a great fellow, ya' know.

Chafin has been credited for having developed complex campaign strategies through the years for numerous candidates in the area and having groomed many of today's local leaders. Even though he has only a grade-school education, local and state leaders for decades have considered him a genius at organizing a precinct. He still occasionally speaks with students at the University of Charleston, at Marshall, and at WVU.

Besides being in the forefront of the Democratic advisory arena, Chafin has also been involved in several political faction quarrels — some having erupted in fistfights behind his house, at precincts, and at the county courthouse. He has worked diligently at devising slates, sometimes having to cut off unproductive candidates and scolding other lackluster officeholders. He quickly admits that he was involved in buying votes, selling out candidates, and stopping at nothing to win an election in the past.

Through wondrous successes and terrible failures, unfounded rumors, and embarrassing scandals, Raymond Chafin has still remained at the helm, as arguably one of the most influential men in the Logan County political arena, guiding the Democratic Party through the second half of the 20th century.

Chapter Thirty-Seven
Ellis Remembers Other Leaders

Claude Ellis says that he remembers well West Virginia Governor Hulett C. Smith, who was governor from 1965 to 1969. According to Ellis, he was a pretty good governor. Ellis worked under Smith's leadership for the Liquor Commission as a store manager at Ellis Addition.

"We were close, and I personally think he did a lot for our region," Ellis said.

Smith, whose father, Joe L. Smith, served in Congress for many years, was defeated in his first gubernatorial race in 1960 against William "Wally" Barron. He was then elected in 1965. According to many, Governor Smith's administration was perceived as weak and unable to render decisions quickly on important issues. Big Daddy saw him differently and was a loyal supporter and friend.

Ellis also recalled working with Arch Moore:

> I also had a good relationship with West Virginia Governor Arch Moore, who first took office in 1969 after Hulett. T.K. Killen was the chairman of the Republican Party in Logan County at that time. I met Arch through T.K., and even though he was Republican, I liked his thinking and his way of doing things. I sort of leaned toward him a little bit, especially when I found out that Bill Abraham was supporting him. I endorsed him after that, too.

According to Ellis, Jay Rockefeller was a "strange, strange man" in person. Ellis said that he'd had the state license plate number 155 for about ten or twelve years before Rockefeller was elected governor. After Rockefeller was elected, Ellis says he took his special license plate away.

> That made me mad. Of course, I let it be known that I was angry about it. I'd been with Jay at meetings and at other functions, but was never able to get the license number back. Apparently there was somebody in the county more powerful that swayed him — probably Red Hager and his boys. Red and I knew each other well, but we were never on the same side politically.
>
> Governor Rockefeller was also against strip mining; and I remember being interviewed by the media and saying, "It's hard to look back and enjoy these mountains when you're hungry." That comment of mine didn't sit well with the governor.
>
> I was for coalmining and jobs. In my opinion, Rockefeller wasn't. From that time forward, we haven't spoken much. So, 'cause of the license plate and a few other things, I never got along too good with Jay — a mysterious man in my opinion.
>
> As far as what he's doing now as our senator, I guess he's getting a few things done. I don't think he's breaking any records, though. I know he was against the United Mine Workers when he was governor, but now he's for 'em. He's working with them, and I guess he's grown and matured a little bit. Maybe.

Gaston Caperton was a good governor, but I wasn't particularly close to him at all. He was an excellent businessman and he did a lot of good things for the state. He became friendly toward me at the end of his administration, and we met on several occasions.

As for Cecil Underwood, I haven't got much to say about him. I didn't support him — he was a Republican. Case closed.

Bob Wise, the governor of West Virginia, has made a great deal of mistakes and will probably go down in history as a lackluster governor. He started out on the wrong foot and never did get his balance.

I guess I have been pretty lucky to be involved with many of these men, and I hope I've had some impact within the state. We've had good governors and we've had men who weren't exactly that wonderful. I've known them all; and our state and region has certainly come a long way in my lifetime.

I've also worked among or against most of the local politicians. There were several I was very close to, like Tom Godby; and there were others, like Red Hager and Jack Ferrell, whom I didn't get along with too well. Of course, Raymond Chafin and I had our battles, too.

From the late 1950s through the 1970s, "Big Daddy" Ellis was known as one of the most prominent, persuasive, and dangerous — if need be — of the political kingpins in Logan County. His foremost rival, Raymond Chafin, now says that "Claude was a hard-nosed bruiser who took care of business when it concerned anyone coming against his faction. I still wouldn't want to tangle with Big Daddy!"

Claude Ellis gave his synopsis of his own involvement in county government and his outlook on politics in general:

Politics in Logan County was and is a tough business. I don't need to kid the people. In my day, I was a tough boy! I knew there was a job to be done; and I did whatever it took to get the job done — and then I let the chips fall where they may. Period.

In a political race, somebody has to win; somebody loses. I tried to better my chances by whatever means seemed appropriate. It often took plenty of thinking and political leverage.

Do I have any regrets? I have a few regrets — certainly some reservations about a number of things I wish I could go back and change or do over again differently. But as for politics, if the laws were still the same, and I was hooked up politically like I was then, and circumstances were similar, I'd do it all the same way again — so my politicians would be successful. Being victorious is important. It's the final outcome that counts. Yes, we may have bought votes and handed out whiskey in pint bottles; but I also know that we were partly responsible for John Kennedy's victory. The outcome was worth the methods we used.

Claude, Dan, and Raymond Still Active

Now at 77 years old, Claude Ellis deals with the harsh effects of diabetes and advanced age with grace. He has a head full of white hair, and his gait has slowed quite a bit. He says he is "now in church" and has turned his life around. He and his wife, Rosemary, live in an attractive dwelling overlooking Logan Post Office within the city limits. He still owns and manages real estate in the region.

He lives his retirement years peacefully. He still dabbles in politics as an elected City of Logan councilman. On some days he can be found in downtown Logan, sitting with several other fellows "chewing the fat at the courthouse square."

Dan Dahill, who is 84, still practices law in Logan County on a limited basis. He seems to always have "several irons in the fire" and "works as he needs money." When weather permits, he spends many hours on the golf course. His enthusiasm for life, quick wit, and boisterous personality persist. He lives with his wife, Jean, at Ethel, outside Logan.

Of course, Raymond Chafin, now 86 years old, still lives and breathes politics. Every conversation with the kingpin will eventually involve the upcoming election or some political issue. He spends his days at Cow Creek, usually on his front porch entertaining company or talking on the telephone.

"Far too many of my ol' friends have passed on. I go to many, many funerals these days," he said.

Chafin continues to have a huge following from the region.

Chapter Thirty-Eight

The Real Reason to Be a Politician

During the 2000 primary election season, a Logan County Democratic faction organized an enormous rally to be held at the Logan County seat, which included a list of important politicians from across the country speaking to attendees at the Logan Fieldhouse on the importance of voting Democratic for gubernatorial hopeful Bob Wise and other Democratic candidates. Senator Robert C. Byrd, U.S. Rep. Nick Rahall, Sen. Jay Rockefeller, and Senator Edward Kennedy were supposed to be the headliners for the event.

The idea of Senator Edward "Ted" Kennedy triumphantly returning to the City of Logan was considered a historic and joyous occasion, since he had once made such a positive impression with the people of the region in 1960 when campaigning for his brother.

Although Ted Kennedy did speak briefly at the 2000 political rally, several Logan residents who assisted behind the scenes have since stated, anonymously, that the blatantly self-important Kennedy refused to mingle with the common people of the region before or after the highly publicized event. It was also said that he was unapproachable and standoffish with local politicians and gave many who attended the rally the impression that he appeared at the function purely for financial gain, as a paid speaker — nothing more.

Those who romanticized the notion that Teddy would once again walk the streets of downtown Logan and captivate the people as he did at the beginning of the reign of Camelot were sorely disenchanted.

Many were equally disappointed that the once handsome, personable, and articulate younger brother of John and Bobby was a different person than remembered. Now bloated, rude, and aloof — a distorted shadow of his perceived former self — he wanted little part of Logan County or her people after his speech was over. Perhaps the years since 1960 have stripped the senator's desire or need to be charming or to connect with the common public.

"I saw him that day, and he didn't even speak," Ellis stated. "After all the moments we had shared in 1960 and all we did for the Kennedy family, he didn't even acknowledge me. Alex DeFobio, who also worked extremely hard for JFK and worked closely with Teddy, was tremendously hurt that day. Alex passed away since then, but I believe he never understood Kennedy's attitude that day."

Ted was a different person and we were all disappointed. Seeing the way he treated the citizens that day, I don't even know why he came to Logan. It's possible that even Bobby and John would have been disappointed with him."

According to Logan County "Godfather" Chafin, a situation like this is just one of the potential hazards or pitfalls of being a long-term successful politician. Chafin explained that the politician who has gained a certain amount of power may also acquire an overblown self-image along the way and become "complacent, too satisfied, or even cynical" about his constituents and admirers. Because of an increased sense of political control and pride, he or she may even lose touch with the working people who once supported the candidate in the first place. The person ultimately becomes "too big for his or her own political britches." Many believe that Ted Kennedy has become one who has just this kind of difficulty fastening his own trousers, so to speak; he has become too liberal, too ultra-leftwing, and too arrogant for the common Democratic voter — or at least the type of voters found in southern West Virginia. Perhaps he may even be too haughty and out-of-touch for his own Massachusetts constituents.

At the time of that 2000 rally in Logan, Chafin did not attend because he was supporting West Virginia's Republican Governor Cecil Underwood and his campaign to win a second term.

Chafin recalled:

> Unfortunately, Cecil Underwood was not able to hold on to his post as governor. He eventually lost to Bob Wise. But I certainly had the local faction scared for a while; and they had to bring in the big guns — Kennedy, Byrd, Rockefeller, and all the rest of 'em — in order to prevail. They were fearful that Wise would stumble in Logan County.
>
> I supported Underwood because he had given me everything I had ever asked for in our county during his first four years in office. Bridges, roads, and favors in Cow Creek were mine for the askin'. I felt like I had his ear and I was going to support him, even if he was a Republican.
>
> Now that West Virginia has gotten their belly full of Governor Wise, I suspect many wish they had listened to me back in 2000. Oh, well, that's politics. I'm now lookin' on to the next election, and I have a firm idea of what I'd like to do.

In spite of the potential drawbacks and setbacks, Chafin maintains that there are still a multitude of reasons for being a politician, with one of the reasons being influence.

> A lead politician can have an amazing amount of influence and authority, as long as he retains control of his or her own faction. There's a lot of good that a politician can do for the people. There are even jobs that can be given out as favors. The more good you do for people, the more the citizens will support you at election time. Simple enough.
>
> So a good politician who wants to remain in office and remain the kingpin has to get results — and provide good works — that people can quickly see. It's all about visability. To be seen, he needs publicity. He has to offer favors to voters who need a helpin' hand and he has to bend over back'ards for his supporters. Every vote counts — 'specially in the local elections.
>
> A politician with influence, who understands the overall game, will be rewarded for his elected position in due season.
>
> John Kennedy understood the value of influence and power on the local level. He knew exactly how politics worked. His daddy, Joe, taught him very well. Joe was a sly ol' dawg behind the scenes, and he knew how to get things done for people, too. He could be helpful, and he could be ruthless — it took a little of both to work.

JFK and his brothers also had a firm understanding of how to pull a grumbling faction together and how to win in a state like West Virginia. The key: cash, and lots of it. It always works.

Chafin reared back his head and laughed, paused for a moment, and then continued:

They said a Roman Catholic would never be president in this country. I doubted it at first, too. Well, a handsome, extremely rich Catholic can make miracles happen.

I think Jackie liked the idea of power, too — you better believe it. I saw that love for control in her the first time I met her. Wow! Even being soft-spoken, she had my attention from the very first! Humphrey, Johnson, and McGovern had that need for power, along with the others — even Clinton and Bush.

Every politician I've made or met liked control, power, and influence. Mark it down. It's a fact.

Today, politics in Logan County is not really any different than it's always been, except for one big change: nowadays, it's hard to get people to get out and vote on Election Day. Money or half-pints of cheap liquor in the ol' days was a nice enticement to vote.

You probably couldn't buy someone into the voting booth nowadays, or even give them enough moonshine to sway them into the precinct house. American people need to take an active role in choosing leaders. Folks need to be serious about votin'.

Claude Ellis told me one time that the difference between him and me was that I spent my Kennedy money; he kept his! But seriously, the Kennedys knew how to play the game and get votes and support. In the ol' days, we could get voters out and we could rally a crowd. It took thousands of dollars, thousands of handshakes, and plenty of corn whiskey to do it, but we got people out to the precincts. Look up the ol' voter turnout numbers. They don't lie.

The way we did things back then wasn't the important thing; the important part was the end result. The final result was President John Kennedy. Where would we have been without his presidency?

Folks need to be passionate enough to fight over their candidate or do whatever it takes to make 'em win — even if it involves buying the election. Believe me, I knows what I'm talkin' 'bout. I wouldn't steer ya wrong — that's for dang sure.

THE END

Raymond And Lillie Unite In Marriage

The day before this book was to be sent to the printers, the author received an early morning phone call at his office from Raymond Chafin. The following chapter was the result of that telephone call and the circumstances which transpired later that day:

By 3:45 p.m. on September 16, 2003, the lobby of the Family Court building on Main Street in Logan was filled with folding chairs and each seat was quickly being taken. In spite of the limited size of the room, a constant flow of people continued to pour through the metal detectors at the front door and into the small waiting area.

It was a Tuesday and Family Court Judge Kelli Codiposti was wearing her black robes and preparing for a civil wedding ceremony. Of course it wasn't just any marriage ritual about to begin — this was the wedding day of Raymond Chafin, 86, of Cow Creek, and Lillie (Meadows) Bowen, 71, of Sandy Bottom.

Chafin was about to tie the knot for the second time in his life. His first wife, Louise, had passed away in the late-1990s. Lillie, also widowed, had known Chafin — or of him — throughout her life; but only in the last few years, did they find one another. After a growing friendship and an extended courtship, the two finally "decided that Tuesday would be their big day."

The room was full of young and old politicians, courthouse employees, family and friends of the couple. County Sheriff Johnny Mendez was there; Magistrate Leonard Codispoti also attended. Deputies were present. Other county officeholders looked on. Even several of Chafin's political adversaries from yesteryear were in attendance, including Claude "Big Daddy" Ellis and Attorney Dan Dahill. Everyone chatted jovially as they awaited the bride and groom's arrival.

While the audience passed the time, Chafin and Bowen were busy applying for their marriage license at the Logan County Courthouse up the street.

"We got a call last night from Uncle Raymond that they had decided to marry," Todd Chafin said as he smiled, before the ceremony began.

By 4:15 p.m., Chafin and his bride-to-be finally arrived at the lobby area and made their way toward the front of the room. Chafin slowly strolled down the aisle way — stopping to smile at, speak to, shake hands with, and hug friends along the way — and looking curiously enough as though he were still playing the part of the politician.

When the more reserved bride and the obviously outgoing groom finally reached the front of the room, they sat down in special leather chairs directly in front of and facing Judge Codispoti. Judges Roger Perry and Eric O'Briant were invited, by Chafin's request, to step forward and address the attendees.

"It's wonderful to find love once; it's especially nice to find love a second time," Judge Perry stated. "Raymond and Lillie, I wish you both the very best and many years of happiness."

After Perry spoke briefly, Judge O'Briant stepped to the front of the room, opened a Bible, and read from I Corinthians 13, known as the "Love Chapter": "Love is patient and love is kind …"

As Judge O'Briant finished his words of inspiration and wished the couple his best, Judge Codispoti took her position and began the traditional civil ceremony.

During the course of the formal procedure, the couple exchanged wedding rings and repeated their vows, which culminated with each saying "I will."

"You may now kiss your bride," the judge instructed Chafin, who immediately leaned over and kissed Lillie unashamedly, while the onlookers laughed aloud, cheered, and clapped. The judge then pronounced Raymond and Lillie man and wife, and presented the couple to the group as "Mr. and Mrs. Raymond Chafin."

Afterwards, as people walked up to congratulate the happy couple, Chafin, who was emotionally overwhelmed by the moment, wiped away a tear as he stated, "It is so nice to have so many of my friends and political cronies here with us today. At our age, this will most likely be our last go around. This is surely a big day for us."

A reception was held in their honor immediately following the ceremony at the Omar Elementary School gymnasium.

***

Earlier in the day on that Tuesday, Chafin had called F. Keith Davis and talked about his wedding plans:

> Lillie is a wonderful person, and Raymond Chafin is a lucky man. It wasn't too hard to talk her into this — it just took time. All of my people — the Chafins — like her, and her family seems to like me, too. We get along so well that this only makes good sense; I am proud that she'll be my wife.
>
> And I couldn't have ordered someone out of a Sears Catalog that would fit better with me politically than Lillie. She's a Democrat and she's active; and of course she means so much to me in so many ways.
>
> Plus, I'm a little bit of a show-off, and she — well, she's calmer than I am. We can work well together.

The couple will reside at his home at Cow Creek. They also plan to do a little traveling over the coming months as they settle into the routine of marriage.

Chafin elaborated:

> Later on, we may even travel to Florida for three months or so, to enjoy the winter in a warmer climate. I believe she will really enjoy it there. Our travel plans sort of depend on how this next election goes.

Chafin spoke about how the two first started talking, and how their relationship slowly blossomed. He also spoke about how they were different in so many ways; but he felt that she has been and would continue to be a great influence in his life.

He explained:

250

For example, Lillie likes to go to church, and certainly I need to go. So, I plan to start attending with her. It sure couldn't hurt me none. She's an awfully good woman.

Even though the actual wedding plans were not finalized until Monday evening, the night before the ceremony, Chafin said that the two of them have been discussing the possibilities for a long time.

Chafin chuckled and then said:

Since I had Lillie in the mood to marry me on Monday, I had to move quickly!

A NEW BEGINNING

Sources

Billy The Kid, A Short and Violent Life, By Robert M. Utley, © *1989 Robert M. Utley*, University Of Nebraska Press, Lincoln, NE

Claude Ellis Collection*, 1960 photos, campaign badges, letters, etc., Logan, West Virginia

Current photos of Raymond Chafin, Dan Dahill, and Claude Ellis, *Historian Martha Sparks*, Logan, West Virginia

Forty "40" Years, Mountain Politics, 1930-1970, By Lester "Bus" Perry, © *1971 Lester "Bus" Perry*; Published by McClain Printing Company, Parsons, WV

John F. Kennedy Library and Museum, Oral History Interviews, CHAFIN, RAYMOND 1917-, West Virginia political figure. 1964. 8 pp. ©

John F. Kennedy Library and Museum, Oral History Interviews, ELLIS, CLAUDE, 1964. 13 pp. ©

John F. Kennedy Library and Museum, Oral History Interviews, McDONOUGH, ROBERT (Paul), Director, John F. Kennedy's campaign, West Virginia primary (1960). 1964, 1965. 64 pp. ©

Just Good Politics, The Life Of Raymond Chafin — *Appalachian Boss*, By Raymond Chafin and Topper Sherwood, © 1994 Raymond Chafin and Topper Sherwood; Published by University of Pittsburgh Press, Pittsburgh, PA

Ku Klux Klan*, The Britannica Concise*, Via Internet © 2003

1960 Campaign and Presidential Photos*: John F. Kennedy Library and Museum*, Audiovisual Archives ©

The Kennedy Men 1901 – 1963, by Laurence Leamer, © *2001 Laurence Leamer,* Published by William Morrow/Harper Collins Publishers

The Logan Banner*, 1940-1970 archives, Logan, WV

Recorded and Non-Recorded Interviews, 2001-2003: Raymond Chafin, Claude and Rosemary Ellis, Ben Hale, James Major, and Dan Dahill

ACKNOWLEDGEMENTS: *I would like to extend my special thanks to West Virginia Senate President and Lt. Governor Earl Ray Tomblin and Administrative Assistant Raamie Barker for their commitment to this project. I am certainly appreciative of Raymond, Claude, and Dan for their openness and generosity during the interviewing process. I also wish to recognize Tim and Renee Fortune, my family and associates at Woodland Press, for their confidence in this project and their encouragement along the way.*

A very special thank you to the love of my life — and my favorite editor — my lovely wife, Cheryl.

Finally, a special thank you Lord Jesus Christ for Your continual love and provision — and for guiding me through this effort, delivering me through cardiac bypass surgery and recovery during the time period of writing this book. I look to You, Lord, with great hope and anticipation of the future. — Romans 8:28.

*DEDICATION: West Virginia Tough Boys is dedicated to the memory of Mr. James Major, a lifelong resident of Superior Bottom, in Logan County, who passed away at age 80 years old on September 6, 2003, while this book was in final production. Major was, among other things, an aggressive community activist, Logan County's first black deputy, and the first black manager of Junior Mercantile in Omar. Major was an inspiration to all who knew him. He will be sadly missed; however, the impact he made in behalf of Logan County people will certainly live on.

Brief Index